IKAT II

Lydia Van Gelder

Introduction by Prof. Alfred Bühler

Unicorn Books and Crafts, Inc., Petaluma California

Revised Edition

This book is dedicated to the memory of my beloved husband, Homer Whitney Van Gelder, who, through our fifty-six years of loving companionship, supported me in all my fiber directions, and I surely went to a lot of his track-and-field meets.

Art:

Front Cover. *Emily DuBois,* Mesa, *(detail). 15" x 46".*

Back Cover. *Gina D'Ambrosio,* Plique Ajour, *Shawl Series.*

Page 1. *Virginia Davis,* Tartan 3, *(detail), 12" x 9".*

Pages 2 and 3. *Ethel Stein, Untitled (detail), Compound ikat, satin damask, indigo dyed silk.*

Pages 4 and 5. *Emily DuBois,* Feather Ghost, *44" x 61".*

Page 6. Geringsing *from Bali (detail).*

Published in the United States of America
by Unicorn Books and Crafts, Inc.
1338 Ross Street, Petaluma, California 94954

Design: J Fay Design, Sausalito, California

Printed in Hong Kong by Regent Publishing Services

First published in 1980
Watson-Guptil Publications
New York, New York

Library of Congress Catalog Card Number:
96-60718

ISBN 0-9625586-5-6

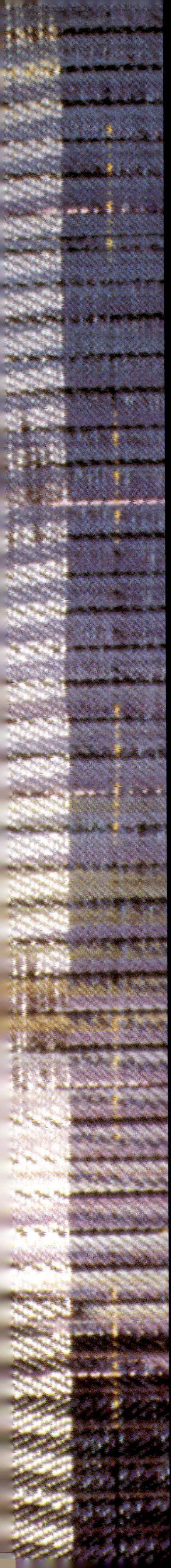

Contents

Acknowledgments

So many people have encouraged, stimulated and supported the preparation of this book that it is difficult to name them all. However, at the top of this long list are the very busy people of the staff at the Museum für Völkerkunde, Basel, who gave so graciously and unstintingly of their time and expertise: Prof. Alfred Bühler, former director of the museum and Professor Emeritus in Ethnology at the University of Basel; Dr. Marie-Louise Nabholz-Kartaschoff, Textiles Curator, East Asia, and lecturer in Ethnotechnology at the University of Basel; Dr. Renée Boser-Sarivaxévanis, Textiles Curator, Africa; Dr. Urs Ramseyer, Curator, Indonesia; Nicole Ramseyer-Gygi, Indonesia; and Elizabeth Eschler, staff assistant.

For the time they spent in interviews, I am grateful to: Ulla Häglund, Textiles Curator, Göteborgs Historiska Museum, Göteborg, Sweden; Marianne Erikson, Keeper of Textiles, The Röhss Museum of Arts and Crafts, Göteborg, Sweden; Inga Wintzell, Textiles Curator, Nordiska Museet, Stockholm, Sweden; Dr. Mattiebelle Gittinger, Research Associate for Southeast Asian Textiles, The Textile Museum, Washington, D.C.; Lois Vann, Museum Specialist and Conservator, Smithsonian Institution, Textile Division, Washington, D.C.

Technical assistance was generously given by: Joseph Fischer, Berkeley, California; Dr. Sarah Gill, San Anselmo, California; Yoshiko Wada, Berkeley, California; Lawrence Moss, Berkeley, California; Dick and Beany Wezelman, Berkeley, California; Steve and Susie Lee, Applied Photographic Laboratory, Santa Rosa, California; Karen Melander, Swedish translation, Santa Barbara, California; Magrita Klasen, French and German translations, Sonoma, California; Dorothy M. Beebee, drawings, Forestville, California; and Kathleen Hastings, who so cheerfully saw me through the long manuscript typing, Santa Rosa, California.

To my many friends who loaned fabrics for photographing or photos for illustrations, my deep appreciation.

And lastly, without the loving support and encouragement of my husband, Homer Van Gelder, through the years of preparation for this book, these words would not have been written.

In addition to the people mentioned above, I would like to express my appreciation to all the friends and colleagues who have assisted me in *Ikat II*, especially Virginia Davis, Mary Walker Phillips, Emily DuBois, and my friend and mentor, Yoshiko Iwamoto Wada.

I would also like to acknowledge Jason Pollen, president of the Surface Design Association, and Professor of Fiber at Kansas City Art Institute, and Charles Edmund Rossback, Professor Emeritus, Design, University of California, Berkeley. As the following comments show, both have so clearly expressed the essence of ikat. Jason Pollen: "Surface doesn't exist without foundation." Ed Rossback: "I think about the wondrous magic of ikat – the fact that a single thread can carry a message that can be revealed as the weaving progresses."

(right) Rio Grande Blanket, Weft Ikat *(detail). Purchased by the Smithsonian Institution around 1900 at Chemayo, New Mexico, this is the earliest recorded example of the ikat technique found within the continental United States. It is woven of handspun wool dyed a dark indigo blue, with some lighter blue and natural white stripes. Of higher quality than the indigenous spinning and weaving, it may have been made by master craftsmen not native to the Rio Grande area. The design of the weft ikat suggests Spanish or Guatemalan influence.*

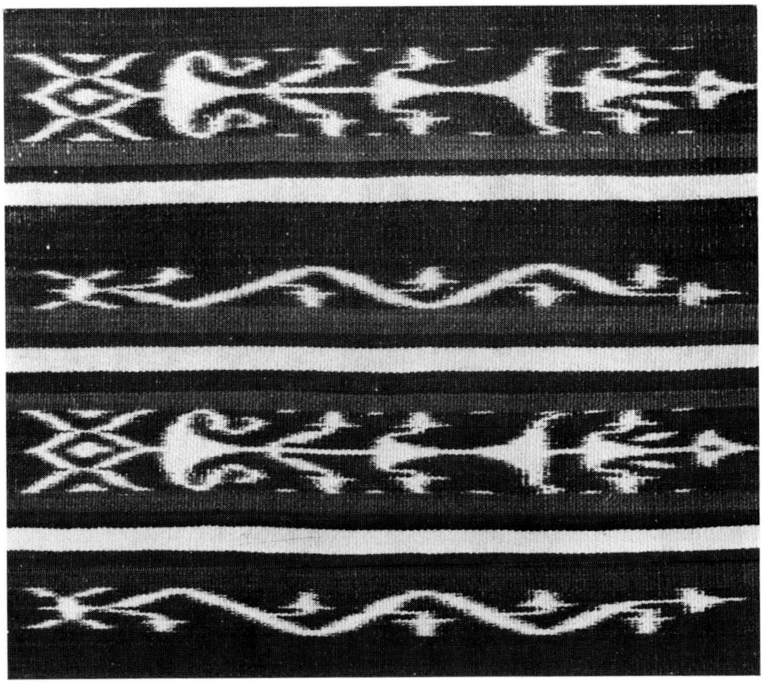

Preface

Perhaps my first awareness of the technique of ikat weaving came during the 1950s. Occasionally I would find references to ikat here and there in articles and books, but it was not until I read "The Ikat Technique" by Prof. Alfred Bühler (published in *CIBA Review* No. 44, Basel, Switzerland, August 1942) that I was stimulated to explore the possibilities of this technique in my own fiber work.

Ikat, in which certain areas of the yarn are bound off to resist the dye and produce a pattern that will be developed later in the fabric, is a very distinctive and challenging technique in that it can employ the full scope of the artisan's skills in designing, spinning, dyeing, weaving, knitting and other fiber techniques. The ikat technique is a means by which we can not only examine the intricate and beautiful ikats of the past, finding great appreciation for the people who created these fabrics before our time, but also explore its possibilities in our own fiber work.

This book is for the textile artist and the weaver with an understanding of the primary functions of a two- or four-harness loom; knitting, weaving and dyeing techniques are not explained except as they pertain specifically to ikat. Since the projects are arranged sequentially, each project building upon experience gained in the preceding ones, it is recommended that you do them in the order in which they are given. This book aims to bring out the basic principles of the ikat technique, and, through the progressive development of the projects, provide you, the contemporary craftsperson, with a means of carrying the techniques into your own creative fiber art.

Figure 1. *(left)* Velvet Warp Ikat, Turkestan. *The sett of this prayer rug, woven in a 3/1 warp twill, is incredibly fine. The silk pile carries the ikat pattern; the weft is cotton.*

Figure 2. *(right)* Japanese Weft Ikat *(detail). the techniques for making* e-gasuri *(picture ikats) like this one require a high degree of skill. The bold geometric double-ikat design contrasts with softer weft-ikat motifs of stylized shrimp and well water. Hirose, Shimane Prefecture, Honshu, mid-nineteenth century. Size: 58 x 13 in. (150 x 33 cm).*

Introduction

A Brief History of Ikat

by Prof. Alfred Bühler

Ikat is a method for coloring and ornamenting fabrics with the help of resist dyeing. This means that the pattern (design) is not applied directly (e.g., by painting or printing) and also not by weaving (e.g., with threads of different colors and/or binding systems) but by protecting parts of the yarn with resists (reserves) during the dyeing process. After the dyeing, the resists are removed and the pattern appears undyed on a colored ground. This process may be repeated, and it may be applied to white or to colored yarn.

Most kinds of resist dyeing are used for the patterning of fabrics. They are based on folding and/or covering parts of the cloth to resist the dye. We distinguish between fold resists, bind resists, tie resists, stitch resists, paste and wax resists, and negative resists. Among the first methods, tie-dye work, or *plangi,* is the best known. Batik is an example of the processes using paste or wax. In negative-resist techniques, parts of the cloth are prepared for dyeing with mordants; the unprepared parts do not take the dye, and thus act as reserves.

Ikat, by contrast, is not a technique used on fabrics. It is, instead, a method of patterning yarn that will be woven into a fabric. It may be applied to the warp, to the weft, or to both parts. Accordingly we speak of warp ikat, weft ikat, compound ikat (if the patterns on warp and weft are independent) and double ikat (if the designs of warp and weft are identical and cover each other). Warp ikat is most frequently found, weft ikat less common, and double ikat the rarest and most complicated form. Figures 1 through 4 illustrate the four types of ikat.

The principle of ikat is quite simple. Sets or bundles of yarn are partially tied with bast fiber, yarn or other impenetrable material such as pieces of paper, rubber or plastic. Then they are dyed and afterward the dyer/weaver removes the reserving material.

Actually, however, the whole process is very complicated, much more so than the processes used for resist dyeing of fabrics. Among the reasons: before it is patterned, the yarn must be arranged as it will be used later as warp or weft. For warp ikat, the single yarns must be divided by a cross, so that when they are mounted in the loom, sheds will be formed during the weaving. For weft ikat, the sequence in which the yarns will be woven must be taken into consideration. To simplify the laborious work, sections of yarn which will be patterned identically in the ikat reserve are joined into bigger bundles for tying and dyeing (and separated again later). Yarns for two or even more fabrics can also be bundled in this way. All parts of the patterned yarn must be carefully fixed in place to prevent them from slipping or being shifted. Otherwise the pattern would become indistinct.

Although ikat techniques are always very similar in principle, each locality has its own peculiarities. These may stem from regional differences in the materials (such as bast fibers, cotton, wool and silk) that have to be patterned. Much more often, however, they are the result of the experience of many generations of workers, each showing a successful way to avoid mistakes. Thus the methods are very different for patterning a whole warp or weft and for setting up parts which must be joined after the patterning.

Each local technique depends as well on the kind of loom used for the weaving. Preparing a comparatively short warp for the type of horizontal backtension loom used in most parts of Indonesia must be very different from the process for a long warp to be woven on the more complicated looms of India or Thailand.

Figure 3. *(left, bottom) Geringsing* Double Ikat, Bali. *In this cloth from the village of Tenganan Pergeringsingan, paired figures between the rays of the large star motif show a little boy paying respects to a royal lady. He wears the characteristic head covering found in depictions of the East Javanese hero, Panji.*

Figure 4. *(left, top)* Compound Ikat, Southern Germany *(detail). This mid-nineteenth-century silk scarf is woven in a combination of weaves, predominantly satin, sateen and twills, and is edged on four sides with gold torchon bobbin lace. The ikat patterns in the warp and weft are independent of each other.*

Figure 5. *(far right)* Plain-Weave Ikat, Japan *(detail). A geometric* kasuri *(ikat) design with* e-gasuri *in the center. Warp and weft yarns are equally visible. Collection, Lydia Van Gelder.*

The structures (construction, binding systems) of ikat fabrics also differ. Apparently warp-faced and weft-faced rep weaves (for warp ikat and weft ikat, respectively) are the most appropriate because the non-ikatted yarn system is not visible in the fabric and consequently the patterns appear identical on both sides of the cloth. However, plain weave, twill, satin and even velvets (from Persia, Turkestan and Afghanistan) with ikat patterns are also known.

As in the mechanical parts of ikatting, we find local differences in dyes and dyeing processes. They often are not the same for cotton as for bast fiber, wool or silk. They are more complicated if one wants to apply more than one color. Generally speaking, the whole process of tying and dyeing must be repeated according to the number of colors. Again, however, ingenious methods of simplifying this part of the technique have been invented. Of course, all dyeing methods also depend on the kind of dyestuffs used. Formerly, when only organic dyes were known, the processes very often were quite complicated. Thus to dye cotton yarn red with certain woods or roots, the yarn had to be prepared for the dye with tanning substances, oil or fat and mordants such as alum. Because of this preparation, and also because the dye solutions were not concentrated, the whole process sometimes lasted ten or more years. Today, synthetic dyestuffs are more and more in use. The dyeing has become much simpler and the time required shorter. These improvements in the process do not always yield adequate results, however.

As with the principle of resist dyeing in general, the idea of patterning bast fiber or yarn by partially tying it is spread all over the world; it is even known by people who have no knowledge of weaving. Techniques of this kind are named *protoikat.* They are used, among many other places, in different localities in New Guinea for decorating fiber skirts of the women.

Genuine ikat, i.e., patterning of yarn to be woven, is also widespread. With the exception of Australia and Oceania (where, apart from a few places, weaving does not exist), it was and mostly still is practiced in many parts of the Old and the New World.

In America it was in use in pre-Columbian times, as proven by finds in Peruvian graves. Nowadays it is still done in some places in Mexico (warp ikat), Guatemala (warp and weft combined), Ecuador, Colombia, Peru, Argentina and by the Mapuche of Chile (warp ikat at all of these places).

Important ikat centers are spread all over Asia. Some are situated in the Near East (Turkey, Syria, Persia – warp ikat) and Central Asia (Turkestan, Afghanistan – also warp ikat). Among the many centers in India are very important places in Orissa and Andhra Pradesh (ikat on warp and weft, compound and simple double ikat) and above all, Gujarat, with its world-famous silk *patola* saris (double ikat). The technique (mostly warp ikat) is also known by tribal people in Burma, Thailand, Cambodia, Indochina, and Southwest and South China.

Figure 6. *(above)* Warp-Ikat, Turkestan. *Warp patterning is clear in the center panel of this very fine silk taffeta* chapan. *The panel is divided in half and designs are repeated on each side and alternated in each row. "Steps" occur in the design where groups of warp yarns were tied and dyed in the same ikat bundle. Collection, Lydia Van Gelder.*

Figure 7. *(right)* Weft Ikat, Thailand. *this silk skirt fabric has a taffetalike quality. The lozenge shape in this detail represents a feather motif; reverse curves at the base of the feather represent the* naga *or dragon symbol. Collection, Dorothy Miller.*

Figure 8. *(far right)* Warp-Ikat Stripes, Turkey *(detail). The ikat bands are alternate stripes of red/white and blue/white between warp-satin stripes of yellow and black. The warp is artificial silk and the weft, cotton.*

In highly developed forms (weft ikat on silk), it is also done in parts of Thailand, Laos, Cambodia and Malaysia. One of the main centers is Indonesia, where ikat is still done in many parts of the archipelago. Bast fiber, cotton and silk are used. Warp ikat is most common.

Weft ikat, mostly made with silk, is done in Palembang, Sumatra, East Java and Bali. At one place only, in Tenganan on Bali, are made the unique double-ikat cotton *geringsing* cloths, like the one shown in Figure 3.

Asian centers of ikat also lie in Japan and its Ryukyu islands in the Okinawa prefecture. Warp, weft, compound and double ikat on bast fiber, cotton and silk are known, and quite a few peculiar techniques were developed on these islands.

In Africa, ikat is known in the western parts and on the island of Madagascar. Warp ikat is very popular among the Yoruba of South Nigeria and the Dyula of the Ivory Coast and Upper Volta, but it is also known by other tribes. In Madagascar (here the technique came from Indonesia), warp ikat is used on bast fiber.

In Europe ikat was done, sometimes up to nearly recent times, in northern Italy, France (Lyon and other places), Germany, Austria and Switzerland. It is still made in Scandinavia (Sweden, Finland – weft ikat), Spain (Mallorca – warp ikat) and northern Greece (warp and weft ikat).

From the distribution of ikat, it follows that different places of origin of the technique may be possible. A first root may lie somewhere in East Asia. From there the technique might have spread over Central Asia, Southeast Asia, Japan, Ryukyu and probably America. India appears to be a second center, from which ikat may have diffused into the regions of the Middle and Near East and Africa. In western Asia there may have existed a third root, which may also have influenced West Africa and may have been the root of most European ikat centers. Archeological finds and old reports throw some more light on the origin of the ikat technique. The oldest sources point to three regions: In Nara, Japan, elaborate warp ikats of silk are kept. They belong to the Asuka period, A.D. 552-644, and very probably were made in China. Wall paintings in the Ajanta caves near Aurangabad, India, show people in cloths which are patterned in warp

Figure 9. *(above)* Mallorcan Warp Ikat. *This traditional linen warp-ikat pattern is dyed a brilliant blue.*

Figure 10. *(right) An example of ikat from Yemen. South Arabia, with inscription.*

ikat. The frescoes belong to the seventh century, i.e., to the same time as the finds from Nara. Excavations in Egypt, mostly at Fostat, reveal the third old center. The warp ikats on cotton found here were mostly made, according to their printed or embroidered inscriptions, in Yemen, South Arabia, during the tenth to twelfth centuries. According to written sources, ikat was known in South Arabia even earlier, as far back as the seventh century.

Thus the three main areas of ikat in our time are confirmed by the existence of three ancient ikat centers of about the same age. They may have originated independently of each other. It is conspicuous, however, that China is not only the oldest center of the three but also the one with the most elaborate patterns, the most highly developed technique. In this connection it is very important that ikat is repeatedly mentioned in old Chinese reports as being used by various non-Chinese tribes of South and Southwest China. These same non-Chinese people knew a few of the other resist-dyeing methods which are technically connected with ikat. It seems probable, therefore, that the Chinese took over ikat, and other resist techniques, from tribal cultures. Hypothetically, this could be the sole root of the technique which may have spread, together with other inventions, from China to the secondary centers. In all of these regions, the technique and the designs were developed locally and thus achieved the forms typical for each region. In most cases warp ikat seems to be the oldest form, followed most probably by double ikat and lastly by compound and weft ikat.

When one thinks how laborious and difficult ikat work is, one understands that ikat fabrics belong to the most precious properties wherever they are made or known. As a rule, they are mostly used at festive occasions, and especially for ceremonial and religious purposes. At these occasions they often play a role not only as clothing but as decorations (hangings, covers) as well. Because they are so precious, they are sometimes reserved for the upper classes or for the courts. For the same reason they often play an important part as bridal gifts. In Eastern Indonesia the dead are wrapped in ikat cloth for burial. At other places, ikats are among the gifts offered to the gods. They are used even as medicine. In Bali, where the double ikats from Tenganan and *patola* (saris) from India are believed to possess healing qualities, pieces of imported Indian *patola* are burned to ashes and then given to sick people. All these customs prove that ikats are highly valued, not only for purely material reasons, but also as objects with supernatural or magical powers.

Figure 11. West African Warp Ikat. *A Dyula dyer and weaver made this cloth for a woman's wrapper in the village of Kong, Ivory Coast. It is embellished with inlay patterns and warp-ikat stripes. Thirteen strips, each 4 in. (10 cm) wide, were sewn together to form a fabric 52 in. (132 cm) wide by 60 in. (152 cm) long.*

Figure 12. *(left) Emily DuBois,* Tsankawi, *54″ x 44″.*

Figure 13. *(right) Marylin Robert,* Architectonic *(detail) Warp ikat.*

Chapter I

Designing for Ikat

Ikat, as we have come to know the technique, is the process of wrapping or binding off sections of yarn to resist the dye during dyeing, before the textile is woven. This wrapping or binding off may be done on yarn to be used for the warp, the weft or both. The unwrapped areas of the yarn absorb the dye, while the wrapped sections remain undyed.

Before you begin to do the projects in this book, and particularly before you attempt to dye and weave an ikat fabric of your own design, it is essential to have a basic understanding of the different types of ikat; the factors such as pattern, color, materials, weave, and the end use of the fabric which will influence the design; and finally, the steps involved in planning, tying and dyeing an ikat so that you will have control over your design.

Types of Ikat

An ikat fabric can be classified as one of four types, depending on which group or groups of threads carry the resist patterning and whether, if both warp and weft are ikatted, the patterns are designed to coincide or exist independently of one another. These four types are illustrated in Figures 18 through 21 on page 20.

A warp ikat is a fabric where only the warp yarns are tied to resist the dye and form a pattern, whereas in a weft ikat, it is the weft yarns that are resist tied. A double ikat is a fabric where the yarns of both the warp and the weft are tied off to coincide with each other in a predetermined pattern. In the fourth category, compound ikat, both warp and weft yarns are tied off but they form independent resist patterns. When the fabric is woven, the warp ikatting has a design feeling of its own, and the weft patterning does not rely on the warp pattern. In traditional compound ikat the warp- and weft-resist patterns are usually placed in separate areas of the cloth, although in rare instances they sometimes do overlap.

Recognizing an Ikatted Fabric

When you look at a fabric for the first time, you may wonder first whether it is an ikat, and secondly, whether it is warp, weft, double or compound ikat. There are clues in the fabric which will help you determine which kind of ikat it is.

Sometimes it is hard to distinguish between a fabric with a printed or painted warp and one in which the warp has been ikatted. Each would have slightly blurred edges in the patterned areas, due to the unavoidable shifting of the warp yarns during weaving. But for ikat, bundles of yarns are tied together and patterned exactly the same — each bundle might include from two to twelve yarns, depending on the degree of fineness of the yarn — and in the woven fabric you would see small groups of identically patterned yarns. These groups are especially easy to see in Figure 6, page 12. On the other hand, if the warp has been printed or painted, the finished fabric will not show these identically patterned groups of yarns; instead, the design will flow more smoothly from one area into another. Other details may also tell you whether or not the fabric is a warp ikat. When you look at a hanging or a length of fabric, if the strong lines of the design run parallel to the selvage edge and the horizontal lines are a little blurred due to the slight shifting of the warp yarns, then you can safely assume it is a warp ikat.

However, if the sharper and more distinct lines in the pattern of a fabric run horizontally, you can assume it is a weft ikat, since these lines indicate that the resists were tied in the weft rather than the warp yarns. In some weft ikats there also may be evidence of adjustments the weaver has made in the positioning of weft picks in order to bring out the design: tiny loops may have been left at the selvage,

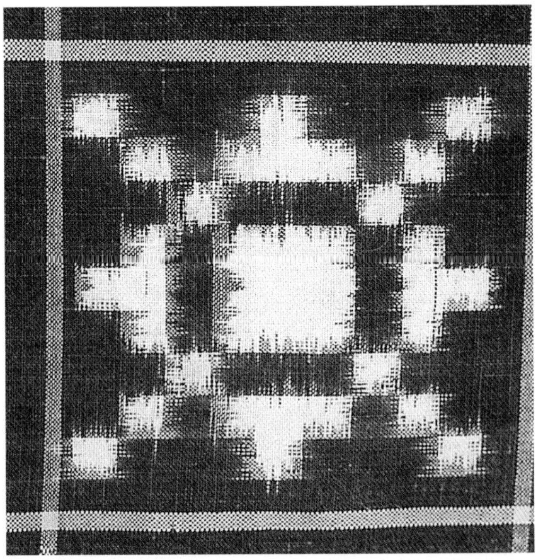

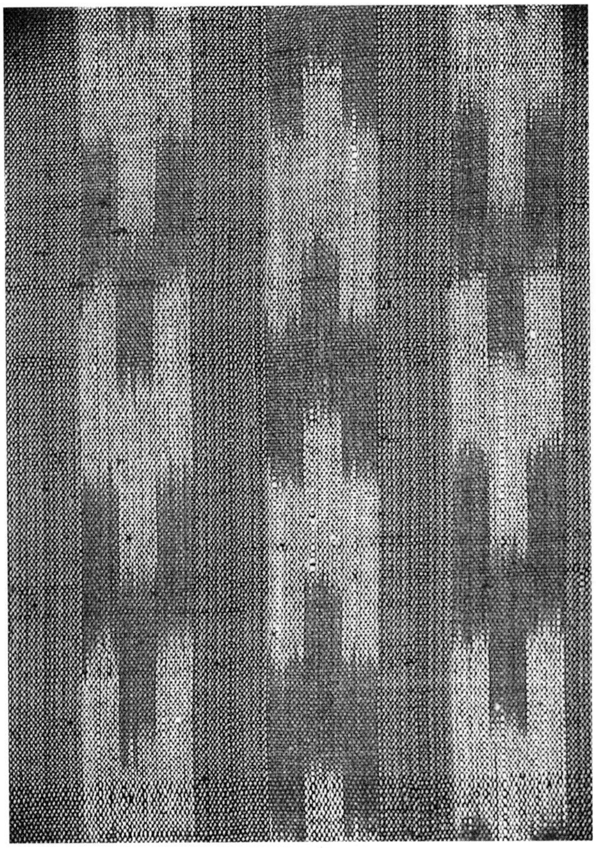

Figure 14. *(top right) An example of double ikat.*

Figure 15. *(above) An example of weft ikat.*

Figure 16. *(above) An example of warp ikat.*

Figure 17 *(page 19) An example of compound ikat.*

or bundles of excess weft yarns turned back and woven into a subsequent shed may have caused lumpiness at the selvage.

You may see fabrics with strong light or undyed units of design against a dark background; often these units are square, though they also may take other shapes. Examine the pattern units carefully. If a square, for example, has tiny legs, or feathery edges, on both sides as well as at top and bottom, then it is a double ikat, since both warp and weft yarns have been carefully resisted to coincide and form the pattern. The legs, of course, are caused by the slight shifting of both warp and weft yarns during weaving. Unevenness also may be the result of differences in the way individual yarns have absorbed the dye or of accidental dye seepage under the resist ties.

A compound ikat can be easily recognized by the independent placement of the warp and weft ikat patterns, which do not rely on each other to complete their design. Even in the rare examples in which warp and weft resist patterns may overlap, they do not coincide exactly to form a single design.

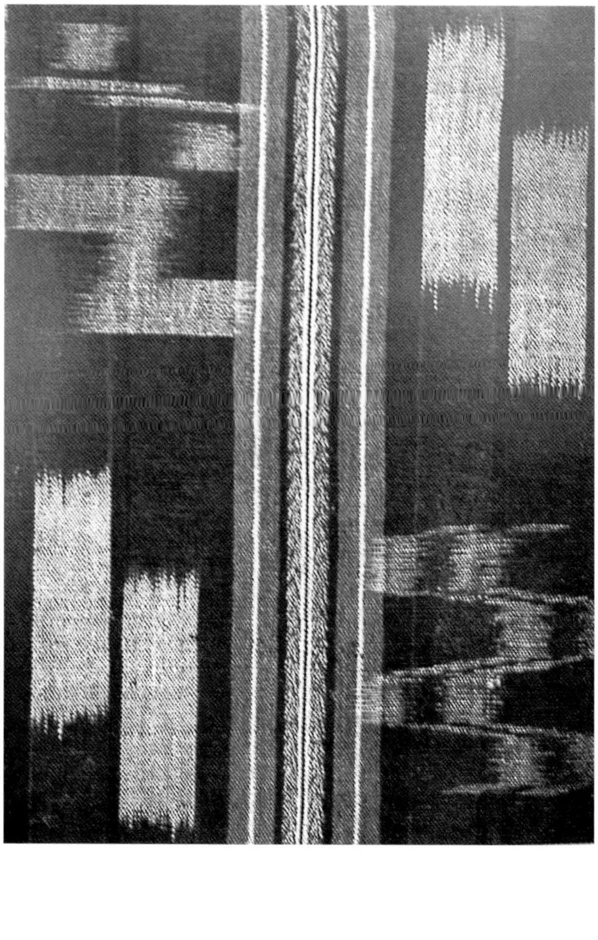

Planning Your Design

The design or pattern in an ikat fabric is of paramount importance, and it requires careful planning. The first step is to think of what you want to say in your design. You can borrow from the traditional designs illustrated throughout this book, or you can develop your own. Will your design have soft, flowing lines as in body outlines and rolling hills, or will it be geometric, with rigid lines and sharp, bold areas? After your design is established, the next step is to decide which of the ikat techniques to use.

The Best Type of Ikat for Your Design. The very nature of warp and weft yarns as they lie in the textile creates design advantages for each type of ikat. A design with strong vertical lines will be most successful if the ikatting is done on the warp yarns. Obviously, it is difficult to control a vertical line in a weft ikat, since even a small shift of each successive weft as it is placed in the shed will distort the developing vertical line. Horizontal lines, on the other hand, would be strongest in a weft ikat; in a warp ikat, they would be weak and somewhat distorted, due to the slight shifting of the warp as it is rolled onto the loom as well as the play of tension during the weaving. The projects describe in greater detail how a design can best be expressed in warp, weft, double and compound ikat, respectively.

Which Weaving Technique to Use. Ikat may be woven in plain weave, warp- and weft-faced rep weaves, various twills, satin and occasionally velvet weave. In ikat, your choice of weave ranks in importance with type of yarn, dye and design (though not necessarily in that order), for all these elements come together when you express yourself in ikat.

In either warp or weft ikat, you can render the pattern most successfully with a warp- or weft-faced *rep* weave in which the opposing threads are completely covered by the patterned yarns. Various warp-faced and weft-faced *twills* may also be used for ikat; they will give you strong pattern definition as well as interesting textures. The opposing yarn system will, of course, show to some degree in a twill weave. The projects explore various warp- and weft-faced weaves, as well as plain weave.

Plain weave can be used for any type of ikat, but it is best suited for double ikat, for it is here that the warp and weft yarns are of equal importance in developing the design. Traditionally, when plain weave is used, there are usually the same number of e.p.i. relative to picks per inch. An exception is the *geringsing* cloths woven in Bali.

For compound ikat, you can use either plain weave or a combination of warp-faced and weft-faced weaves (this is accomplished by varying the sett of the warp yarns in the reed). Combining weaves for compound ikat is discussed further in Chapter VIII.

Although this book does not include projects using satin and velvet weaves, both weaves are suitable for ikat. *Satin* weave is usually woven with a minimum of five harnesses; eight harnesses will give better results with fine warps. *Velvet* weave is a warp- or weft-pile technique. The weave structure

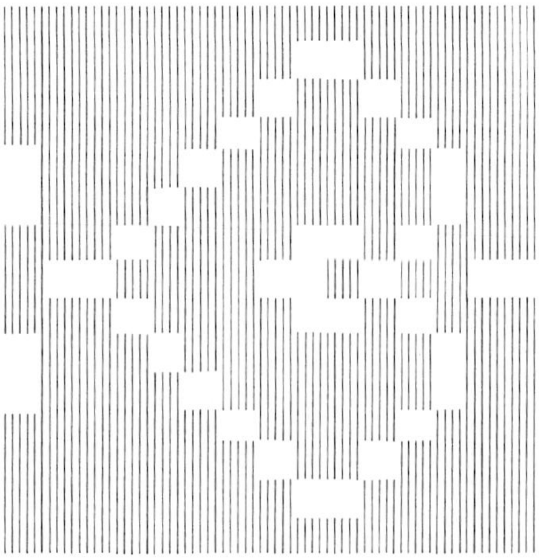

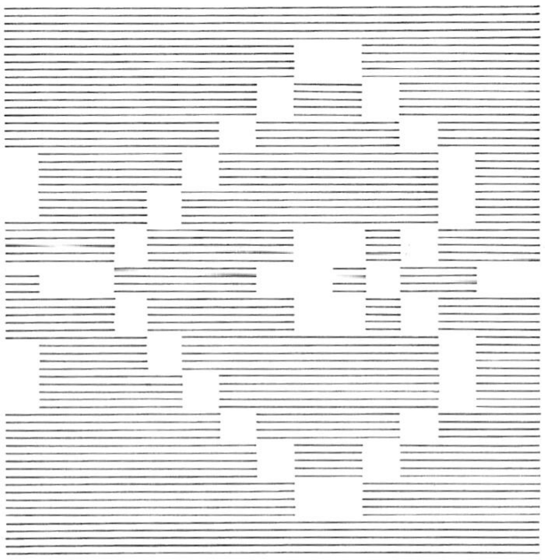

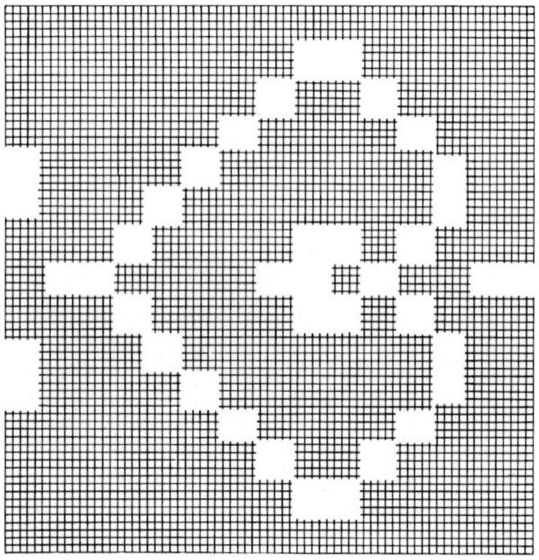

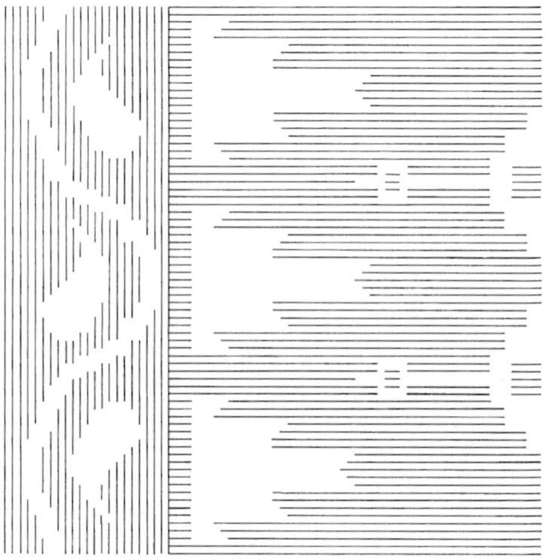

Figure 18. *(top)* Warp Ikat. *The vertical lines in this diagram represent the wap yarns; white spaces indicate where resists would be placed to achieve a warp-ikat pattern. The motif shown is the betel leaf, a popular pattern in India.*

Figure 19. *(bottom)* Weft Ikat. *Resists would be tied on the weft yarns, represented by the horizontal lines, to achieve the betel-leaf design in weft ikat.*

Figure 20. *(top)* Double Ikat. *In double ikat, the resist-dyed warp and weft yarns cross each other, the resists having been planned to coincide exactly in order to produce one motif.*

Figure 21. *(bottom)* Compound Ikat. *The lines in this diagram show how the ikatted patterns in the warp and weft, which are independent of one another, pass through unpatterned yarns of the opposite yarn system.*

of a warp velvet is composed of two warps on separate beams and one common weft. A plain warp is woven into the foundation or background cloth, while the warp that is patterned with ikat forms the loops in the pile.

The important thing in selecting a weave for ikat is to choose one that will enhance the qualities you want your piece to have. Do you want only the ikatted yarns to be visible, or do you prefer that the opposing yarns show, and if so, to what degree? The texture of the weaving will also affect your ikat design.

Choosing Appropriate Materials. Ikat can be used in many ways, and it is a good idea to take a few moments before designing a project to consider what you want to express with the technique. Will you be weaving fabric for clothing, a large wall decoration, a small wall hanging or, perhaps, a rug? Possibly something in an off-loom technique is anticipated. Although the majority of projects in this book are limited to woven pieces, ikatted yarns could also be used to make a basket, a knitted garment, a tatted piece, items in the sprang technique or even a raffia skirt.

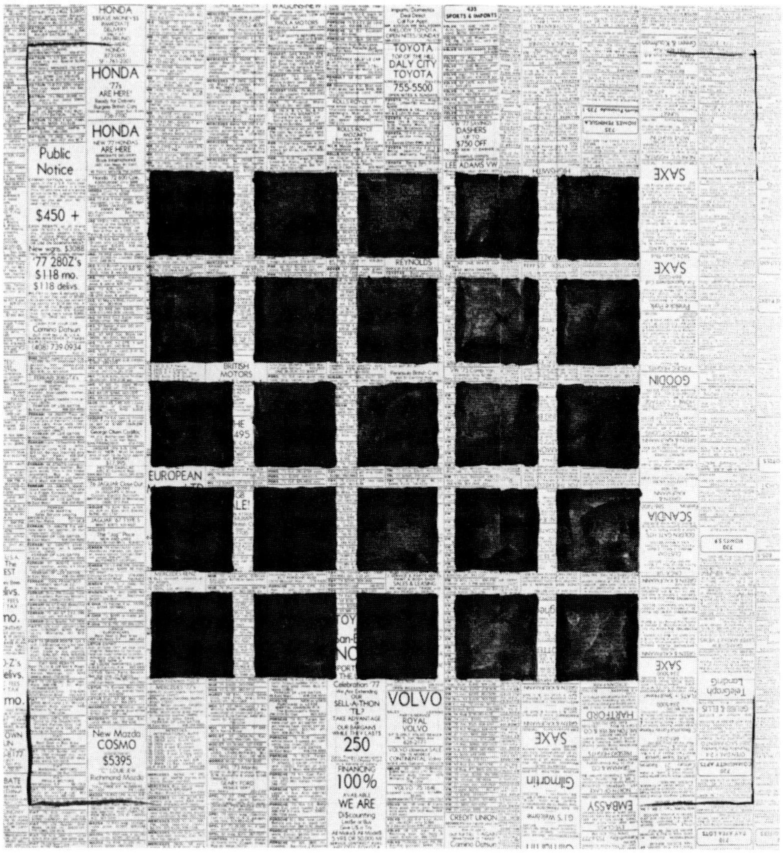

Figure 22. Paper Cartoon. *From a rough first sketch, this cartoon was developed to describe the measurements and placements of overshot areas (represented by the black squares) for the contemporary wall hanging in Project 9. The four outer corners of the piece are indicated as well.*

Any craftsperson knows well that one of the prime considerations is choosing a material to suit the purpose. Weaving a heavy outer garment like a poncho or jacket would normally call for wool, and the sett would be chosen according to the weight of the fabric desired. A body garment, on the other hand, would be best woven of a supple material to give and flow with the body's movements. A finer, softer yarn such as a fine wool, cotton, silk or blends of these would be appropriate. Many garment patterns are designed for a minimum of waste when cutting handwoven fabric; these can be purchased as patterns or found in books on weaving garments.

A rug must have good wearing qualities and lay well on the floor, calling for yarns of sturdiness. Wool and linen come to mind first. Cotton is also usable, but cotton fiber shows soil easily, and it is difficult to wash a rug. A weft-faced or warp-faced rug would have the best wearing qualities, but an ikat yarn used in a rya knotted technique or a velvet weave should not be overlooked.

With wall hangings, the sky is the limit. Here is an area where you have the most latitude. Soft, sheer, open weaves, sculptural wall decorations, or a hanging of strong design could be most striking. The selection of yarns for wall hangings offers limitless possibilities.

Color. In ikat, the particular color you choose is not as important as the value of that color. For good pattern definition, a very pale pink would not be as successful as a deep, dark red. Likewise, a pale yellow will not work as well as an intense, perhaps grayed yellow that is darker in value. In the traditional ikats of the past, there are some lighter shades, but mostly we see dark tones. Contemporary examples use many brilliant, intense colors, which carry the ikat beautifully. For ikat, the best choice is usually a color that will contrast strongly in value with the lighter undyed, resisted parts.

Developing a Cartoon

Many contemporary ikats woven in the United States today use a very casual, random placement of resists. Some of these pieces achieve very charming results. If you have tried ikatting before, perhaps this is a direction you have taken. However, in this book I will be directing your work in a more disciplined way so that you will know how to control your design.

Before you place the first resist tie, you must know just where it will lie in relation to the subsequent ties. Although you should chart out your design in some manner, this does not necessarily mean that you must always draw it on paper — it might be as simple a procedure as making notations on your working sheet, as you will be doing in the first warp-ikat project. In such a project, where you plan to tie off a few inches of resist between evenly spaced lengths of unpatterned weaving, you need only measure the approximate distance between resists.

The complexity of your design is probably the most important factor in determining whether or not you need to make a complete cartoon. When you are designing an ikat that has symbolism, complex detail or an abstract pattern in which the ikat areas must be in proper scale and position relative to one another, you will need to follow a cartoon in order to have your design come out as you wish in the finished weaving. In Bali, where the complicated *geringsing* ikats are made, beginning weavers must rely on a previously woven fabric as a guide, while experienced weavers can tie off the patterns from memory. The same principle applies to our own weaving as well. If we were to repeat the same design again and again, after a while we could tie it off from memory. But modern weavers tend to be impatient, and we rarely repeat our designs, so I advise the beginner and the experienced weaver alike: If you want anything more than a random ikat pattern, you should work up a cartoon of your design to follow for tying the resists.

I like to begin by first drawing a rough sketch on paper with a soft brush and water-base poster paint. You might prefer to use a soft pencil or charcoal stick; anything which allows you to work freely is suitable. I find that the newspaper classified-ad section is wonderful paper for drawing preliminary sketches (see Figure 22). Whereas plain paper sometimes seems lifeless and sterile, newsprint simulates a textural quality that is in sympathy with weaving. With my brush, I quickly make blobs of paint to establish my design feeling on the paper. Then, from my first rapid sketch, I make another drawing, to refine the design and, if I am working full scale, develop it to the size and proportions I want my finished piece to be. This drawing is my working cartoon, similar to the traditional tapestry-weavers cartoon. The size of

Figure 23. *Lydia Van Gelder.* Face-Mask Motif, Warp Ikat. *The design for this piece was first charted in graph paper. It is the best way to transfer a realistic or symbolic figure to your warp with a certain degree of accuracy.*

the weaving and the complexity of the design determine whether the cartoon should be drawn full size or reduced. Until you are more comfortable with ikat techniques, you will probably find it easier to use a full-size cartoon.

Transferring Your Cartoon

From your finished cartoon, you will tie the resists. Visualize the cartoon translated into positive and negative areas. The positive areas will be the parts where the yarn has been dyed, and the negative areas will represent the resist-tied parts. Your method of transferring the design to the yarn and tying the resists will depend on whether you are making a warp, weft, double or compound ikat.

Transferring for Warp Ikat. After the warp is wound, the ends are left uncut, because the next step is to insert rods through these loops at each end of the warp. The warp is placed under tension in some manner by tying the rods to something sturdy. This can be achieved by tying the warp to a frame, in the case of a short warp, or stretching it between stationary objects in your studio (doors, table legs, chair legs) or out of doors between posts, if it is a long warp. The warp should be placed flat, either on a tong table or on the floor or ground (although this is rather hard on the back sometimes), with the warp spread evenly on the rods to approximate as closely as possible the planned e.p.i. of the warp on the loom.

The cartoon can be placed either directly underneath the wound warp for tying or beside you as a visual reference. Then you must decide where you want the pattern to fall in the finished piece, taking care to allow sufficient length of warp at both ends of the design for the tying on to the loom, front and back.

The last step is to tie the resists. If you laid the warp on top of the cartoon, the warp yarns must be spread to the same number of e.p.i. as will be in the reed when you dress the loom. If you tie off too few ends per inch, your design will be condensed when it is woven; if too many, the design will spread out when you weave it. Finally, the ties are placed where you want the yarn to resist the dye in your design.

Transferring for Weft Ikat. Weft yarns are tied for resists in small skeins, based on a calculation of the estimated number of ends and lengths you will need. These small skeins are usually tied right on the weft-skeining device. In weft ikat, there are specific procedures for transferring the design and tying the resists which are particular to each weft-ikat technique; these are discussed in detail in each of the weft ikat projects. General methods of calculating and winding the weft are described at length in Chapter III.

Transferring for Double Ikat. The methods for transferring and tying the design on warp and weft yarns are combined for double ikat, but this technique requires greater exactness in all of the processes in order to achieve the best results in the woven piece. First the design is established and developed into a working cartoon. The warp is then resist-tied according to the cartoon. The weft is calculated according to the number of picks per inch in both the patterned and unpatterned parts, as well as the width of the finished piece plus an allowance for takeup in weaving. The weft resists are planned so as to coincide exactly with the warp resists when the piece is woven. The adjustable weft-winding device in Figure 32, is especially suitable for this. In traditional double ikats — whether they are made in India, Indonesia, Japan or Okinawa — great care is taken in winding and tying off both warp and weft yarns, and the same care should be taken by the modern weaver as well.

Transferring for Compound Ikat. As with double ikat, precise placement of both warp and weft resists is important, even though the patterned areas are independent of one another on the fabric. For traditional compound-ikat patterns, a band of warp ikat is tied along the selvage edges, leaving the rest of the warp unpatterned. The warp which will have the ikat stripe is wound, and the plain warp put on separate warp chains. A previously prepared design is then laid beside the wound warp or underneath it, depending on the weavers preference, and the resists tied. This tied warp is laid aside. Then the weft pattern is tied so that it will fall within the area of plain, unpatterned warp. The weft skeins are wound and tied according to a predetermined design, allowing for plain, unpatterned parts which will weave through the warp-ikat stripe. Whether or not you use the traditional, bordered placement of warp and weft patterns, you should try to plan their placement in relation to the fabric as a whole.

The Graph-Paper Method

Suppose you wish to translate a representational or symbolic figure into an ikat weaving. In order to represent the image in your weaving without distortion, you will need to know precisely where and how to place the resists to achieve a likeness. I recommend two methods: the Japanese picture – Ikat method for *e-gasuri,* described in Project 7, and the following procedures using graph paper.

Designs may be charted on graph paper for any of the four types of ikat. Each square of the graph represents X number of e.p.i. and picks per inch, which you determine by weaving a sample in the yarn and weaving technique you plan to use for your piece.

First you will need to draw your figure on paper, refining your drawing until it conforms to the image you want to achieve. Use curved lines in this sketch if you wish. Next, place a sheet of carbon paper between your drawing and a sheet of graph paper and trace the lines of your design with a pencil. Now go over these lines on the graph paper; where there is a curved line, stair-step the line to conform to the squares on the graph. The line will retain its curved appearance, but it is now broken into squares representing the groups of warp yarns that will be tied off in bundles later. The gracefully curved lines in the *geringsing* ikat shown in Figure 3, page 10, are an excellent example of the amount of control that can be achieved by using graph paper.

The graph-paper method can be used for charting a drawing of your own for ikat. However, it is a good idea to first try charting the simple face-mask design in warp ikat shown in Figure 23. For this exercise you will need a soft lead pencil and graph paper. I prefer to use paper with as large a grid as possible; four squares to the inch is usually a good size, but you can also use a finer grid if you are charting a very large design. Generally, I use the kind of graph paper without the heavier grid marks at one-inch intervals, as these are distracting to me; however, you might prefer them as an assist. If you decide to go on and weave the face mask, you will also need a smooth white cotton yarn such as carpet warp (or a cotton yarn of similar size and texture).

Figure 24. Warp Ikat Shawl, Sawu *(detail). These stylized floral motifs and serrated stripes, separated by bands of plain stripes, are typical of Indonesian shawls woven for the tourist trade. Collection, Dorothy Miller.*

Charting the Design. There will be a total of 176 ends in the width of the pattern warp for this motif, which will be done in multiples or divisions of 8, and in this particular exercise, each square on the graph paper will represent 8 warp ends. Numbers in **bold type** in the list below indicate the number of warp ends to be tied in the resists; for every 8 warp ends, fill in one block on the graph paper. For example, for 32 warp ends you would fill in four squares on the graph. Numbers in regular type indicate the number of warp ends left untied, which would receive the dye.

Referring to Figure 23 as often as necessary to visualize the face-mask motif, start at the top with the blocks representing the hairline. Read from left to right, filling in only the squares on the graph paper indicated by numbers in bold type as they relate to the number of warp ends:

Row 1.	Hairline: 28, **8** and 8 (7 times), **8**, 28
Row 2.	No resists: 176 ends
Row 3.	Brow line: 24, **128**, 24
Row 4.	Upper nose: 68, **40**, 68
Row 5.	Nose center only: 84, **8**, 84
Row 6.	Eye line: 36, **32**, 16, **8**, 16, **32**, 36
Row 7.	Pupil eye-line: 36, **16**, 8, **8**, 16, **8**, 16, **8**, 8, **16**, 36
Row 8.	Repeat row 7, twice
Row 9.	Repeat row 6
Row 10.	Repeat row 5
Row 11.	Upper nostril: 56, **12**, 16, **8**, 16, **12**, 56
Row 12.	Repeat row 11, once
Row 13.	Lower nostril: 68, **40**, 68
Row 14.	Repeat row 2, twice
Row 15.	Mouth: 56, **64**, 56. Repeat this row once

Winding the Warp. If you weave the face mask in Figure 23, determine the length of your warp by allowing for an 18-in. (45-cm) weaving length plus takeup plus loss to the loom tie-on. The 18-in. (45-cm) length would allow for the mask design, which is 3 in. (9 cm) wide and 4 in. (11 cm) long, plus some border above and below it. Wind the two undyed selvage bands in separate bundles of 20 ends each, tie the cross and end loops, and lay them aside. Then wind 176 ends for the pattern warp. It is advisable to make a cross at both ends of the patterned warp for reference during the tying. Tie the crosses and end loops. Transfer the pattern warp to a tying frame or other device – you could simply run a dowel rod through each end of the warp – and hold under tension. Spread the warp out so you can easily count and pick up the yarns. You will be tying by yarn count, following your cartoon on graph paper, not by the sett on the loom.

Tying the Resists. Next decide where you want your design to be positioned in the finished weaving, allowing, of course, for loom tie-on at both ends of the warp. Picking up the warp ends from the cross, count the ends and tie the resists according to your chart on the graph paper. (A note here: Sometimes I insert two lease sticks into the cross, and slide the sticks down as I tie. If you do this, be sure you put the ties of the cross back in their original position for use in sleying onto the loom.) Pick up and wrap the number of warp yarns that seems suitable; bundles of 8 to 12 ends would be about right for this yarn. Make your resist ties on the warp yarn only the length indicated on the graph. You will notice that some rows repeat, as does row 7; this wrap will be three times longer than row 6. As you look at your cartoon and Figure 23, you will see certain vertical resist areas, such as the center of the nose; these verticals may be tied in one long continuous wrap. This will reduce the number of ties and will also make better resists than series of small resist ties. Using your cartoon as a guide, combine as many vertical wraps as possible. After the resists are completed, dye the patterned warp. Remove the resist wraps.

Dressing the Loom. Add the selvage stripes to the patterned warp on the rod and tie onto the warp apron. Sley and dent from back to front. Dent the warp through the reed to weave at 36 e.p.i. Tie onto the cloth apron and weave, using a white weft yarn. The weave will be a warp rep, with 36 e.p.i. in the warp and about 8 picks per inch in the weft.

Figure 25. *(left)* Weft Ikat, Japan. *A narrow fabric with the "interlocking circles" pattern, ikatted in the* e-gasuri *technique, was carefully seamed to match the repeats for this* futon *(bed-covering) fabric from Kurayoshi. Collection, Yoshiko Wada.*

Figure 26. *(right)* Equipment. *Arranged in the picture at right are several articles you will need and some that are advantageous to have. On the left are balloons and raffia, both good resist-tying materials. Within the raffia coil are artist's canvas-stretcher bars, which can be used to build frames for ikatting. String is always handy to have. The rolls of plastic tape are some of the best tying material available. Adjacent are plastic wrap, dowels, C-clamps, metal braces, rulers, a brush and a jar of water-base paint for sketching designs.*

Chapter II

Equipment and Materials

Proper equipment is essential to the making of an ikat. Most of the devices you will need are very simple ones that a weaver would have anyway, but some are unique to this technique. Figure 26 shows a collection of materials discussed in this chapter.

Warp-Winding Devices

In the warm, humid air of India, much of the work of weaving takes place out under the trees. Figure 27 shows weavers from the village of Nuapatna, district of Cuttack, Orissa. Walking back and forth, the weaver winds the required length of warp between sturdy poles. Lightweight sticks hold the warp and also establish the cross. The warp for a fabric such as a sari 6 yards (5.5 meters) long is easily wound on this arrangement of poles and sticks, a method rather widely used throughout the world.

Also used in Orissa is a frame that looks much like our warping boards, except that it is placed flat on the ground rather than hung on a wall. The pegs around which the warp is wound are set a little more than a yard (one meter) apart, and the maximum length of the warp is about 12 yards (11 meters), or enough to weave two saris. The weaver sits on a low stool with the peg frame on the ground by her side. Folding and tying a warp this long requires an extraordinary amount of skill and patience.

Figure 28 shows a warping frame from Borneo (which you could adapt for winding and tying both warp and weft). The device has been described in several places as a loom-tying frame or an ikat frame. Actually, it is primarily a warping frame and secondly, with the warp remaining in place, a tying frame.

The frame is constructed from two long wooden rods held rigid by three cross braces, one at each end and one in the center. The two cross bars on which the warp is wound and tied are suspended from top and

Figure 27. Warp Winding in India. *A sari length is wound between sturdy poles out of doors, a widespread method of winding long warps.*

bottom braces by simple loops of material. (Notice the clever tightening arrangement on the loops at the bottom.) To use the frame to wind warp, you would connect the cross bars at either side with temporary loops of cord the exact length of your warp, then wind the warp in a continuous circle between the two cross bars. Notice how the group of warp yarns is divided at the lower center, and how the division coincides with a separation in the ikat pattern. The top and bottom layers of yarn can be tied as a unit for the ikat design. In Borneo, this continuous warp is transferred to a backtension loom for weaving. Your own contrivances for winding the warp (or weft) will vary according to the length and amount of yarn to be wound. A contemporary weaver usually has a warping board or a warping reel. These are by far the best warping devices because they not only hold the warp rigidly for an even tension, but in some instances they may be used to hold the warp or weft under tension while the resists are tied.

For special projects (~such as Projects 3 and 4, Chapter V), you can build a warping and tying frame from canvas stretchers and dowels, using as a guide the frame from Borneo (Figure 28). This type of frame, however, is useful only for short warps.

Weft-Winding Devices

The people of India have worked out three simple but highly functional weft-winding devices for fast, accurate work. In Figure 29 a villager from Jhilminda, district of Sambalpur, Orissa, works on a frame made in the following manner. Two steel spikes are driven into the ground at either end of a piece of wood cut to the length of the weft yarns. Attached to this dividing wooden bar is a second piece of wood into which several sticks have been set. The grouping of the weft yarn as it is wound around the upright sticks establishes crosses. Before removing the weft to the tying frame, lease cords are tied around all the crosses formed between upright sticks. A portable variation of this device is also used, with the spikes driven into a wooden frame instead of the earth. Figure 30 shows a semicircular frame used in the Indian village of Pochampalli and other places in the district of Andhra Pradesh. The weft yarn is wound in sequence from the single peg on one end to the peg on the semicircle. This portable frame has a tension-adjustment device: shims that are inserted under the cross bar of the warping-frame structure. Lease cords are tied in the cross before removing the weft to the tying frame.

From Finland comes a weft-winding and weft-tying device called an ikat stick, shown in Figure 31. It was also used in other Scandinavian countries. The carved and notched stick or rod is approximately a yard (meter) long with a diameter of about 1¼ in. (3 cm). The weft is wound around two sticks that protrude through the holes drilled in each end of the rod, and the resists are tied to coincide with the notches. Notches on each side of the rod are a little different in placement and measure, so that two different weft patterns can be tied on one rod. The sticks at the ends of the device are removable and additional holes for the sticks can be used to change the length of the weft skein.

For your own weft winding, any arrangement that will hold a specific length of weft taut and allow the skein to remain under tension for tying is all that

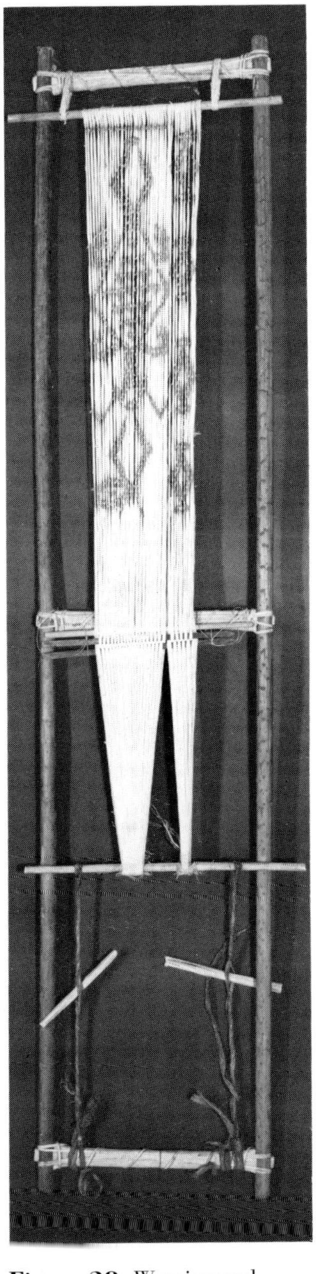

Figure 28. Warping and Tying Frame from Borneo. *Undyed warp yarn has been wound continuously around the two cross bars and resist ties for a design partially completed. The four lozenge shapes on the right represent birds; the crocodile is complete enough for us to see most of the design, though its tail is still to be finished.*

is necessary. Even winding your yarn on a niddy-noddy and then leaving it there while you tie the resists will work.

The easily made device shown in Figure 32 is one that I have found to be the most helpful and accurate in winding and tying weft skeins. Get two blocks of finished lumber, each 1½ x ¾ x 6 in. (4 x 2 x 15 cm). Drill a hole in each block to accommodate a 3⁄8 in. (1-cm) dowel, 6 in. (15 cm) long. Glue this dowel into the hole and then sand to remove any rough spots in the wood. Secure the blocks to the table with C-clamps. As you can see, the weft is wound between the two dowels and tied under tension. By adding another block, you can make a portable warping board as well. Take another block of finished lumber of similar measurement but 12 in. (30 cm) long, drill and insert three dowels, evenly spaced about 4 or 5 inches apart (10 to 12 cm). These three dowels are used to wind the cross in the warp. With C-clamps, attach both the weft and the warp blocks to a table at appropriate distances, and wind your warp.

Tying Frame

You won't always need to transfer your warp or weft to a special frame to make the ties. Most often, the resists can be tied right on the warping board or warping reel, or directly after winding the weft skein. However, in India, weavers transfer the weft and sometimes the warp to special tying frames.

Figure 33 shows a tying frame that you can make quite simply. Choose a piece of 2 x 4 (5 x 10 cm) lumber longer than the weft you wish to wind. Wrap the lumber with brown paper and drive a pair of finishing nails into one end; drive a similar pair of nails into the other end, so that the distance between the pairs of nails is precisely the length of your weft. By using two nails, you will leave room to tie cords around the loops before you take the weft off the frame. These ties help in straightening out the skein after it has been dyed. On the paper, you can mark just where you want to place your resists. Precise methods for calculating weft length and using this frame for tying the resists are discussed in Chapter III.

Figure 29. Weft-Winding Device, India. *This weaver from Orissa sits on a low stool to wind weft yarns around upright sticks on a frame between steel spikes. The sticks, which establish the crosses, will be replaced by lease cords before the weft is removed to a tying frame.*

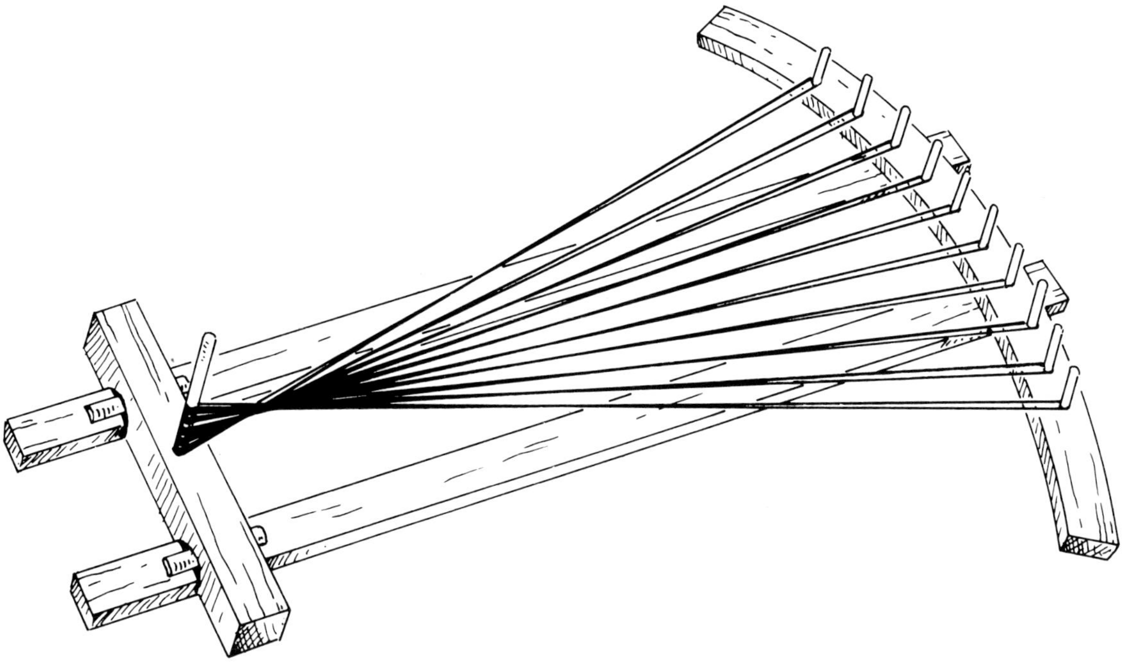

Figure 30. (top) Semicircular Weft-Winding Frame. *This unusual frame, also from India, is used in a manner similar to the device in Figure 26.*

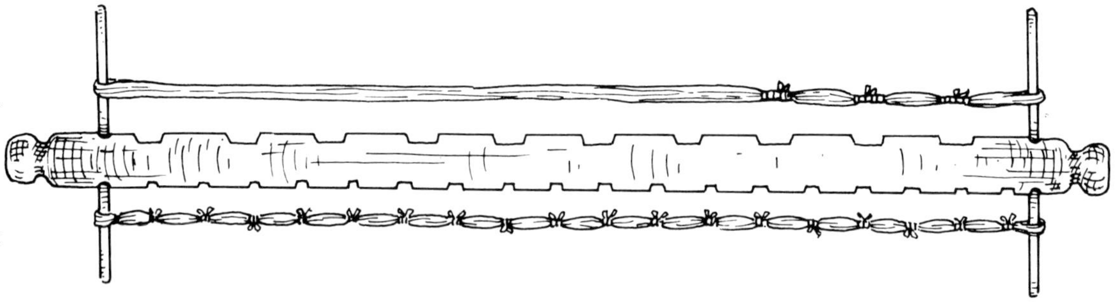

Figure 31. *(middle)* Ikat Stick. *An adaptation of this traditional Finnish weft-winding and -tying device, with carved notches to guide your tying, can be made easily.*

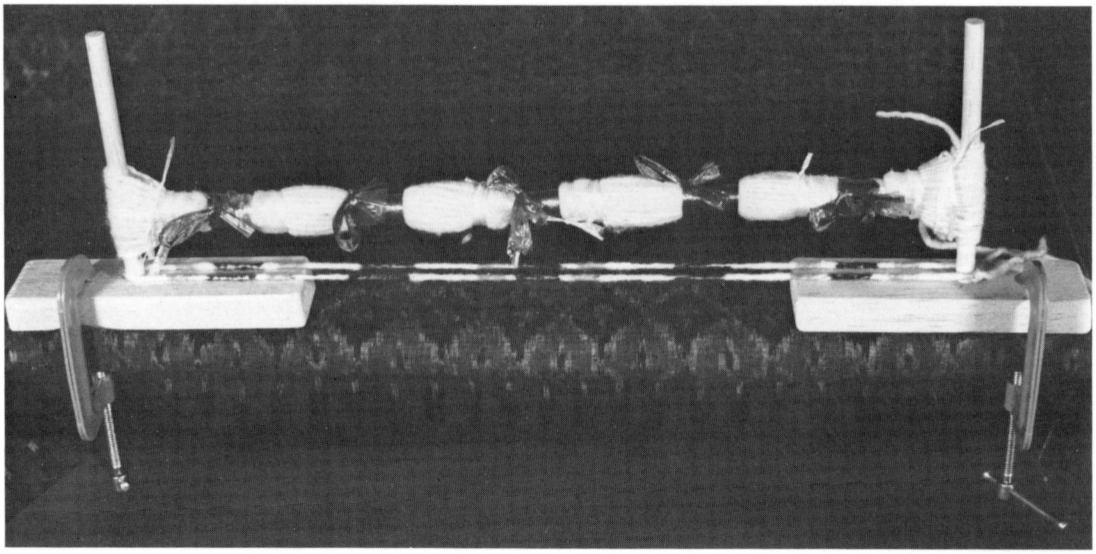

Figure 32. *(bottom)* Adjustable Weft-Winding Device. *Made with lumber and secured to a table with C-clamps, this frame is useful for both winding and then tying the weft. Its simple construction is an advantage.*

Resist-Tying Materials

Plastic tape manufactured in Japan and sold through suppliers in the United States is perhaps the best tying material of all for the resists. It comes in several colors, in rolls 2 in. (5 cm) wide and 610 yards (560 meters) long. While one roll lasts quite some time, it is helpful to have two or three rolls of different colors. Changing the color of the tie assists in designating a certain color sequence in dyeing. The plastic tape can be used as it comes off the roll or it can easily be torn lengthwise into narrower strips. Natural untreated raffia is comfortable to handle, and I have used it from time to time. But it is not as suitable as the plastic tape because the raffia does not overlap as easily. However, bast fibers were used as ties in many parts of the world (and are still used in some places today) before man-made materials were available. Balloons and rubber bands, wrapped and tied tightly, serve well for quick work if you do not have very many ties to make. They are good for short resists. But it is difficult to wrap a long resist with them and not have some dye seep between the bands. Plastic wrap from the grocery store, first wrapped around the yarn and then tied with string, works very well for longer resists. You can also take several strands of string bundled together and use these for resist tying. Just how many strands of string you will have to put together is something you will have to determine. Too few, or a single fine strand, would take too long to tie. One very heavy string does all right if it is just a short tie.

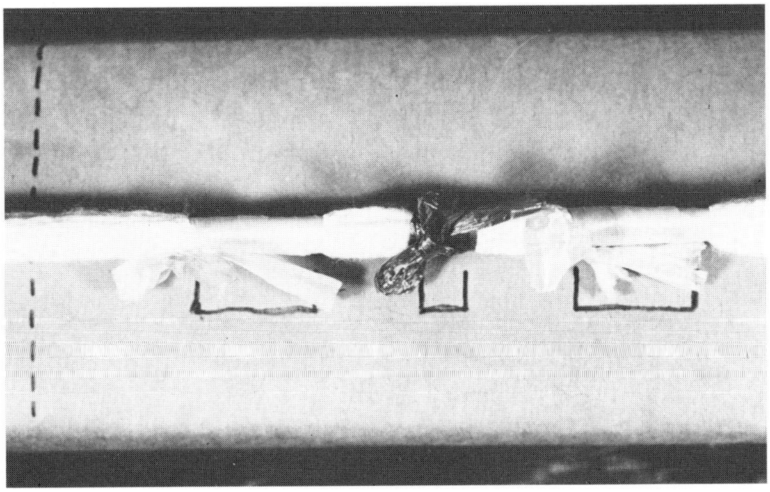

Figure 33. Weft-Skein Winder, 2 x 4 Lumber *(detail). Marks on the paper guide the placement of resist ties; the dotted line represents the center of the fabric.*

Yarn

The traditional ikats were woven with natural yarns such as cotton, linen, hemp, silk, wool and the bast fibers, such as raffia, banana fiber and abaca. They were chosen for their suitability to the end product and because they were available in the region where the ikats were woven. The modern fiber artist can use not only the traditional fibers but also a wide array of synthetics and blends.

Any yarn which is suitable for the techniques of weaving, knitting, crocheting or tatting may be ikatted. The bast fiber raffia, which takes natural dyes so beautifully, is a material that remains relatively unexplored in contemporary weaving. Ikatted yarn has also been successfully used in coil basketry. Let the nature of your end product be your guide in selecting an appropriate yarn (see the discussion of yarns in Chapter I), and select a dye that is compatible with the type of fiber you have chosen.

Dyes

There are many kinds of dyestuffs available, and each type has its own special properties. In choosing a dye for ikat, there are two main criteria to be considered. You will, of course, want to select a dye that works well on the kind of fiber you are using; books listed in the Bibliography provide detailed information on using both natural and commercial dyes, and the manufacturers instructions on dye packages explain how to use their products to best advantage. Secondly, some dyes are better for ikat than others, as dyes vary in the way the color is developed and fixed and in the amount of seepage under the resist ties.

Natural Dyes. Perhaps my first love is ikatting yarns of silk and handspun wool with natural dyes. These dyes are sometimes called vegetable dyes, a term that is not wholly correct, since they include, besides those from plant sources, the cochineal insect found on cactus plants in Mexico and the mollusk known for Tyrian purple, to name only two.

Natural dye materials can be gathered from plants or natural weaving supply shops. The beauty and richness of color of the natural dyes used in older ikats is an inspiration to try to obtain this quality in our own work. The more or less slow absorption of natural dye by the fiber is well suited to ikat.

Vat Dyes. Vat dyes give the sharpest and strongest resist patterns of all dyes, and they will dye a range of fibers, including cotton, wool, silk, linen and rayon. A major advantage of vat dyes is that the color is not fixed until the yarn is taken from the vat and oxygen in the air interacts with chemicals in the yarn. This reaction works only on the fiber exposed to air, thus protecting the resist. You can also blend and overdye beautifully with vat dyes. CIBA vat dyes in paste form are available in a beautiful range of colors, and I find that these plus a natural indigo vat dye and the CIBA Kiton dyes give me all the latitude I need. The CIBA Kiton dyes have worked very well for me on wool, silk and nylon.

Other Dyes. Procion and all the package dyes made from a Procion base are fiber-reactive dyes. Because of this, sometimes Procion will follow the fiber right along under the ties, ruining the resist. If you do use Procion, work fast and do not leave the yarn in the pot longer than necessary. My experiments with all-purpose package dyes purchased in grocery and variety stores have not been very satisfactory, and I do not recommend these dyes for ikat.

Inko dye has given me beautiful colors, and it is useful for spotting, but again I do not recommend it as a major dye for ikat. A colorless liquid that needs either sun or heat to develop the color, it works well on flat fabric surfaces, but it is difficult, with the sun method, to obtain good results on ikat. The sun does not easily penetrate the bundle of yarn between resist ties, and spreading the bundles out without disturbing the ties is difficult unless there are long stretches of color between the ties. Developing Inko color with heat also has its drawbacks, as too much heat may affect the plastic resist ties. If you do experiment with Inko dye, try to use a resist-tying material other than plastic, and develop the color with heat.

Dyeing Supplies

Equipment for dyeing need not be complicated or expensive — simple household items will usually do. For ikat, the following basic dyeing supplies will probably be sufficient:

- Two large 4- to 6-gallon (15- to 20-liter) canning kettles with lids; all kettles and pots should be made of enamel, stainless steel or glass, not aluminum or cast iron
- Two smaller 2- or 3-quart (2- or 3-liter) pots with lids
- Stirring rods made of glass, plastic or wood
- Measuring cups and measuring spoons of plastic, stainless steel or glass
- A small 4- or 8-ounce (approximately 100- to 300-gram) balance scale of the type sold by dye suppliers and health food stores
- A thermometer made of glass that registers as low as 100° F (38° C)
- Assorted plastic dishpans or buckets to wash and soak yarns
- A plastic colander for straining natural dyestuffs and draining yarns after the dye bath
- Rubber gloves
- A stove

A few general comments on dyeing equipment and procedures are needed here. You will notice that I recommend using kettles and dyepots made of non-reactive materials such as enamel, stainless steel or glass. If you were to use kettles made of aluminum, iron or tin, the metal would react chemically with the dye materials and alter the color. Using nonreactive materials prevents this added chemical action. In handling all dyes and chemicals, it is important to protect yourself and others. The first rule is to use utensils reserved only for dyeing; do not use any that are also used for the preparation and storage of food. It is advisable to work in a well-ventilated room or outdoors. Wear rubber gloves if you put your hands in any chemical liquids – remember that natural dyes are chemicals too – and a face mask to prevent your inhaling any fine powders. Generally speaking, all dyeing procedures are completely safe if a reasonable degree of precaution is taken.

Figure 34. *(left)* Picture Ikat, Japan *(detail). This charming sparrow, made in the* e-gasuri *technique, shows how successfully line drawing can be translated into an ikat weaving, It is made of cotton, resist dyed in indigo. Collection, Yoshiko Wada.*

Figure 35. *(below) Barbara Shapiro,* African Strip Weaving.

Figure 36. *(left)* Brushing and Drying the Warp, Bali. *The continuous warp for a* geringsing *double ikat has been dyed, and the weaver has inserted a barge roller to separate the yarns and a smaller one at the bottom to weight them. After brushing and aligning the wet yarns, she will leave the warp to dry under tension.*

Figure 37. *(right)* Warp Preparation in India. *Weavers from the village of Kuntpal in Orissa, India, take great care to maintain the Cross throughout the warping process and keep the warp yarns in meticulous order. The man on the right is shouldering a brush which he will use to straighten out the yarns after the sized warp has been stretched under tension.*

Chapter III

Methods

Many of the methods discussed here are only reflections of good weaving habits. But in ikat, attention to such fundamentals is essential if you are to achieve the results you desire.

Warping for Warp Ikat

For the most part, warping for ikat is no different than for any other weaving, and you can use the method you are most comfortable with. At a few places in the process, however, it is important to follow certain procedures that will prepare the warp for ikatting at a later stage.

Winding the Warp. Figure the length of your warp as you would for any other weaving, including extra length for loom waste and takeup. Wind it in the manner you are most accustomed to using. Accurate counting of warp ends and an absolutely perfect cross are even more essential in warp ikat than in normal weaving. In Figure 37, showing weavers in the Indian village of Kuntpal, observe the great attention given to the maintenance of the cross in the warp. Some weavers feel the need to have a cross at both ends of the warp. If that is most comfortable for you, that is the method you should employ. I use a single cross, and that is the method described here. Work with an even tension on the yarn while winding the warp and use a counting string to keep track of the number of warp yarns wound. Frequently you will divide your warp into sections and wind it in separate bundles that will be treated differently in the tying and dyeing stages.

Tying the Cross. Before removing the warp from the warping board or reel, the cross and the uncut loops at both ends of the warp should be tied. When doing ikat, it is best to make these ties long enough to function as lease cords when you dress the loom, so that the cross is maintained. For your lease cord, use a piece of string a different color from your warp and one that will not bleed onto your yarn during the dyeing, as this tie

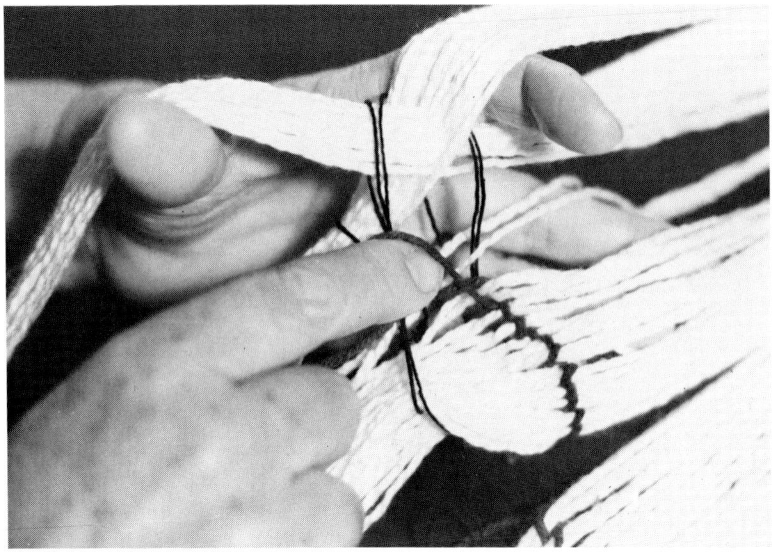

Figure 38. Twining. *The thumb and index finger of the left hand open the cross in the warp, and the right hand works the twining cord. Two warp yarns are picked up, one from the top and one from the bottom of the cross, and caught within each twist of the twining cord.*

will remain in your warp until you put it on the loom. Make the string long enough to allow you to spread your warp flat when you wrap the resists. Tie the ends of the string together, then make a soft finger-chain loop (later to be released) in the string near the cross. It is important in ikat to leave the loops at each end of the warp uncut so that dowels can be inserted to manipulate the warp when you tie the resists. Here, too, it is best to make the holding strings that go through these loops of a generous length.

Twining. The cross, of course, separates your warp end-by-end, but you will rarely tie an ikat resist on a single end. You need to divide the warp into sections, each containing several warp ends. Twining is the traditional and best method of doing this.

The number of ends caught in each twist of the twining cord is usually one warp end from the top and one from the bottom of the cross, but this is arbitrary and depends on your ikat design. Also, you will normally twine across only the section of the warp that will be tied for resists.

Frequently, you will leave the twining cord in the warp when it is dyed, and it will form a faint line where the yarn beneath resists the dye. Your row of twining should therefore be placed as close to the end of the warp as possible, so it won't interfere with your ikat pattern.

If you are not familiar with the process of twining, experiment as follows: For righthanded people (reverse the process if you are lefthanded), hold the warp at the cross in your left hand (Figure 38). Open the cross and place the thumb of your left hand on one side of the cross and your index finger on the other side of the cross as shown in this picture. Do not remove the cord holding the cross. In your right hand, take a twining cord folded in half of a contrasting color that won't fade in the dyeing. Work from right to left. Pass one end of the cord over the top of the first two warp yarns (one warp end from the top of the cross and one warp end from the bottom); pass the second end of the cord under the paired warp ends. Slide the two warp yarns along the twining cord to the right. Now give the two ends of the twining cord a twist so the cord on the bottom becomes the top cord, and the top cord moves to the bottom, reversing their original positions. Always twist the cord in the same direction. As you work, each pair of warp ends will be encircled between each twist of the twining cord. Continue across the warp, picking up two warp ends from the cross and twisting the twining cord once between each pair of warp ends. Tie the twining cords together when you have finished working across the width of the warp.

Although the yarn is usually held in the hand while twining, it is also possible to twine when the warp is under tension on the tying frame.

Calculating Weft Length for Weft Ikat

Since the positioning of the weft is crucial in weaving weft ikats, in order to bring out the design, the length of the weft and the placement of the resists must be calculated before the yarn is tied and dyed. While estimating the length of the weft is unique to certain ikat methods and will be dealt with in greater detail as it comes up in specific projects, here are two methods that can be adapted for most weft ikats.

Estimating. One way to calculate your weft is to simply add to the planned width of your fabric the amount you estimate will be taken up by shrinkage during dyeing, plus the takeup in weaving and enough for the shifting weft (if you are doing this weft technique).

Determining the X Measurement. Perhaps a more precise way is to adapt the Japanese method of calculating the width of the weft, called the X measurement. To do this, put your warp on the loom ready for weaving. Size all your weft yarn and dry under tension. Allow at least four or five hours to thoroughly dry the yarn; overnight is best. Now load a shuttle with undyed weft yarn and weave at least 3 in. (8 cm), or until you have established the beat and true weaving width you will use later in weaving your piece. (You may want to go on and weave the entire shuttle in order to determine how far one full shuttle will weave.)

Count the number of picks per inch and record this in your notebook. With a water-soluble felt-tip pen, mark the weft yarn as it turns at the selvage for 5 to 8 picks, to indicate the length of each weft shot. Unweave this weft and measure under tension as follows: Mount graph paper on a Celotex board and stick a heavy-duty pin on one of the lines of the paper. Wrap the end of the weft around this pin until you reach the first mark. Use a tension equal to winding the weft skein and stretch the weft in a straight line across the graph paper until you reach the second mark. Insert a pin so that this mark is on the outer edge of the pin. Wind the weft several times between the pins, making sure the marks line up exactly. Measure the distance between the pins to get your X measurement, or the amount of yarn needed for each shot of weft in order to get the finished weaving width you want. Many things will influence this measurement: the weight of the yarn used, the number of dents in the reed, the width of the weaving, tension on the warp, and, of course, the weaver.

Tying the Resists

Particular methods of designing for ikat, charting the design and transferring it to the yarns for wrapping are explored in Chapter I and in the projects throughout this book. However, the basic principle of wrapping the resists is the same for every ikat method: You wrap to prevent the dye from penetrating the yarn under the tied area; therefore, for your design to emerge as you have planned it, you must wrap and tie accurately and tightly.

The yarn is *always* held under tension during tying. This applies to both warp and weft. You can nearly always leave the warp on the warping board or reel as you tie, eliminating the need for a separate tension device. An ikat weft can be both wound and tied under tension on a weft-winding frame. Here is a good rule of thumb to follow in winding skeins for weft resists: The closer together the resists are to be tied, the thinner your skein should be; the wider the spaces between resists, the thicker the skein may be.

The Japanese Method. Figures 39 through 42 on page 38 illustrate the Japanese manner of wrapping and tying resists that Yoshiko Wada introduced to me. It is the method I use most frequently. Cut a length of plastic tape. It needs to be long enough to wrap and tie the section you are working on, but too long a piece is apt to be cumbersome and awkward. After you have wrapped several sample ties, you will be able to judge the length of tying material you will need for each resist.

Hold about one third of the tape in your left hand (reverse the directions if you are lefthanded) as shown in Figure 39. This tape should be at least 3 in. (8 cm) longer than the length of the wrapping area. If your wrap is going to be 2 in. (5 cm) or longer, wrap the plastic tape held in your left hand in a spiral flatly around the area to be resisted, to give you added insurance in covering the yarn. The longer end (in your right hand) is the working end; bring it under the yarn toward you, at the same time clasping the tape in your left hand very firmly to the yarn.

Wrap the working end up and away from you as shown in Figure 40, pulling it tightly each time you wind around, and let the tape overlap with each turn around the yarn. Always wrap toward your left hand. When you have wrapped the area to be resisted, make a couple of turns more with the tape, pulling very firmly each time. The finished wrap must have a hard feel, not soft and spongy. On the last wrap of the working end, catch your left thumb in the wrapping; bring the tape around your thumb in a clockwise direction, completely encircling its tip (see Figure 41). Hold this last loop down with your left thumb as you complete the next step. With your right hand, reach behind your left thumb and pull the beginning end of the tape firmly from left to right. Fold it into a loop and, with

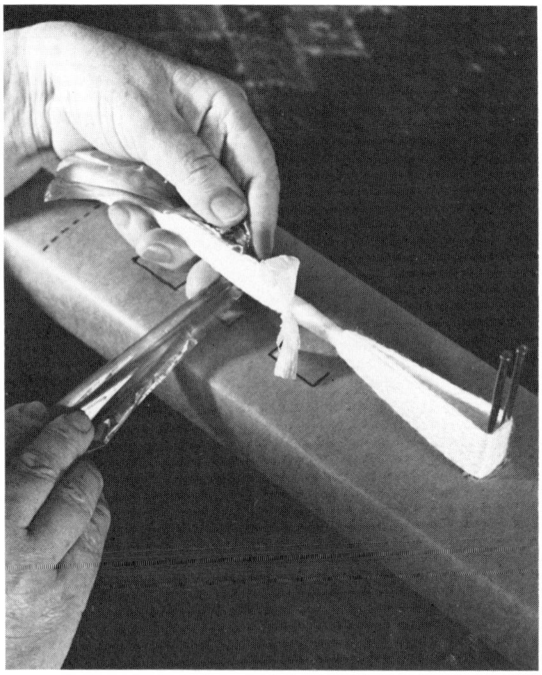

Figure 39. Japanese Method of Tying Resists, Step 1. *To begin, hold one end of the plastic tape firmly to the yarn with your left hand. Pull the working end, in your right hand, under the yarn and toward you.*

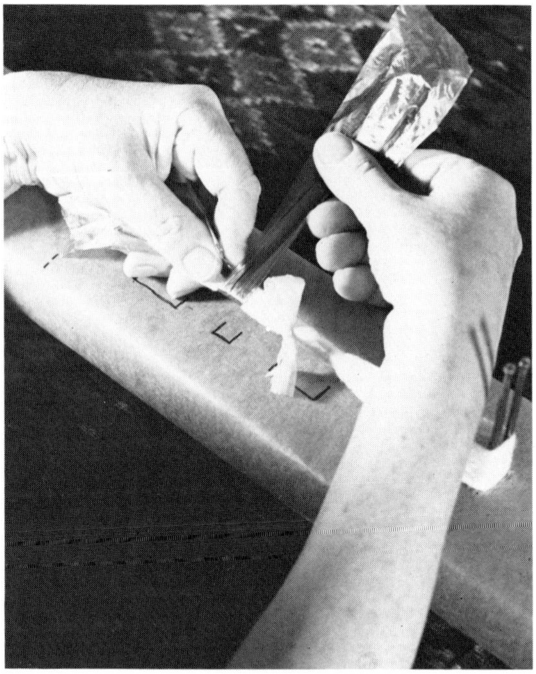

Figure 40. Step 2, Wrapping. *Next, wrap the working end of the tape up and over the yarn, away from you. Continue wrapping for the length of the resist.*

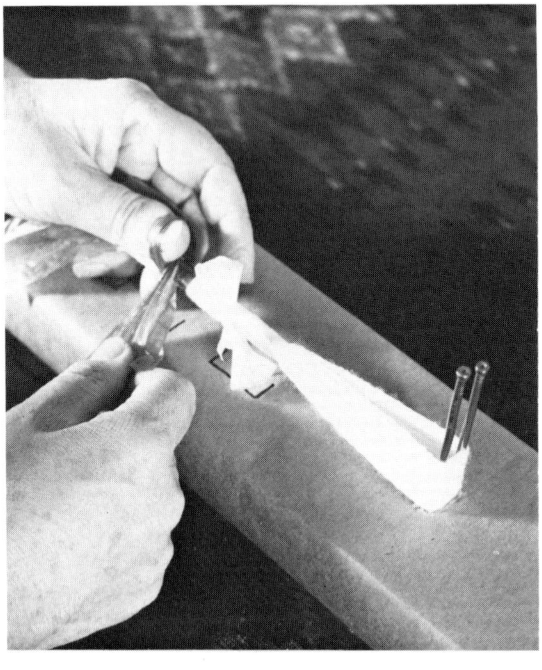

Figure 41. Step 3, Beginning the Knot. *On the last wrap, encircle your thumb with the working end.*

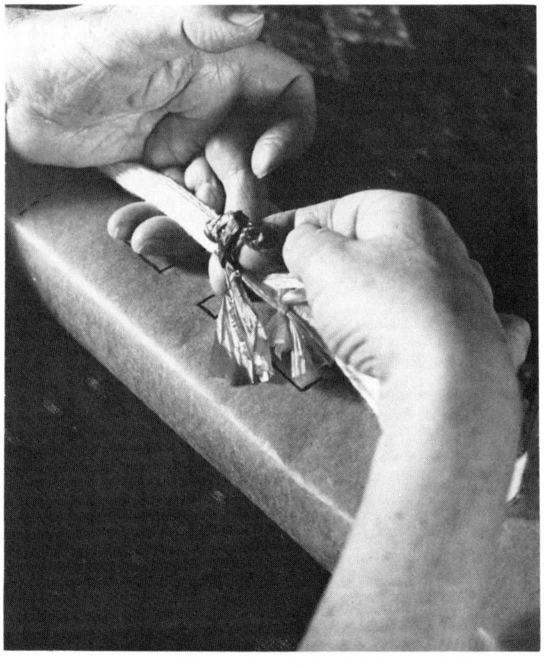

Figure 42. Step 4, Completing the Knot. *Make a second loop with the beginning end and push it through the loop on your left thumb to make half a bow knot. Pull down sharply on the working end to tighten the knot.*

your right index finger, push this loop through the loop on your left thumb. Hold this second loop with your left hand as you give a sharp tug on the working end to secure the knot. When finished, you will have a tight half-bow that you can untie quickly after you have dyed the yarn (see Figure 42). Cut the end forming the loop short, about ¼ to ⅜ in. (0.7 to 1 cm) long. Cut the working end a little longer (about ½ in., or 1.3 cm), so there is a noticeable difference in length between the two ends. After you have completed the dyeing, a quick tug on the shorter end will release the knot. This knot is much quicker to untie than a square knot and is especially useful when you have many tied resists.

When you use this plastic tape, you can shrink and tighten the wraps further before dyeing, by putting the resist-tied yarn in cool water and bringing the water to a simmer for ten minutes. With wool yarn, of course, you would skip this simmering to shrink the wrap.

An Indonesian Method. Figure 43 shows a detail of an Indonesian silk weft tied and ready for dyeing. A square knot has been used, and the plastic tape has been torn to a width of approximately 3/16 in. (0.5 cm) to facilitate the fine tying.

Long Resists. Another method of wrapping has been developed in several parts of the world to simplify the work of tying long resists. In Orissa, India, the kya leaf is neatly cut and wrapped around the yarn and the ends are then tightly tied with thread. A similar method combining a leaf and ties is used in Japan. Figure 44 illustrates a very useful adaptation of this traditional method for long resists, say from 3 to 8 in. (8 to 20 cm). First wrap several layers of plastic wrap around the yarn, making sure to use plastic that won't melt in the heat of the dyepot. Plastic bags or the plastic wrap that is sold in grocery stores will do very well, and the latter clings nicely as you wrap several layers around the yarn. The plastic bags used for freezing and cooking food right in t he bag are another choice, and are sure to withstand the heat of the dyepot. Either slit the bottom of the bag open and slip the bag over the folded skein of yarn and tie, or slit the bottom and one side and wrap the bag several times around the yarn before you tie it with string. When you have wrapped the plastic material around the yarn, fold a length of string in half and make a larkshead knot around the plastic and yarn at the start of the resist. Tighten the string and wind it tightly for about ½ to ¾ in. (1 or 2 cm) at the beginning of the resist. Then space the wrapping more widely but wrap tightly, until you reach the other end of the resist. Finish off with the same tight band of wrapping as at the start, tie and cut the string ends.

Dyeing Procedures

Prof. Alfred Bühler has condensed some of the most pertinent information on primal dyeing in his article, "Dyeing Among Primitive Peoples" (*CIBA Review* No. 68). This background material, which includes numerous source references, will interest the serious student of the subject and provide a deeper understanding of the dyeing methods used in traditional ikats. There is also much excellent material currently available on contemporary fiber dyeing, and so the subject is covered here only as it relates to the ikat technique.

Preparing the Yarn. Yarn should be cleansed before dyeing, since any kind of grease or dirt will repel the dye. For washing wool yarn, I recommend a mild liquid detergent because after rinsing a detergent will not leave a residue. Soap is apt to leave a soap curd in the wool, and this may show up in spotty dye absorption. When washing wool yarn, have an even temperature in the wash and rinse baths to prevent shrinking the yarn. Cotton yarn is tied into skeins and put in a hot bath of a small amount of soap flakes and washing soda (¼ cup [60 ml] each of soap and soda per pound [0.5 kg] of cotton yarn). Boil it in the soapy solution 20 minutes, rinse and dry. This also preshrinks the cotton yarn. This is particularly necessary for white or natural cotton yarn. An already dyed cotton yarn can be presumed to be clean and preshrunk.

Dyeing. Once the resists have been tied, dyeing procedures are the same as for any yarn dyeing, and vary according to the type of yarn and dye material used.

Rinsing. As soon as you remove the yarn from the dyepot, rinse out as much of the excess dye as possible to prevent crocking (a rubbing off of the excess dye not absorbed into the yarn). Remove the resist ties, and lightly wash the yarn again to clean

Figure 43. An Indonesian Method of Tying Resists. *Square knots have been used to tie the weft pattern for this contemporary silk piece from Java. Note how the twining across the weft was used to separate the yarns into groups for tying. Collection, Lydia Van Gelder.*

and fluff the yarn that has been under the ties. If you are going to size the yarn, do so at this time; then dry under tension (suspend the warp or weft skeins with weights in some manner so they are taut while drying).

Sizing. It may seem bothersome, after all the work done up to this point, but you will find it most essential to size the warp and, in some projects, the weft. The weaving really goes along much more

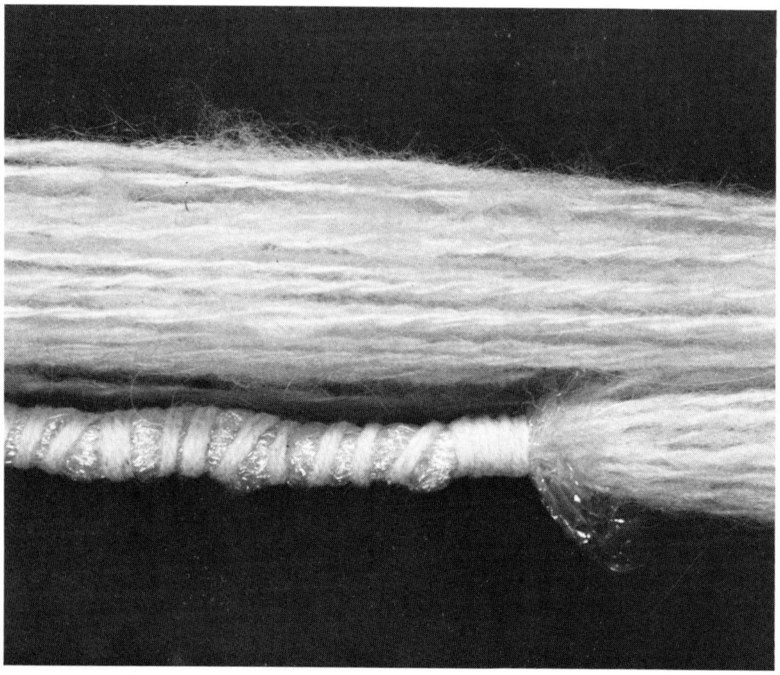

Figure 44. Tying Long Resists. *Grocery-store plastic wrap, tightly tied with string, works well for longer resists.*

nicely if the yarn is sized because there is less play or shifting of the yarn.

Figure 45 shows sizing being done in the village of Jhilminda, district of Sambalpur, Orissa, India. The yarn is sopped in a vessel containing a thin solution of rice starch and water, the starch liquid is squeezed out and the warp is stretched out tightly. This man is brushing the warp to straighten the yarn. When it is dry, the warp will be taken to the loom. The Japanese use a thin mixture of ogre starch, water, wheat flour, and a few drops of vegetable oil to size the warp as well as the weft. (Ogre starch, recipe and instructions are available from the Kasuri Dye Works [see Suppliers List].)

A dilute animal glue solution works well on wool (if your local craft store does not stock this type of glue, see the Suppliers List for sources). Linen does best with a sizing of boiled flaxseed which has been strained and thinned with water. For cotton, I have used a liquid household starch (purchased in the grocery store), diluted about half with water. A thin solution of paperhanger's wheat paste (obtained at a paint store) also works well on cotton and wool. No matter what sizing you are working with, the warp or weft is soaked in the solution and then squeezed to remove the excess liquid. It is always dried under a little tension with the individual yarns more or less neatly in place. When dry, the warp is ready to be put on the loom. After the weaving is completed, you may wish to wash the fabric to remove the sizing, especially if you intend to wash the fabric as part of its normal care.

Special Effects. Many interesting results can be achieved during the dyeing process with multiple wrappings, overdyeing and spot dyeing.

With multiple wrappings, a technique used frequently in traditional ikat, you can get several tonal variations from a single dyebath. You might plan a piece, for instance, with an ikat design of light blue and white on an indigo background. In tying the resists, you would use one color of plastic tape to wrap the white sections and a second color of tape for the

Figure 45. *(above)* Sizing the Warp in India. *This man is brushing the warp yarns, wet with sizing, to untangle and straighten them.*

Figure 46. *(left)* Dyeing the Yarn, India. *This dyer's sari has a border of ikat.*

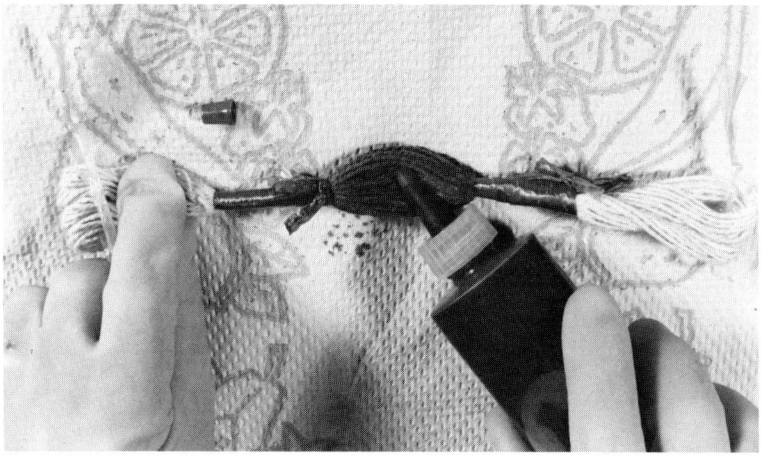

Figure 47. Spot-Dye Method. *This is a convenient way to apply dye if you want only small areas of color against a white background.*

light blue sections. All the yarn would then be dipped in indigo and exposed to the air several times to develop the dark background color. When the background was almost as deep a tone as you wanted it, you would remove the resists wrapped in the second color of tape and then put everything back in the dyebath once or twice, until you had the right shade of light blue. Traditional Sumbanese ikats are often dyed in this way.

More complex mixtures of color can be obtained by adding overdyeing to the process. For a four-color piece, three of the four colors could be tied for resisting as just described. You might first dye the piece in red and then unwrap the sections slated to be dark blue, and wrap over those sections you wanted to remain red. A few dips in indigo would develop the dark blue sections and create a deep-toned background where the indigo overdyed the red yarn. Finally, the sections marked for light blue would be unwrapped and the whole dipped again in indigo. The white areas that had remained wrapped throughout the dyeing would add a fourth color to the final piece.

A more contemporary approach to tonal variation is the one I used in a weft ikat dyed in two colors. I wrapped some sections of the resist rather loosely, so that a little dye would seep under the tie. With practice, you can control the amount of dye penetrating these sections.

To become familiar with the possibilities, try this experiment. Tie a weft skein in five different places and dye it yellow. Remove the wrappings from two of the resist parts and wrap off a section of the yellow just dyed. Allow the skein to dry, then dye the skein blue. When all the wraps have been removed, you will have a skein that shows the original white plus areas of yellow, blue and green. If you started with a colored yarn instead of white, your palette would, of course, be still different.

I have had a lot of fun playing around with two research projects involving spot dyeing of small areas, a technique used in parts of India and Japan. In India, they either spoon on the dye or dip-dye small sections between ties to get a beautiful multicolor weft.

My spot-dye method is shown in Figure 47. I apply Procion (3 tsp.), mixed with salt (2 Tbsp.) and warm water in a squirt bottle, to cotton yarn which has previously been tied and then saturated with a washing soda solution (about ½ cup [120 ml] soda to 1 gallon [4 liters] of water) and dried. First I dry the skein and then, while holding the undyed parts of the skein, I wash only the dyed spots in hot soapy water; I rinse these spots and remove the ties. When this weft is woven, I have spots of color against a white ground. This spot-dyeing technique can also be carried out in multicolors. Using natural dyes, I applied successive solutions of iron (3 Tbsp. ferrous sulphate to 1 cup [240 ml] of hot water), tannic acid powder (3 Tbsp. to 1 cup [240 ml] of hot water) and washing soda (½ cup [120 ml] soda to 1 gallon [4 liters of water) to cotton yarn. First I wound the yarn and tied the resists. Next I soaked the yarn in the washing-soda solution and let it dry. Then I dabbed on a solution of tannic acid, then iron and finally, iron on top of the tannic-acid spots. The reaction with the washing soda gave me these results: the tannic acid alone resulted in a light celery green; the iron alone gave a good, rich medium brown; and the iron over the tannic acid created an intense, dark brownish purple. All the colors sun-tested very well in ten days of California sun. They have the richness I admire in natural dyes.

Figure 48. *(right)* Double ikat, silk. *Probably from Patola region, India.*

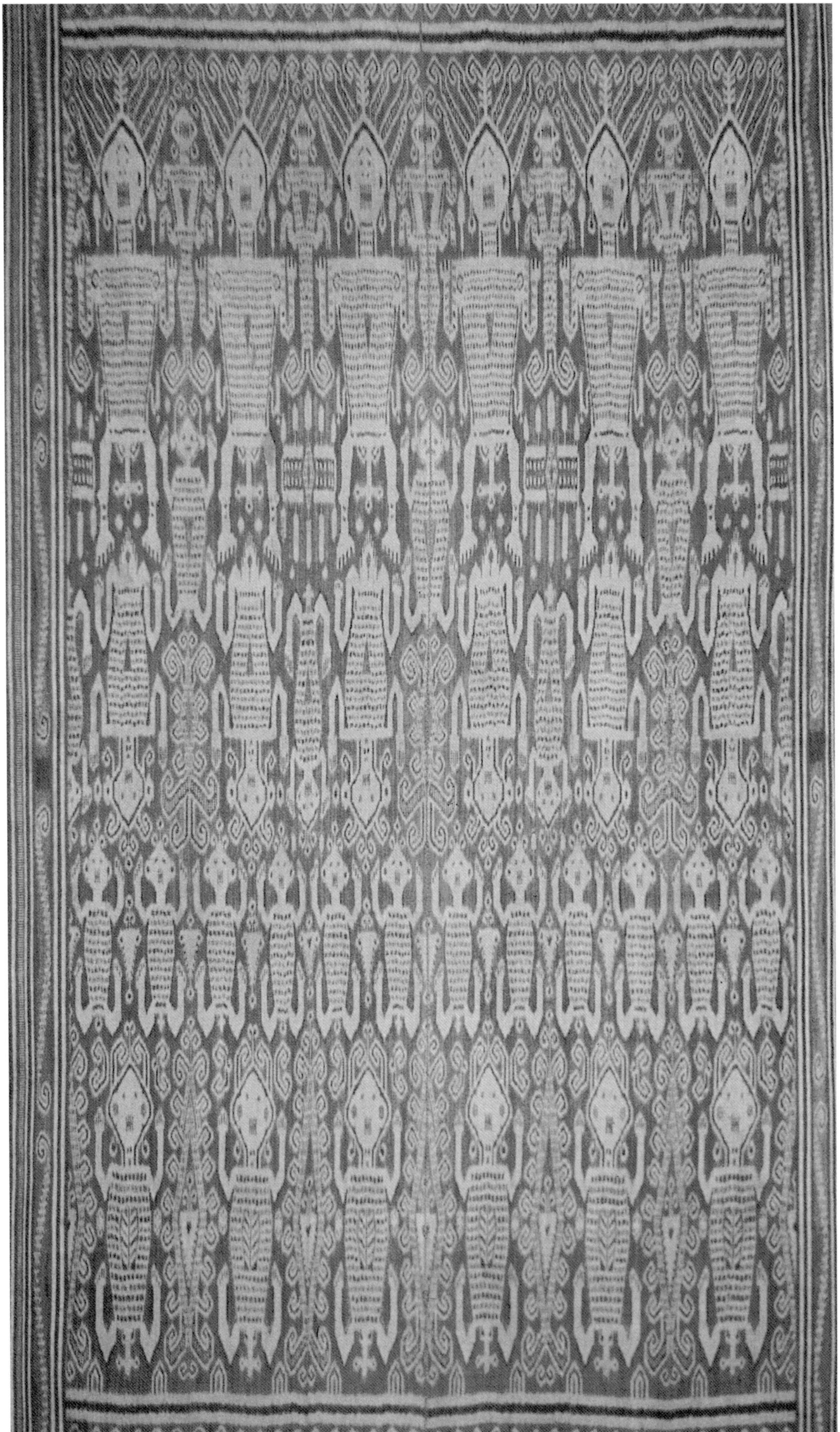

Figure 49. *(left)* Sea Dayak, Sarawak, Borneo. *This ceremonial hanging is an elaborate example of warp-ikat patterning. 102 x 49 in. (259 x 125 cm). Collection, Dr. Sarah Gill.*

Figure 50. *(right)* Prayer Rug, Turkestan. *The silk warp pile carries the ikat resists. The cypress tree under a prayer arch is a recurring design in these rugs, which exhibit beautiful, precise craftsmanship.*

Chapter IV

Warp Ikat

Since the warp of a primitive backtension loom is structurally a major part of that loom, it is not surprising that the patterning of the warp, rather than the weft, has received the greatest attention and development from earliest times, and that warp ikat is, even today, the most common of the four types of ikat. It is also true that once the warp yarns have an ikat pattern, it is a fairly simple matter to weave the fabric, whereas weft ikat requires greater skill during weaving. Figures 49 through 50 illustrate a selection of warp ikats from various world ikat centers.

Ikat has reached its highest development in Asia (Central and Southeast Asia, India, the Middle and Near East). In her research and writings, Dr. Renée Boser-Sarivaxévanis has traced the development of ikat techniques in Africa. There, ikat is practiced in only one small area on the western edge of the continent, south of the Sahara. Dr. Boser's hypothesis is that there may have been Asian craftsmen among the people returning to Mali after the pilgrimage to Mecca in A.D. 1324-35 of the Manding king, Kango Moussa, and that they introduced warp-ikat techniques to the Dyula. The Dyula transmitted the methods to a group of the Baule and the Yoruba of southern Nigeria, and the Yoruba, in turn, introduced a simple form of ikat to a small fraction of the Nigerian people. Only warp ikat is practiced by these African groups. Nowadays the Dyula people of Upper Volta produce ikat textiles almost exclusively on order and you rarely see them in the markets. In the Ivory Coast, however, the demand for these expensive cloths is much broader. They have been adopted as official and festive vestments by Baule chiefs and the well-to-do, but the Baule ikat dyers and weavers have also been able to commercialize them on a larger scale. Figure 51 shows a detail of a Dyula warp ikat.

In Europe, the very fine silk taffeta chiné in Figure 53 was woven in Lyon, France, during the Louis XV period; the floral motifs against a creamy white background are bolder than later French silks. An incredibly

Figure 51. Woman's Wrapper, Dyula *(detail). Ikat blocks, divided by a characteristic red stripe, form the all-over chessboard pattern of this fabric from the Upper Volta. The dark patterned border on the left was woven separately in long strips.*

fine silk velvet warp-ikat prayer rug from Turkestan is shown in Figure 50. These rugs were so expensive to weave that they were reserved for only the most affluent. They are presumed to have been woven only in Iran, Turkey, western Europe and Turkestan. This prayer rug uses silk in the ground and pile warps, has a cotton weft and is woven in a 3/1 twill. A deep wine-red background sets off green cypress trees. Blue, red, green and the natural color of the silk are used in the borders.

Among the hill tribe Karen, who live in highland Southeast Asia (Burma and northern Thailand), married women wear red cotton sarongs with warp-ikat stripes. The fabric for these is woven in two strips that are sewn together at the selvage. The two ends are then sewn together to make a tube skirt, with the vertical warp stripe now running horizontally. In the detail of a sarong shown in Figure 52, notice how the white resist stripes are interrupted by two yarns resisted only at the beginning and end of the motif, allowing the dye to penetrate in the middle. This unit was combined to make a larger motif, a method that can be easily adapted for contemporary weaving.

The Sea Dayak hanging from Borneo, shown in Figure 49, combines design elements of carved figures, lozenges, bamboo shoots and rotan leaves. The Sarawak people, ordinarily very shy about their person, produced this ikat depicting the male (with penis bones) and female figures in positions of copulation.

In Indonesia, many different types of ikat are still being produced, among them the very famous East Sumba warp ikats which are discussed in Projects 3 and 4.

Bold warp-ikat patterns like the one in Figure 54 are woven in the ponchos of Bolivia, Peru and Ecuador. The indigo and white warp-ikat shawls of northern Peru and Ecuador are made of cotton; generally speaking, they carry a small allover design, usually resembling tiny flowers. They are distinguished by a very long, elaborately knotted white fringe, usually starched. The fringe is kept out of the dyepot and extra undyed yarn is added to the warp ends to make a substantial fringe.

Mention must be made of the warp ikats woven with bast fibers, such as the abaca fiber woven into fabric by the T'boli tribe in the mountain regions of southern Mindanao in the Philippines. Also notable are the fast-disappearing raffia weavings from the island of Madagascar, off the coast of Mozambique, Africa. It is possible that the designs in these weavings were influenced by the Yemen people from the north or by other peoples they may have traded with long ago. These long, narrow raffia cloths are woven on a horizontal continuous-warp loom with a fixed heddle, similar to the type used in adjacent Africa.

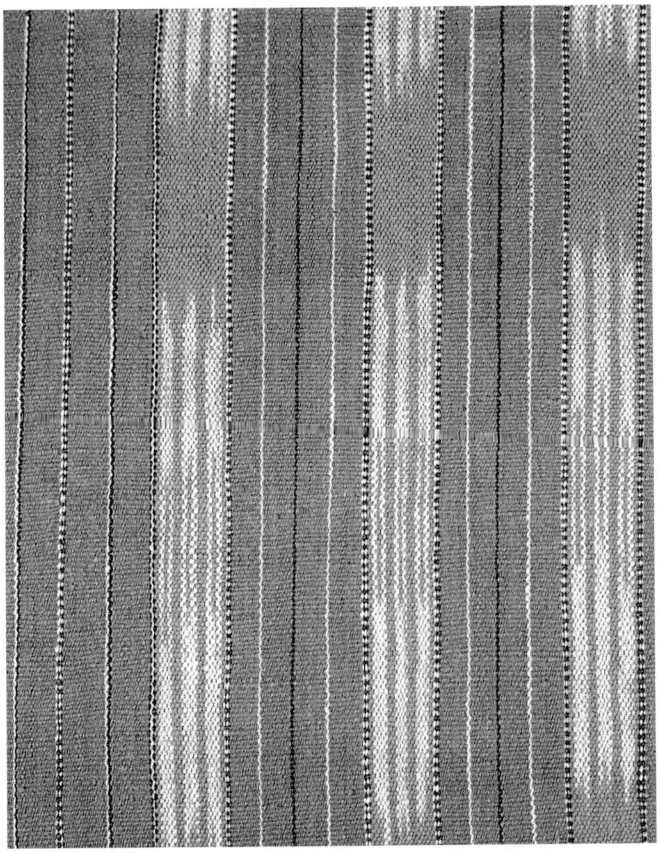

Figure 52. *(left)* Sarong Fabric, Karen, Southeast Asia *(detail). This skirt is worn pulled across the back, folded in front and tucked in at the waist. The fabric suggests design possibilities for contemporary warp ikats, particularly in the way the white resists have been handled. Collection, Lydia Van Gelder.*

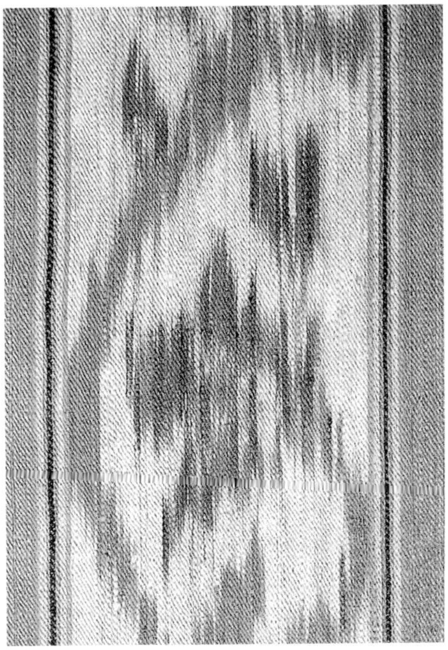

Figure 53. *(right)* Silk Taffeta, France *(detail). This chiné fabric exemplifies the floral patterns popular during the Louis XV period. The warp-faced weave accentuates the design of the warp ikat.*

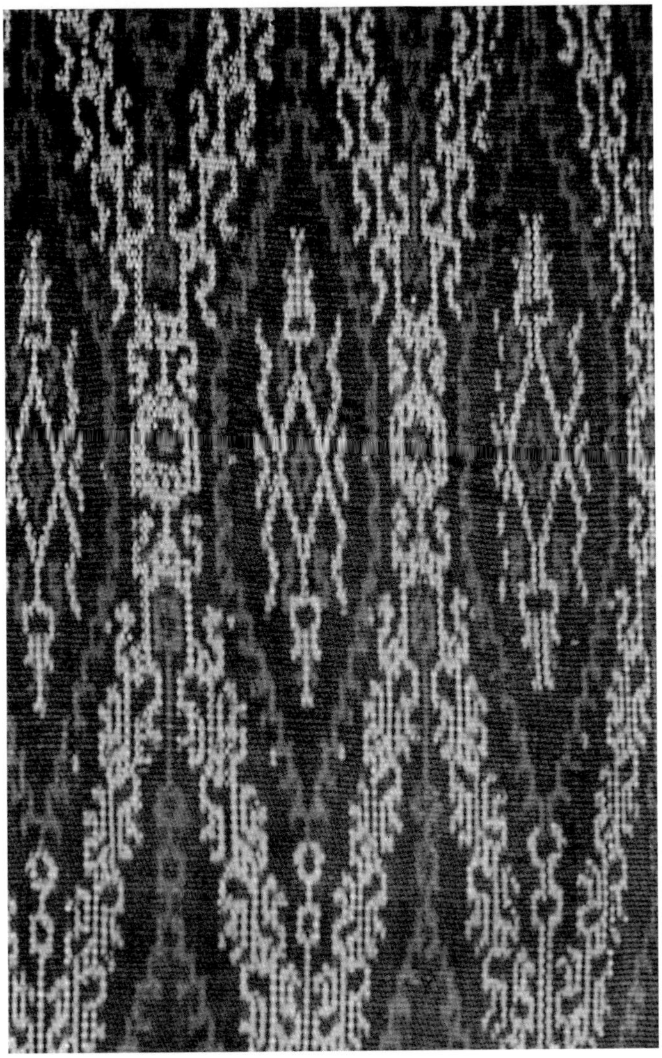

Figure 54. *(left)* Warp Ikat, Philippines. *The T'boli people of southern Mindanao use abaca fiber for elaborately patterned ikats like this one. However, the abaca fiber requires such extensive preparations in order to be suitable for weaving that these highly prized fabrics are usually reserved for bridal-gift exchanges and ceremonial occasions. Collection, Lydia Van Gelder.*

Figure 55. *(below)* Poncho, Peru *(detail). A stylized step design borders this poncho on two sides; the band of alpaca fringe was woven separately and then sewn around all four sides of the completed poncho. Collection, Janet Van Gelder.*

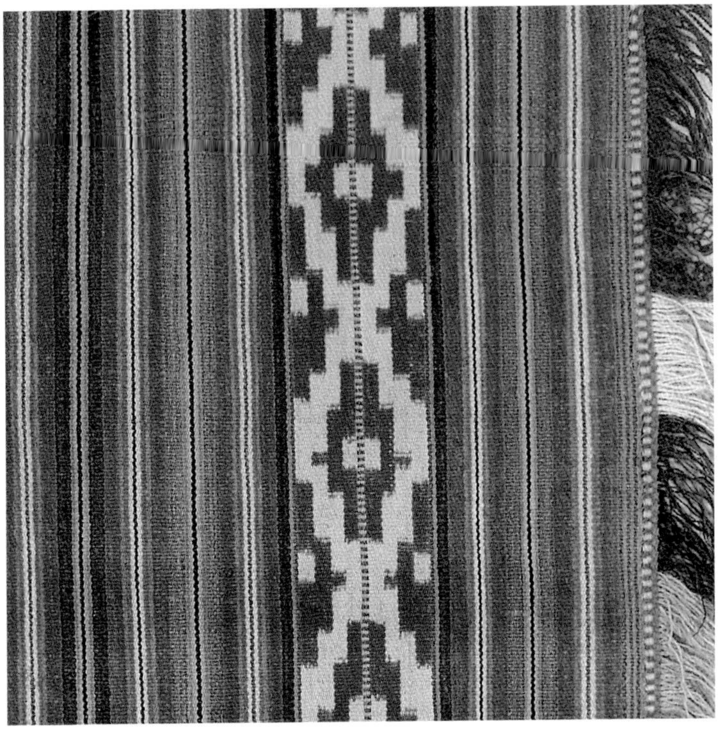

Figure 56. *(above left) Charcoal drawing.*

Figure 57. *(left) Painted white ovals.*

Figure 58. *(below) Painted black ovals.*

Figure 59. *(bottom left) Warp placed over design sheet.*

Figure 60. *(above middle) Tied warp bundles.*

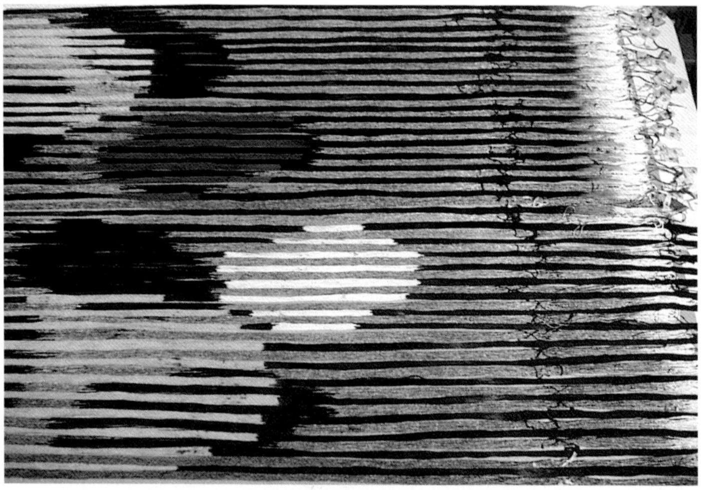

Figure 61. *(above right) Partially dyed warp.*

Figure 62. *(below middle) Warp bundles numbered.*

Figure 63. *(bottom right)* Interlocking Ovals I *on the loom.*

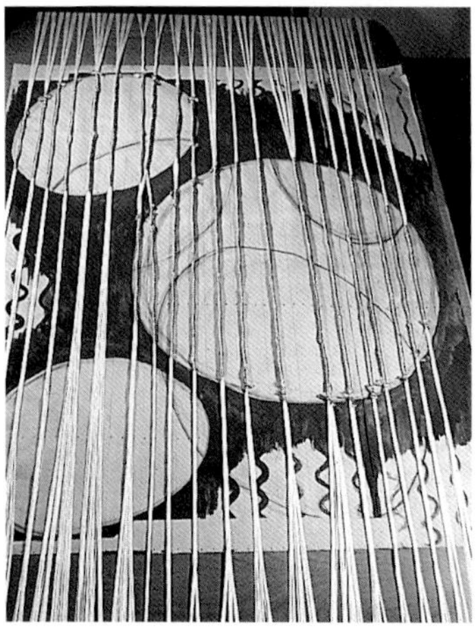

Figure 64. *The artist/author with* Interlocking Ovals I.

Warp Ikat

Interlocking Ovals

The warp ikat wall piece "Interlocking Ovals I" (Figure 64) exemplifies how a design idea first sketched on paper can transfer and reveal itself in a final woven design statement. Ovals were used as the motif in this weaving because they are more easily drawn and woven than circles.

On a sheet of paper 4½ ft. (135 cm) x 3 ft. (90 cm), six interlocking ovals of various sizes were drawn with charcoal (Figure 56). From this sketch, ovals were selected and painted in white with black background (Figure 57) and black with white background (Figure 58) on separate sheets to full scale. The warp for the first panel was wound in separate bundles with the proper number of warp ends for a 1-in. (2.5-cm) stripe; the cross was tied in each separate bundle. Similarly, another group of warp bundles were wound and laid aside for the other panel.

One of the design sheets was placed on a table and the warp laid on top, under tension, with correct yarn count equal to the width of the oval (Figure 59). The areas of resist in the design were tied into the warp. These warp bundles were grouped together to go, ultimately, into their respective dyes (Figure 60). Some of the yarn was left exposed to receive the dye.

At this point, it was very important to number each bundle (on the top end) within the panel: for the left panel, L-1, L-2, on through to L-30. This was important later when some of the bundles were turned upside down but needed to be maintained in sequence. (see Figure 62.)

On the loom, the weaving was done in a sateen weave, raising one harness against seven. (It is easier this way as this was a "rising shed" loom and the patterned warp ikat should show strongly on one surface when it is displayed.) First one panel and then the second was woven (Figure 63). They were joined together with an invisible handsewn seam. The design revealed itself when the weaving was hung with sturdy rods across top and bottom hems (Figure 64).

Chapter V

A Gallery of Ikat

Until the industrial revolution in the nineteenth century, fabrics were manufactured by hand; but with the development of mechanization, handcrafted fabrics gradually gave way to cheaper mass-produced, mill-woven, machine-printed fabrics. However, in the twentieth century, fiber artisans in industrialized countries such as our own have found a new appreciation of handcrafted fabrics and of fiber materials in general – an awareness that has inspired the commercial fabric industry to produce more beautifully woven and colored fabrics. Dyes and dyeing processes – particularly those involving resist-dyeing techniques – have traveled a parallel path. With the development and availability of commercial dyes, there was at first a movement away from the traditional natural sources of animal, plant, and mineral dyes; but now, along with the continuing use of synthetic dyes, there is also a returning interest in natural dyes.

There is also renewed interest in resist-dye techniques, and in particular, ikat. Two people – Prof. Alfred Bühler of Basel, Switzerland, and Prof. Ed Rossbach, University of California, Berkeley – have, each through his own independent research, writing, and teaching, encouraged the study of fabric construction and dyeing. They have been particularly instrumental in opening the door to our knowledge of traditional ikat techniques the world over. Modern fiber artists are becoming aware of the electric potential of these beautiful techniques. The traditional museum tapestries have long been considered the ultimate in woven wall decoration. Now fiber artists are once again doing large commissions for public and private buildings, stimulated by research in new fibers, natural fibers used in new ways and the exciting possibilities of new dyes and dye techniques – all expressing our fast-moving culture.

It is my hope that you will not only enjoy the traditional and contemporary examples pictured in this gallery of ikats, but will also use them as reference material and inspiration as you use this book, do the projects and design your own ikats.

Pages 50 and 51:
Hillary Steel. Of Ancient Cloth *(detail).*

Page 52:
Virginia Davis.
X. *Double Ikat.*

Page 53:
(above) Tetsuo Fujimoto. Untitled.
(right) Shigeo Kubota.
Pacific Overture.
Warp Ikat.

Page 54:
Louaine Elke. 10:30 AM.
Weft ikat.

Page 55:
(left) Lia Cook. Untitled. Collection, Morrison and Foerster.
(below left) Lydia Van Gelder. Ikat Wedding Basket. Collection, Mr. and Mrs. Roger Von Rosenberg.
(below right) Lydia Van Gelder. Bobbin Lace Ikat.

Page 56:
(left) Double Ikat with Picture Ikat, Japan. Collection, Yoshiko Wada.

Page 57:
Twice-Dyed Warp Ikat (detail), Dyula, Ivory Coast.

Page 56: *(right)*
Jan Janeiro.
Ikat Feathers #2.

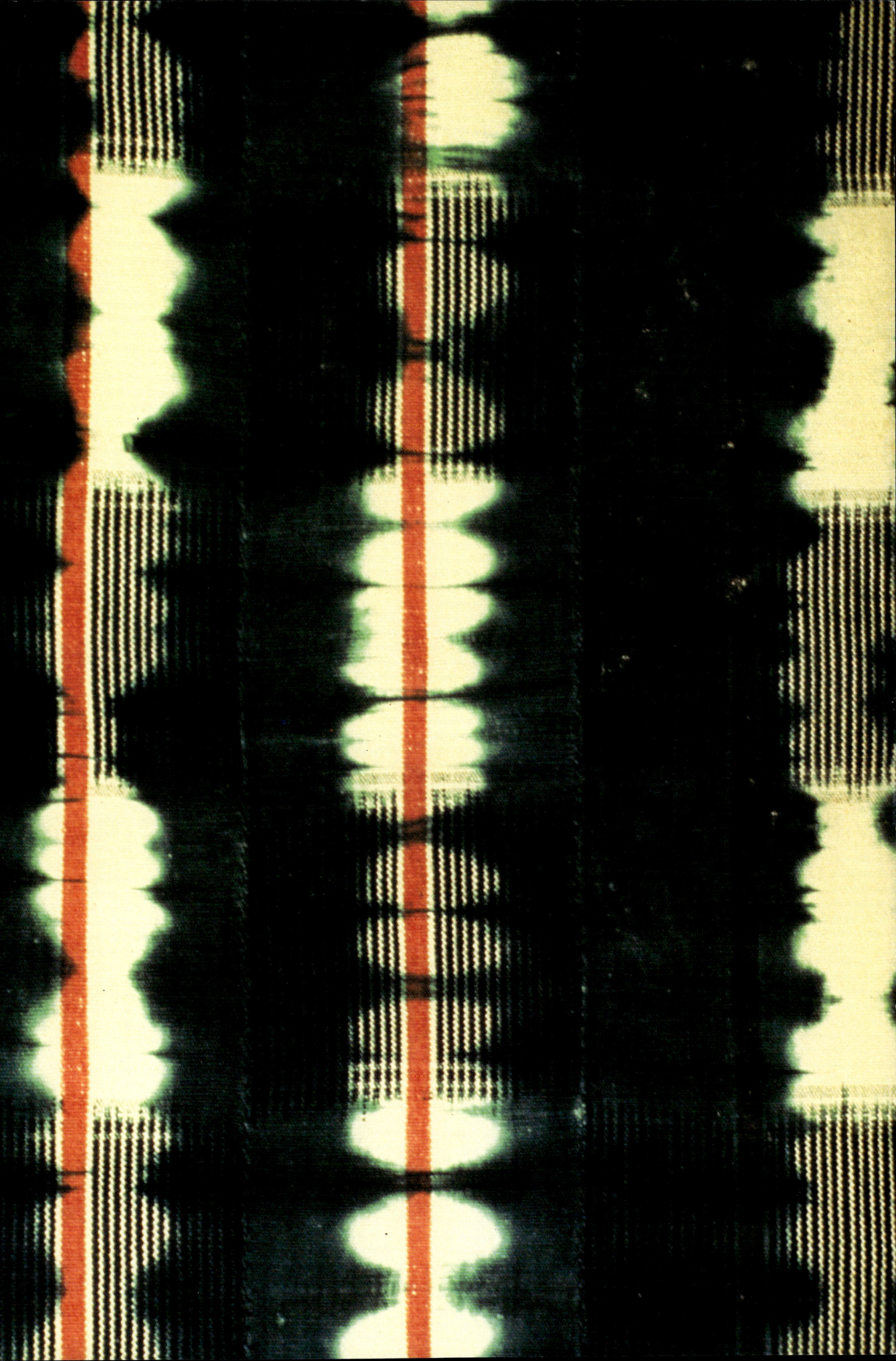

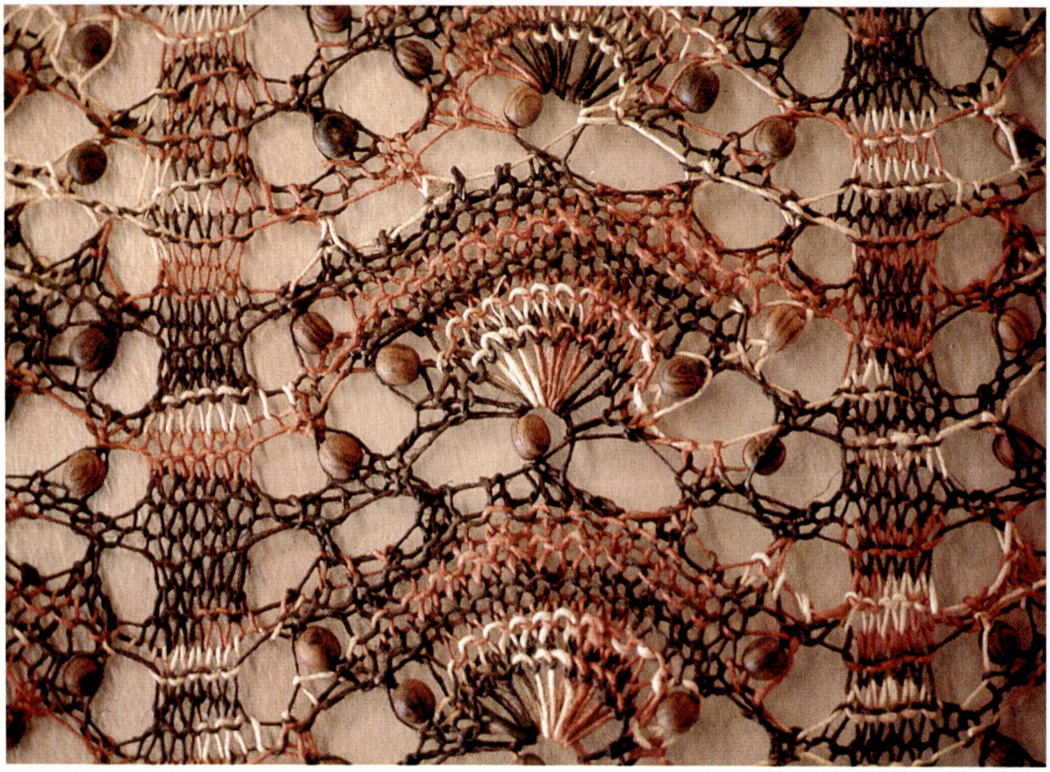

Pages 58 and 59:
(top left) Emily Dubois. Kerkes.

Page 58:
(bottom left) Mary Walker Phillips.
Fans with Beads *(detail). Silk ikat, knitting.*

Pages 58 and 59:
(bottom) Lydia Van Gelder.
Tatted Ikat.

Page 59:
(below right) Lydia Van Gelder.
Twice Dyed #8. *(detail).*

Page 60:*(above) Silk Kimono, Japan (detail). Collection, Dorothy M. Miller.*

Page 61: *Warp Ikat, Philippines (detail). Collection, Lydia Van Gelder.*

Page 62:*(above left) Sumba Warp Ikat (detail). Collection, Glen Black. (below left) Lydia Van Gelder.* Three Ovals. *(detail).*

Pages 62 and 63: *Hillary Steel.* Migration Patterns *(detail).*

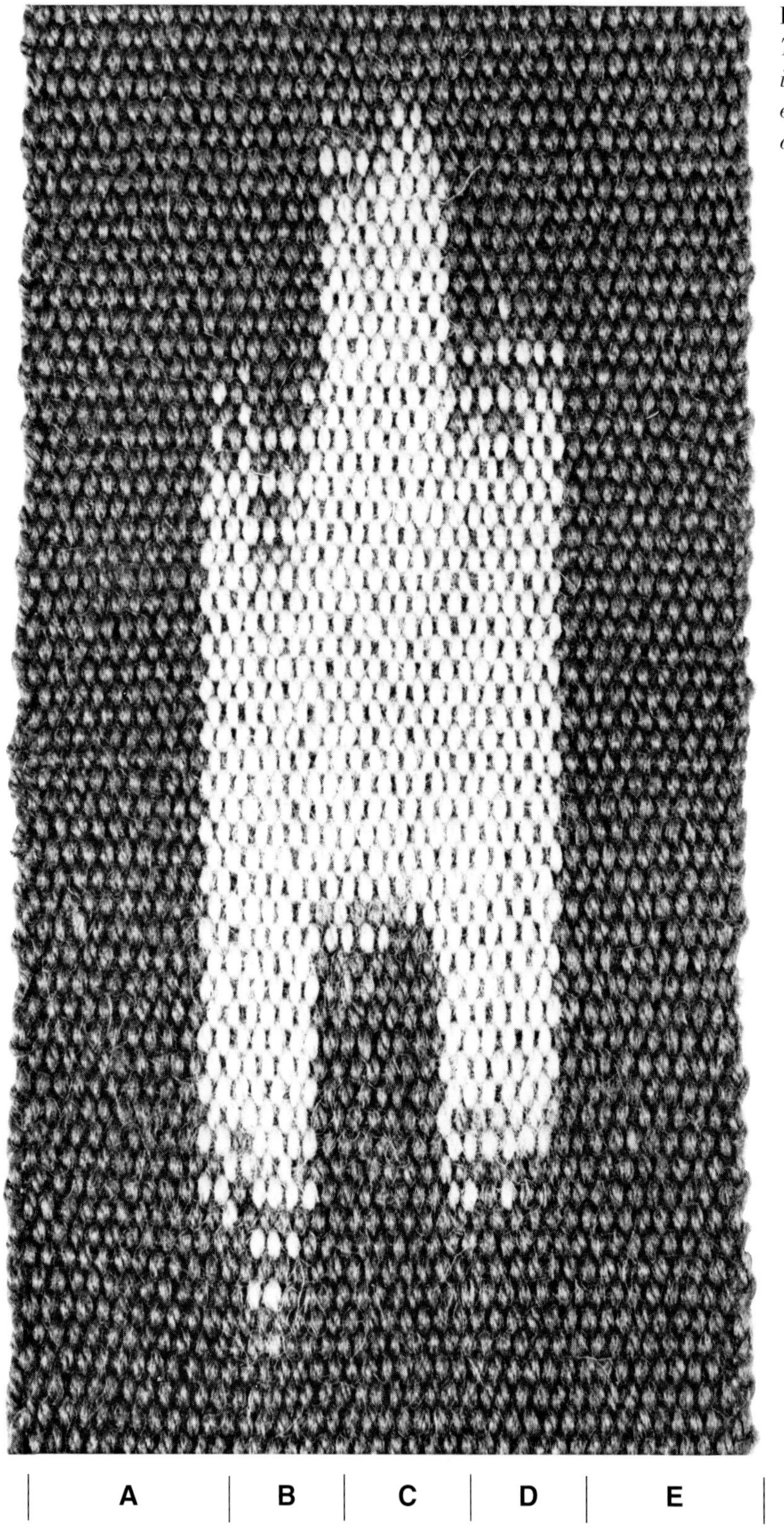

Figure 65. Flame Motif. *The lettered sections indicate groups of warp ends to be wound separately and dyed or ikatted.*

Figure 66. Contemporary Japanese Ikat. *The white ikat-resist areas were shifted in opposite directions on a warp-shifting frame to develop the feather motif, which is crossed with resist-dyed weft yarns to make a double ikat. Warp-shifting also created the chessboard pattern of the dark bands. Collection, Lydia Van Gelder.*

Project 1

Flame Motif

In this first project, you will weave several samples of a motif that illustrate how one simple resist tie on the warp can be manipulated as you dress the loom to create not a stripe, but a more complex flame or arrow motif when you weave the fabric. Figure 65 shows the finished motif.

Materials

1. Warp and weft yarn to weave 2 yards of fabric 4 in. (10 cm) wide; sett 24 e.p.i., 10 picks per inch

2. Four-harness loom, 12-dent reed, warping board, and standard weaving equipment

3. Plastic tape for the resist ties

4. Dye material to suit your yarn

5. Two dowels about 12 in. (30 cm) long and ½ in. (1.3 cm) in diameter

Methods

Winding the Warp and Weft. You will wind five separate warp bundles. For the selvage stripes (sections A and E in Figure 65) wind two bundles, each 20 ends. Tie the uncut warp ends and the cross and lay the two bundles aside. Next, as Figure 68 on page 67 indicates, wind and leave on the warping board three separate bundles: 13 ends for stripe B; 14 ends for stripe C; and 13 ends for stripe D. These will form the flame motif during weaving. Tie the cross and end loops of each bundle separately. With a plastic tie around all three bundles, mark the places where you will be wrapping resists. As you wrap the resists, treat these three bundles as a single unit – you will separate them again when you dress the loom. Make each resist wrap 3 in. (8 cm) long

Figure 67. Weaving without a Reed. *Notice the empty beater, and the use of a sword to beat down the weft.*

and leave 8 in. (20 cm) of warp between resists. Allowing for loss to loom tie-on at each end of the warp, tie at least 4 resists, one for each sample you will weave for this project (or more, if you wish to experiment). Figure 69 shows some of the resists wrapped and tied.

Wind enough yarn for the weft into a skein. Secure the two selvage warp bundles, the design warp bundle and the weft skein with large, loose figure-eight ties, in preparation for dyeing. Dye all the warp and weft yarns together in the same pot, to ensure color matching. After dyeing, follow the routine instructions outlined in Chapter III, to prepare the yarn for dressing the loom.

Dressing the Loom. To create the flame motif, you will shift some of the warp ends before you dress the loom, using a simple method that works well for small projects. Use of a Japanese frame to make more complex shifts in warp placement is explained at the end of this project. Lay the five dyed warp groups out in the sequence illustrated in Figure 65. Run one of the dowels through the uncut loops of warp bundles A, C and E and tie the dowel to the warp apron. Next run the other dowel through the shed formed by the warps on the first dowel, at the same time sliding bundles B and D onto this second dowel so that the sequence A, B, C, D, E is preserved. Tie the second rod holding bundles B and D securely to the first rod (Figure 70).

Following your normal procedure, draw in, using a 1-2-3-4 draft. For the first sample, do not sley the reed; remove the reed from the beater and tie directly onto the cloth apron.

Weaving. For your first sample, weave a warp-faced fabric. Figure 67 shows that when the warp is not restricted by the reed, the weft is drawn up tighter than usual and the width of the warp narrows, resulting in a very firm weave and strong pattern definition. Many exciting effects in ikat can be achieved by weaving without a reed. Figure 71 shows the weaving off the loom, and you can see the close sett of the warp. Work in tabby and weave at 36 e.p.i. and 7 picks to the inch. Weave until you complete the first flame motif. After you finish this first sample, cut it off the warp, replace the reed and sley the warp at 24 e.p.i., with two warp ends in each of the two outside dents for the selvage.

Weave the next motif in tabby, at 9 picks to the inch. Figure 65 shows how this sample will look. Notice how changing the sett of the warp affects the design. Even though the warp at 24 e.p.i. is quite close together, you can now see the weft just a little bit.

Next change your treadling and try some warp-faced twills. Figure 72 shows a 2/2 twill woven at 16 picks per inch. Figure 73 shows a 3/1 twill. Contrast this to the 2/2 twill you just wove. See how the white pattern yarns are more pronounced. The reverse side (Figure 74) shows the lesser dominance of the white

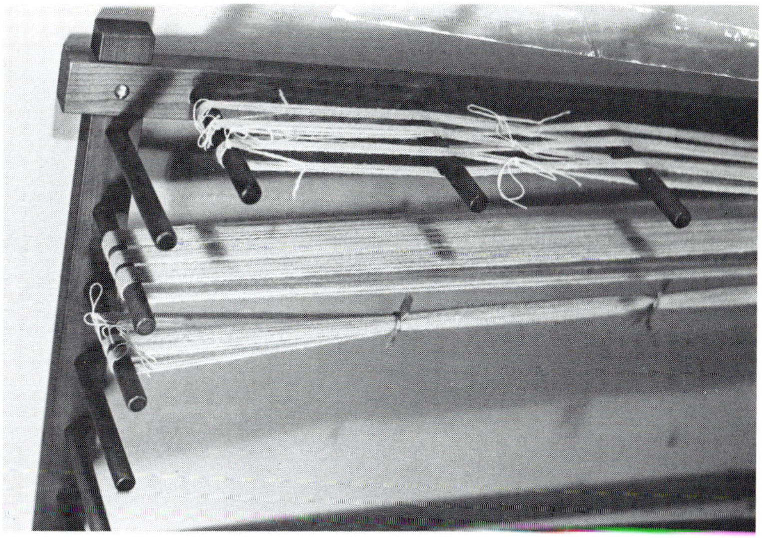

Figure 68. Winding the Warp. *Three separate groups of warp yarns are wound and tied individually. Note the plastic ties marking where the resists will be wrapped.*

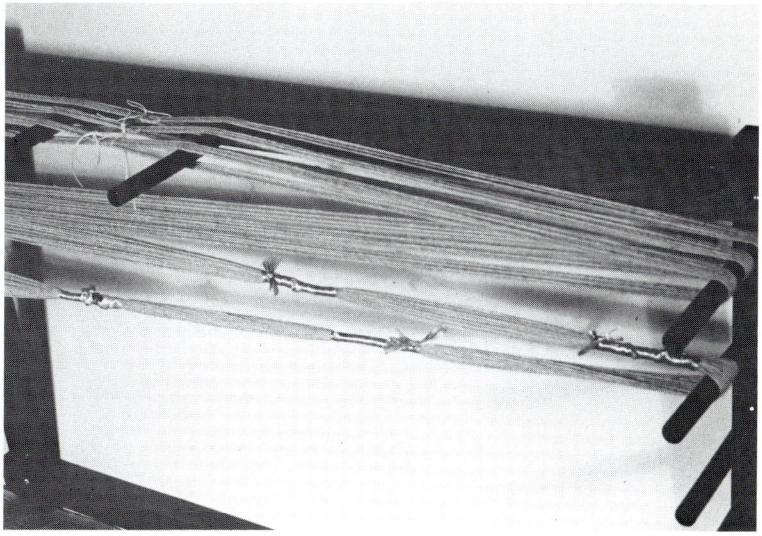

Figure 69. Wrapping the Resists. *The warping board can be used as a tying frame; simply leave the ward on it and begin tying. Note that a single wrapping encircles all three warp bundles shown here.*

Figure 70. Dressing the Loom. *One dowel has been run through warp bundles A, C and E and secured to the warp apron. A second dowel, holding bundles B and D, is run through the shed formed by the first dowel and tied to it.*

Figure 71. Warp-Faced Cloth. *The finished sample shows the result of weaving without a reed. The warp, which has drawn in, completely covers the weft.*

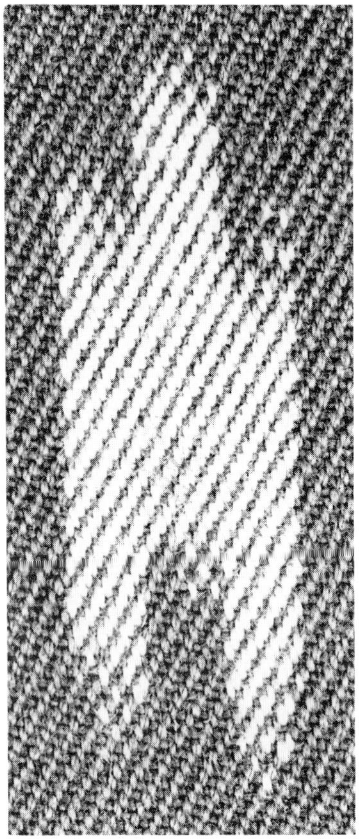

Figure 72. Flame Motif in 2/2 Twill. *Changing to a balanced twill changes the surface texture. Warp and weft are equally visible.*

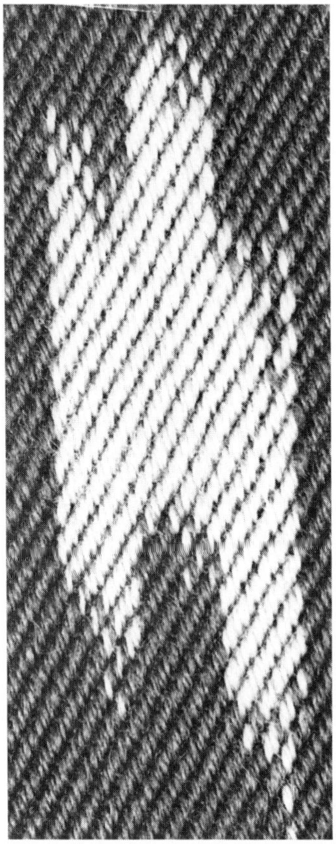

Figure 73. Flame Motif in 3/1 Twill. *A 3/1 twill creates a longer warp skip in the motif and increases surface texture.*

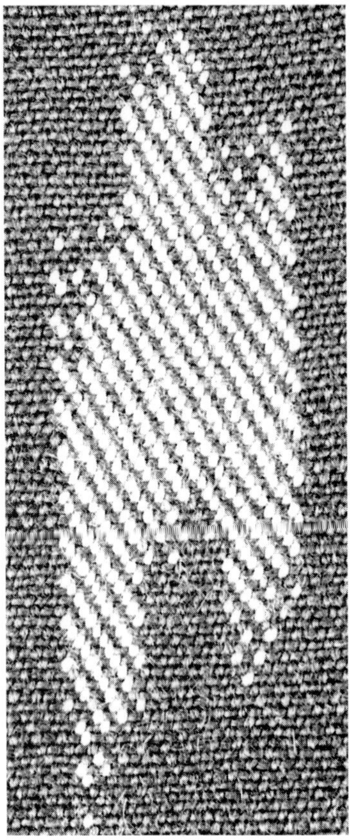

Figure 74. Flame Motif in 3/1 Twill, Reverse Side. *On the reverse side of the fabric, the weft is more dominant.*

ikat-resist yarns because on this side of the fabric the weft has the longer float.

In the four samples of warp ikat that you have just woven — warp-faced, plain weave, 2/2 twill and 3/1 twill — you can see how the weave affects surface texture and the pattern.

Warp-Shifting Frame

In Japan, a warp-shifting method is used to create variations of geometric designs from an ikat warp tied and dyed in straight bands, like the warp you ikatted for the flame-motif samples. Certain groups of warp ends are lifted higher than others by the simple device shown in Figure 75. The loom is then dressed, and the result is a shift in the ikat pattern. The warp-shifting frame was used in making the Japanese warp ikat illustrated in Figure 66.

You can construct your own warp-shifting frame using the drawing in Figures 75 and 76 as your guide. It is simple to construct from materials readily available at any lumber or building-supply store. The following rule of thumb is helpful in estimating the amount of warp needed for a piece in which you plan to shift the warp: For every three yards of finished fabric you want, allow an additional yard for the collapse of the warp yarn when it is released from tension, takeup in weaving and the loss from shifting and tying onto the loom. The following instructions are taken from material in Yoshiko Wada's booklet, *Japanese Ikat: Warp, Weft, Figure.*

After the warp has been ikatted and is ready to go on the loom, the warp-shifting device (without its rods) is placed on the loom between the harnesses and the back beam. The front end of the warp with the cross is pulled through the device and tied to the cloth beam. Lease sticks are put in the cross and secured to the loom, in front of the heddles. The warp is then spread in the raddle and wound onto the cloth beam until the back end hangs down to the warp beam.

Now the warp-shifting device comes into play as groups of ikatted warp ends are lifted to create a pattern and held in place by rods on the device, as shown in Figure 75. All the warp yarns pass under the lower rod closest to the warp beam, to keep the warp under an even tension as it is tied to the warp beam (the yarns will vary in length according to how far they have been shifted). The raddle and warp shifting frame are left in place while the warp is wound onto the warp beam, and then removed before it is sleyed and tied onto the cloth beam.

Figure 75. Warp-Shifting Frame. *Using an adaptation of this Japanese device, you can shift the placement of ikat patterns on the warp as it is being put on the loom.*

Figure 76. *Another view of the warp-shifting frame.*

Figure 77a. *(left) Lydia Van Gelder.* A Pattern of Life.

Figure 77b. *(right)* Twice-Dyed Ikat, Dyula Ivory Coast *(detail). After strips of this fabric were woven, a second resist pattern was created by sewing all along the lengthwise stripes, and the fabric was dyed a second time. The strips were then cut and sewn together at the selvages. 158 x 120 in. (401 x 305 cm).*

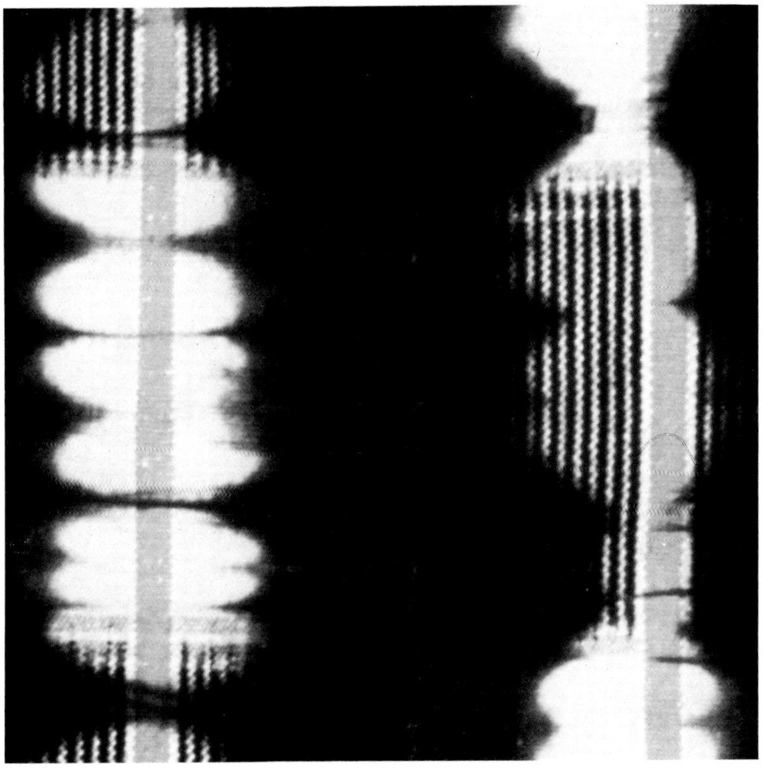

Project 2

Twice-Dyed Ikat

Twice-dyeing is a traditional West African method used not only on ikats but on other patterned cloths as well. After a cloth is finished, sections are resisted and the piece is dyed once again, adding another layer of pattern and color to the textile. It is one of those very simple methods of resist dyeing that gives really exciting results. Figure 77b shows a detail of a twice-dyed fabric woven by a Dyula weaver at the village of Kong, in the Ivory Coast. The cotton cloth is probably a woman's wrapper and is composed of 12 strips of weaving 4 in. (10 cm) wide that are sewn together to make up the piece. Both the ikatted yarn and the second dyeing were done with indigo. In this piece, it appears that the running stitch establishing the resist fold was done on the narrow red stripe.

This project is based on the African fabric, but you may also use the twice-dyeing technique on other fabrics for special design effects. All of the instructions that follow are for one narrow width of 186 ends.

Materials

1. Yarn for warp and weft, enough to weave one width of 186 ends. This yarn should be fairly fine – 20/2 would be suitable – and soft, not firm.
2. Yarn for a narrow red stripe of 14 ends; you may dye some of your warp yarn red, or purchase an already dyed yarn of the same size.
3. Two-harness loom, warping board and standard weaving equipment
4. Plastic tape or wrap for the resist ties
5. Dye to suit your yarn (vat dye if you are using cotton)
6. Large needle, heavy sewing thread, scissors

Methods

Winding the Warp. To weave a single strip of fabric 4 in. (10 cm) wide, you will need to wind 186 warp ends. Decide how long you want your warp to be, then wind the following groups of warp for this strip.

Group 1. Wind 60 ends of white yarn, tie the cross and the uncut loops at each end of the warp, remove from the board and lay aside. (These warp ends will be unpatterned.)

Group 2. Wind 14 ends of red yarn, tie the cross and end loops and lay aside.

Group 3. Wind 112 ends of white yarn to ikat, tie the cross and end loops.

Tying the Resists. On the bundle of 112 ends to be ikatted indicate, with temporary string ties, where you want the resist blocks of white to fall, measuring so they will fall in an even repeat in the weaving. (In the African cloth, these resist blocks are almost the same size as the dyed parts, forming a checkerboard of ikat blocks against plain warp.) Bind these resists together in one bundle if your yarn thickness allows. (If the bundle is too thick, say, more than ½ in. (1.3 cm), divide into smaller bundles but tie them all the same.)

Dyeing. Dye the bundle of 112 ends that you have just tied in the resists. Use a dye suitable for your yarn; wash and dry.

Dressing the Loom and Weaving. Tie the warp onto the warp apron in the following order, being careful not to shift the ikat-patterned yarns and thus distort the pattern.

4 ikat yarns, 2 white yarns;	13 times
4 ikat yarns	once
4 white yarns	once
14 red yarns	once
4 white yarns	once
4 ikat yarns	once
2 white yarns, 4 ikat yarns;	13 times

Now insert lease sticks in the cross of each group of yarns (in the above order) and wind the warp onto the warp beam. Sley from back to front. Tie onto the cloth apron and weave a warp-faced cloth.

Twice-Dyeing. Thread your needle with heavy thread and make long running stitches (a stitch no longer than ½ in. [1.3 cm]) through the red stripe. Draw the stitches up very tightly and secure the thread so it will not loosen. Dye the entire strip again. The weight of the strip you have woven and the size of your running-stitch resist will determine the strength of the dye pattern. Wash the cloth after dyeing; remove the stitches and wash lightly once more, then dry. You may press the fabric or, if you prefer, leave the interesting textural crinkle left in the fabric by the stitches. Cut the strip of weaving into equal lengths and sew them together at the selvages as shown in Figure 77b.

Figure 78. *Virginia Davis.* Starshine *(detail).*

Project 3

Sumba Warp Ikats

By folding a warp many times before you tie the resists, you can create a series of mirror images. In addition to achieving vertical and horizontal repeats in a design, this method also facilitates tying the resists. Fabrics ikatted in this way on the island of Sumba are ranked among the finest of Indonesian ikats, both technically and artistically. Preparation of a traditional Sumbanese ikat might take as long as ten years to complete, so complex are the techniques used in the resist tying and dyeing. These fine cloths are a warp-faced plain weave, with a sett of approximately 120 e.p.i., woven at 22 picks per inch. The handspun cotton yarns traditionally are dyed red, from a plant source, and indigo. The background is an overdye of red on the blue, producing a rich, warm brown-black. Occasionally Sumbanese cloths are dyed only with indigo.

The East Sumba ikats are most distinguished by their design repeats of animal figures, as in Figure 79. These animal figures often have religious significance; in some cases they might denote animals revered by the family and thus not slain. Symbols of horses or buffalo represent wealth, and food animals such as cocks, chickens and ducks are often depicted. Sometimes the sea (fish, crabs, crayfish) and animals for the hunter (deer, monkeys, birds) are represented.

Color and value changes are emphasized in this *hinggi* (man's shawl or waistcloth) in Figure 79. The light and dark horizontal bands of animal figures are assisted in their color and value changes by the weft that is used. In the lighter bands of horses, a red weft yarn was used; at the light line dividing the bands, the bobbin on the shuttle was changed and a dark blue was used. In this manner, color and value changes in the weft were employed to subtly enhance the changes in the horizontal bands of the warp. Because of the great care that goes into producing these beautiful cloths, they are usually worn only for special occasions or ceremonial fetes.

The intricate, repetitive patterns of Sumba ikats are made possible by folding the warp into layers before tying pattern resists. Briefly, the Sumba weavers wind a continuous warp around two rollers; the distance between the rollers is half the length of the finished cloth and twice its width. At this point there are two layers of warp, the top of the continuous warp and the bottom. (One end of the warp will be eventually cut and the weaving unfolded to full length for the fabric.) If the warp were to be patterned at this stage, the horizontal stripes on either side of the geometric band at the center of the ikat in Figure 79 would be mirror images.

The Sumbanese weavers continue folding, however. Their first move is to split the number of warp yarns in half and place one half of the warp precisely on top of the other. (Later, each half will be woven separately and then sewn together at the selvage to form a wide cloth with exactly matching repeats.) Their next step is to fold these four layers of warp lengthwise several times (twice, in this ikat), so the warp width is now much narrower than it will be when it is put on the loom. They can now tie resists for a single design through all the layers of warp at once, which will form multiple repeats in the dyeing.

In this project, the lengthy Sumba ikat techniques used to create mirror-image repeats have been simplified for contemporary weavers. However, the methods you will use are, in essential respects, very close to the traditional ones. The two pieces you will weave for this project are designed to show you how to layer your warp in this way, but are confined to a single width of warp. Once you have learned to handle the layering of warps, you may wish to ikat two warps at once. After dyeing, you would put one warp on the loom and weave it, then dress the loom with the second warp and weave it. You would have two cloths with identical placement of ikat patterns.

Figure 79. Sumba Warp Ikat. *This* hinggi *is composed of two identical cloths. The warps were folded, layered and resist-tied together but woven separately, and the finished cloths were then sewn together along the selvages. 109 x 46 in. (277 x 117 cm). Collection, Glen Black.*

Sumba Squares

Take a look at Figure 80 and notice that the motif of squares is formed by folding the warp both lengthwise and widthwise along the white lines, then tying resists for only one pattern. In this step-by-step procedure, you will develop the vertical and horizontal reverses for this pattern. The warp for this piece is for a single cloth, rather than the double warps of traditional Sumba ikats.

Materials

1. Warp yarn for a finished weaving 23 x 60 in. (60 x 75 cm); sett 12 e.p.i. (Soft, shiny rayon was used in the sample illustrated.)
2. A fine weft yarn (about 14/1) to weave with a beat of about 10 picks per inch. (A fine linen was used in the sample.)
3. Two-harness loom, 12-dent reed and standard weaving equipment
4. Four ½-in. (1.3-cm) dowels 12 to 18 in. (30 to 45 cm) long; two 1-in. (2.5-cm) dowels 12 to 18 in. (30 to 45 cm) long; two 1-in. (2.5-cm) dowels 36 in. (90 cm) long; two C-clamps and four short metal strips
5. Two pairs canvas stretcher bars, one pair wider than your work, the other pair longer
6. Plastic tape for resist ties
7. Natural indigo vat dye or any dye to suit your yarn

Methods

The Working Cartoon. Plan your design and draw it out on paper as shown in Figure 81. The cartoon for this project was done to half scale because of its simple pattern. Figure the length, width and e.p.i. of your warp according to the design and yarn to be used. For this project, the paper cartoon was drawn out to show the proportions of its full design, but only one quarter of the design was drawn in detail, since only one motif will be tied (the result will be four motifs in the finished weaving). In the detailed section, the small white blocks are totally wrapped to resist the dye. In the striped portions, two wrapped warp ends alternate with two dyed ends.

Winding the Warp. Nowhere is it more important to employ good weaving practices than in the preparation of a warp for the Sumba method. The warp must be wound with an even tension; the cross

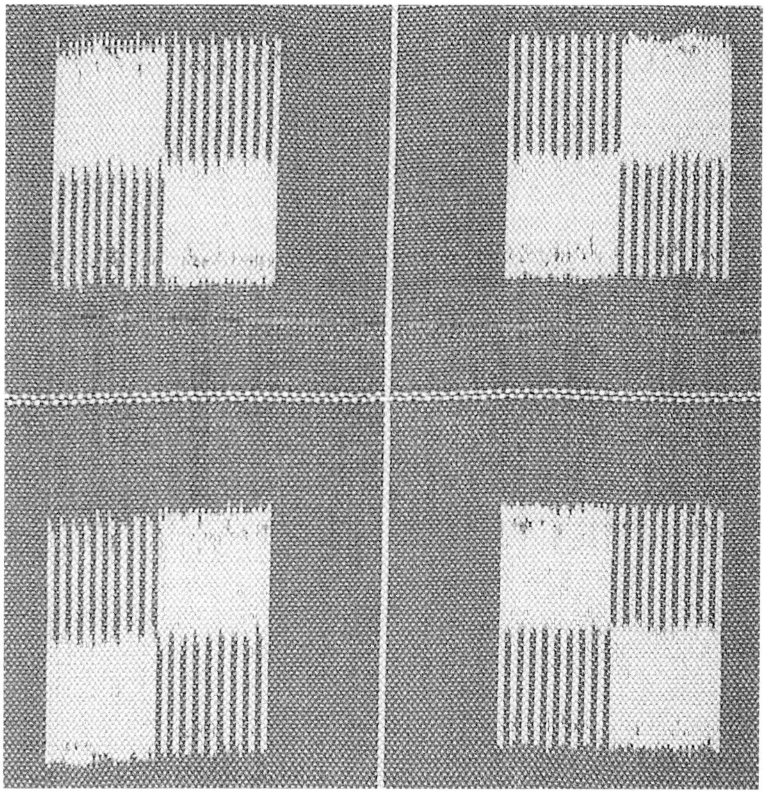

Figure 80. *(above left)* Sumba Squares. *To achieve the mirrored reversal of the design in this warp ikat, you will fold the warp twice before tying the resists. 23 x 30 in. (60 x 75 cm).*

Figure 81. *(above)* The Working Cartoon. *The entire piece is sketched out on paper, but only one of the blocks is drawn in detail showing the exact placement of yarns to be tied with resists.*

tied; the ends of the warp left in a loop, uncut; and a cord or string run through the loops at each end to keep them from getting tangled and to facilitate inserting rods or dowels as you fold the warp and tie the resists. The strings that run through the cross and loops at the ends of the warp groups must be of ample length to allow the warp to be spread out generously on the rods while tying the resists.

Wind the warp in the following separate groups. Remove each group from the warping board (but don't chain it) and stretch it between the two long rods by slipping the dowels through the uncut end loops.

Group A. Two groups of 36 ends + 2 to sley the two outside dents with double yarns for the selvage = 38 ends in each group

Group B. 72 ends in each group
(wind two groups)

Group C. 36 ends in each group
(wind two groups)

Group D. One group of 2 ends

In the working cartoon, shown in Figure 81, you will see where these groups lie in relation to the design.

Work in sequence as you wind the warp, starting with the first group A; wind, tie the cross and end loops and transfer the group to the rods, laying out the warp carefully so as not to tangle or twist the yarns. Next, wind one group B, tie it, remove it to the rods and place it next to the first group A. Wind one group C and transfer it to the next place on the rods. Then wind and transfer a second group C, a second group B and finally a second group A. Wind and put aside the two white ends in group D, as they will remain undyed; you will not need them until you are ready to dress the loom.

Twining. Leaving the warp on the rods, stretch it out on a long table or the floor and put it under just enough tension to hold the yarn flat and even. To maintain the tension on the yarn, tie the rods to stationary objects like door knobs, table legs, or, if you work outdoors, to posts or trees. Now you will twine across the portion of the warp that will be resisted to help keep the yarns in the proper sequence for tying. You should twine near the end of the warp, well away from the main design, as the twining will remain throughout the dyeing and may leave a slight resist-dyed line. Very often this line will fall in the fringe area or even in the loom waste, completely away from the finished woven piece. In this particular project it is not necessary to twine across the entire warp, but only in the B groups where you will tie resists. Work from the cross to make sure the yarns are in the proper sequence, and catch two yarns, one from the bottom and one from the top of the cross, in each twining loop.

Layering the Warp by Folding. This is the first step in the Sumba technique that distinguishes it from other warp-ikat methods. Up to this point, you have held the warp on two long rods to maintain both the tension and the sequence of yarns. Now exchange the single rod at one end for two shorter rods, dividing the warp at its center, between the two C groups (Figure 82). Also do the same at the other end of the warp. Be sure to keep the warp groups in the same order when you transfer them to the new shorter rods. You have divided the warp exactly in half lengthwise. Now fold the warp vertically so that one half of it lies on top of the other half, making sure that one group A falls on top of the other group A, and so on. Align the rods and the groups exactly at each end of the warp (Figure 83). Next, holding this vertically folded warp, fold these two layers exactly in half in a horizontal, or weft, direction. Slip one of the long rods into the center fold. You should now have a single long rod at the horizontal fold of the warp and four separate rods at the other end. Clamp these four rods together securely as shown in Figure 84. It is important to make sure that when the rods are clamped, the warp sections are of equal length. Run your fingers up through the warp groups to reposition any yarns that may have gotten out of place.

Tying the Warps Together. You will need to attach the warp to a tying frame, to hold it under tension as you connect the layers of warp and tie the resists. With the canvas stretcher bars, make an adjustable tying frame, as described in Chapter II. Figure 85 illustrates how this is to be done. Now return to section B and begin to join all four layers of warp into one layer, so that this pattern section can be wrapped as a single unit. You have already twined across section B on all layers, in preparation for this step. Start with the two top layers of warp, at one side

Figure 82. Folding the Warp. *Divide the warp in half vertically, with short dowels running through the uncut loops at the ends. Then fold the warp over upon itself.*

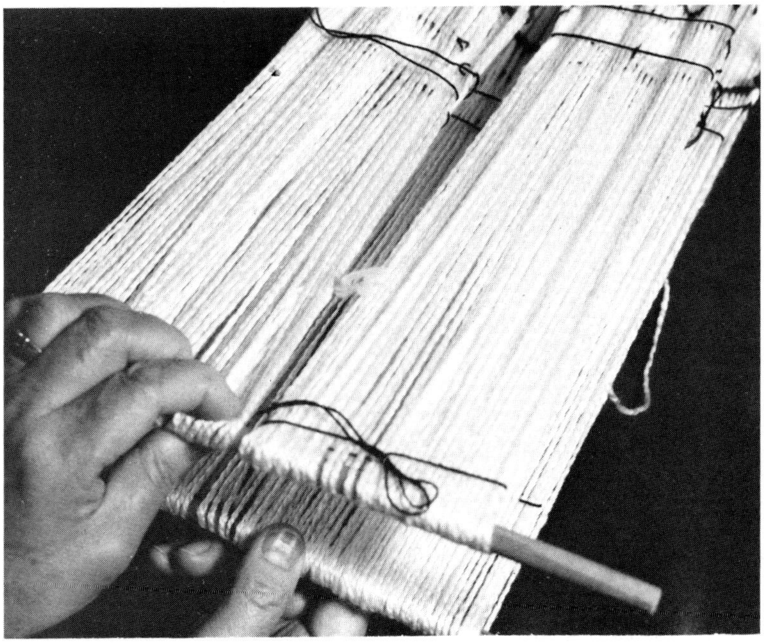

Figure 83. Completing the Vertical Fold. *As you align the two layers of warp, make sure that each group falls on top of its corresponding group. Next you will fold this layered warp in half horizontally.*

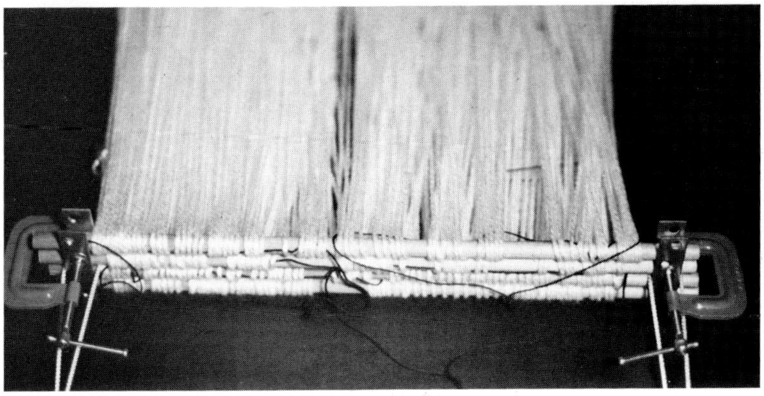

Figure 84. Clamping the Layers. *When the horizontal fold has been made, align the dowels between pairs of metal strips and secure them with C-clamps as shown.*

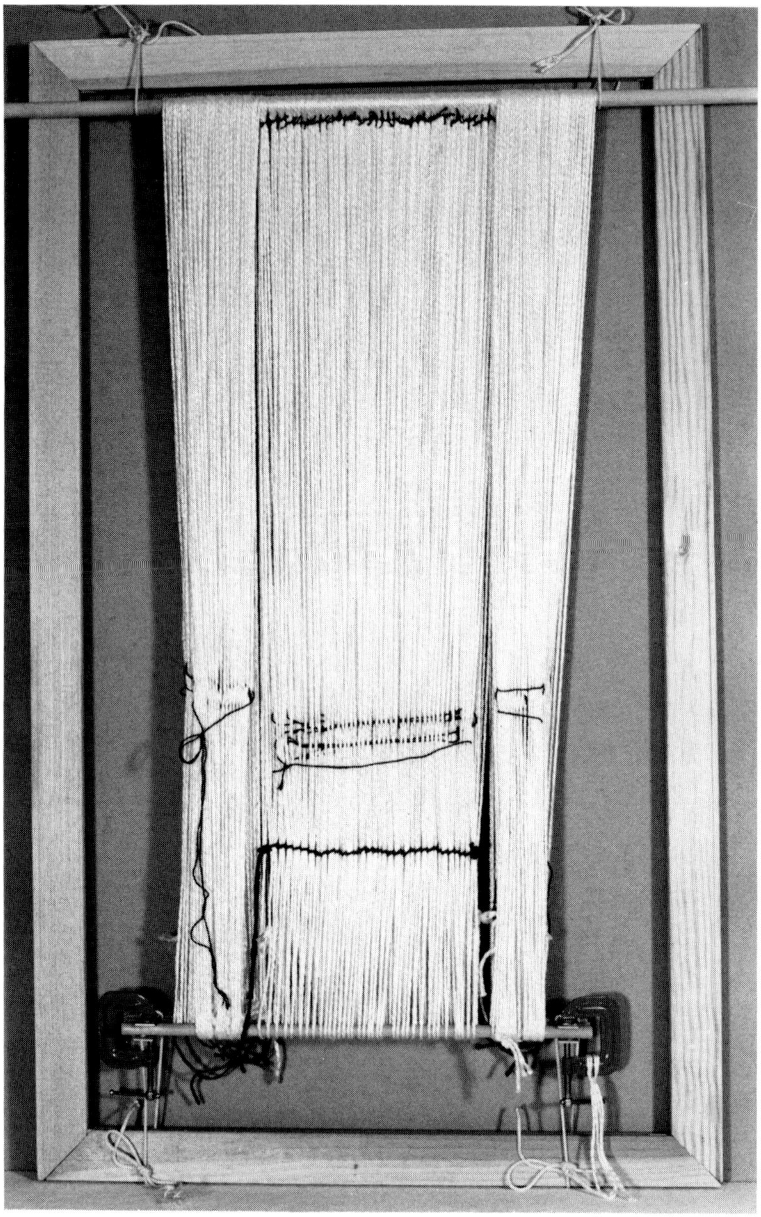

Figure 85. Placing the Warp on the Frame. *Attach the warp to a tying frame with cords. The group of yarns in the center is the one to receive the resists.*

Figure 86. Tying the Warps Together. *Having counted and tied these yarns together greatly facilitates tying the resists.*

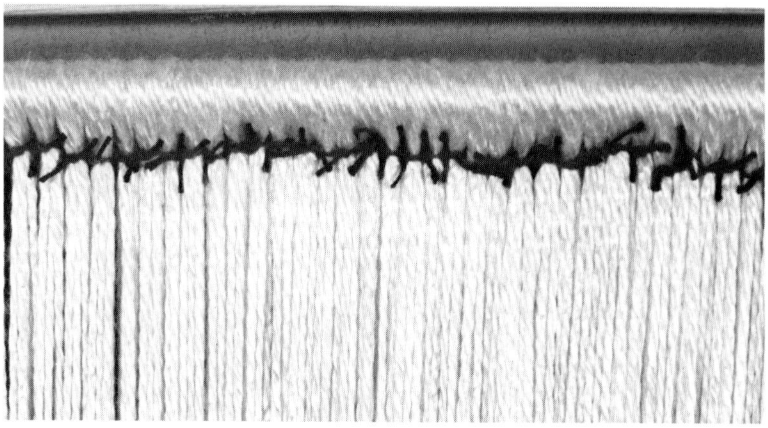

Figure 87. Tying the Resists. *The tied bundles of eight yarns help to keep the proper sequence of yarns. To keep the horizontal resist-dye line true, use a ruler as you tie.*

Figure 88. Detail of the Resists. *This close-up shows the alternate groups of wrapped yarns that create the stripe effect — a technique used frequently in Sumba ikats — and the solid resist blocks that will show up as a solid white.*

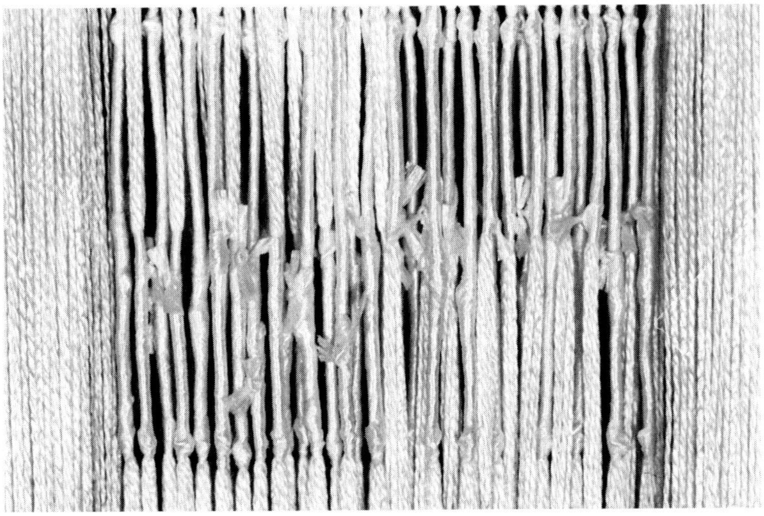

Figure 89. Dressing the Loom. *Before the yarn is drawn through the heddles, check to see that the ikat design on the warp is properly aligned and make whatever minor adjustments are needed.*

of the design area (group B): Take the first groups of twined yarns from these two layers and follow the four threads with your fingers to the top of the frame. Holding the group with one hand, run the fingers of your other hand up over the top of the rod and grasp the same threads on the back. Tie all eight threads together with a square knot as close to the rod as possible. Continue across the design area, tying bundles of eight threads together. Check frequently to make sure you are picking up the right sequence of threads, for if any are picked up out of order, it will show up as a mistake in the pattern. Figure 86 shows how the bundles of twined yarns are tied together.

Tying the Resists. Lay the frame on a table and place your paper cartoon either under the warp or nearby, where you can refer to it frequently. As you wrap the resists, measure the horizontal lines with a ruler for accuracy. You will see how having tied the bundles of eight threads speeds your work now (Figure 87). Follow the markings on your cartoon as you wrap each bundle independently. The detail in Figure 88 shows the finished wrapping. Notice how every group is wrapped for the solid resist blocks, while every other group is wrapped in the striped areas.

Remove the knots (Figure 86) that held the layers of warp together at the center fold, to avoid any slight resist line during dyeing. Leave the cords in the cross, as well as the cords that go through the end loops of the warp. Remove the warp from the frame and follow the preparation and dyeing procedures described in Chapter III. If you want your weft yarn to match the warp in color, skein and dye it with the warp.

Dressing the Loom. Lay the warp groups out in sequence, A, B, C, D, C, B, A, adding the two undyed white ends (D) between the two C groups. Before removing the ties from the uncut ends and the cross, place a rod through one end of the warp loops and tie it to the warp beam. Place the lease sticks through the cross in the warp. Make sure the two white yarns, D, go over and under the lease sticks in a cross. Now remove the cords that held the warp ends and the cross. Stand in front of the loom and give the warp a few gentle tugs to smooth out the yarns. If any yarns have gotten out of place in the ikat design, now is the time to adjust them (Figure 89). Roll the warp onto the warp beam. Heddle and sley the warp from the back to the front of the loom. Tie onto the cloth beam and weave.

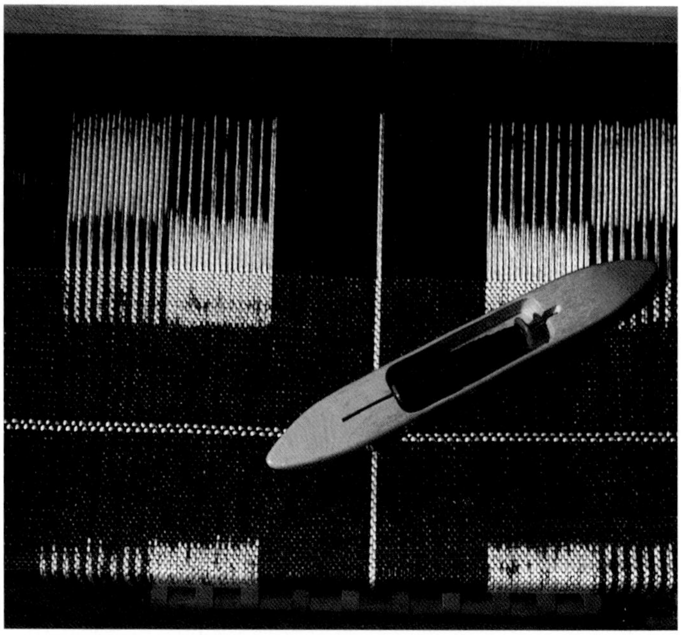

Figure 90. Weaving in Progress. *Two white weft picks have been woven in to balance the two white warp ends. An even beat of the weft is important for this piece.*

Weaving. Work for a good even beat to the weft. Remember that in a warp ikat the warp should dominate. Although this project is not warp-faced, the heavier warp yarn keeps the warp dominant. Notice in Figure 90 that two shots of white weft have been woven to correspond to the two white warp yarns. After you have finished your weaving, you will see how the striped sections change position in the center, and each block of stripes finishes with a white stripe on the outer edge. This stripe treatment is typical of Sumba ikats.

Figure 91. Sumba Arrows *(detail). A contemporary approach to ikat — wrapping loosely — created the mottled background.*

Project 4

Sumba Arrows

The ikat shown in Figure 91 is produced in much the same way as the Sumba squares. Now that you have completed the Sumba squares, you will bc able to ikat this bolder motif. This small wall hanging has a pattern that reverses from left to right and top to bottom. The horizontal center band is treated with a resist pattern typical of the Sumba ikats.

Materials

1. Warp yarn for a finished weaving 23 x 60 in. (60 x 155 cm); sett 12 e.p.i.
2. Very fine weft yarn to weave at 12 picks per inch
3. Two-harness loom, 12-dent reed and standard weaving equipment
4. Four ½-in. (1.3-cm) dowels 12 to 18 in. (30 to 45 cm) long; two l-in. (2.5-cm) dowels 12 to 18 in. (30 to 45 cm) long; two l-in. (2.5-cm) dowels 36 in. (90 cm) long; two C-clamps and four short metal strips
5. Two pairs canvas stretcher bars, one pair wider than your work, the other pair longer
6. Plastic tape for resist ties
7. Dye to suit your yarn
8. Three thin plastic dowels to weave into the ends, to stabilize the hanging

I used a soft two-ply silk in the warp and a very fine gold gimp for the weft (it was so fine as to be seen only as a soft glint of gold).

Methods

As for the Sumba squares, wind the warp, make the warp ties in the cross and uncut end loops, remove the warp from the board and place four short rods through the uncut loops, two rods at each end, dividing the warp in half vertically. (A note: In the illustrations you will see a single rod at each end of the warp; however, I do not recommend this, as the warp is more apt to shift.) Now fold the warp in half vertically and then in half horizontally, with a single longer rod through the center fold. Secure the warp to the tying frame as you did for the Sumba squares.

Twining. Twine across the full width of the warp near the bottom – the design will cover the entire width of the fabric. Using the established cross, pick up the first two yarns from each of the four warp layers and enclose these eight yarns in one twist of the twining cord. The twining should be placed well away from the design area and left in during the dyeing. Tie these eight yarns together at the top (Figure 92), as you did in the last project.

Tying the Resists. You may use a paper cartoon or, if you have the design clearly in mind, work without one. Use a few pieces of colored string to sketch out with temporary ties (to be removed as the tying progresses) the outline of your design. Remember you are tying one quarter of your design, which will have vertical as well as horizontal repeats when it is finished. The completed wrapping is shown in Figure 93. The strong diagonal edge of the arrow and the spaced tying along the selvages shows up once you have finished tying the resists. In this piece, you will see how to achieve an absolute repeat of a line such as a diagonal.

It is easy to achieve a strong vertical stripe, either in a single line or in a block of stripes. Look at the solid dark lines framing the motif and on the selvage of the piece (Figure 91). These lines were accomplished simply by leaving four yarns unwrapped for the desired length. The blocks of striped pattern in Figure 95 and the Sumba squares were made by alternately wrapping and not wrapping pairs of yarns. In the traditional Sumba ikats, where very fine cotton yarns are used at a sett of 100 e.p.i. or more, six or more yarns are tied in alternate groups.

One bit of tying remains, to create the staggered feathery band at the center fold, typical of Sumba ikats. Slip the rod at this fold out of the warp, leaving the knots in place. Referring to Figure 91, make a few short wraps on the yarns above the knots to form a pattern.

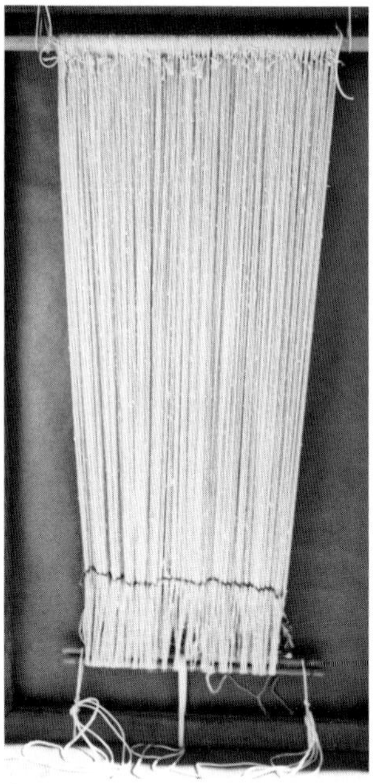

Figure 92. Twining the Warp on the Tying Frame. *When the warp is on the tying frame, twine across the full width of the warp; at the top of the frame, tie bundles of eight yarns together as shown.*

Rather than the usual dyed-undyed ikat, this piece has an additional contemporary resist treatment that creates a mottled effect in the background. Notice how, at the edge of the arrow, the background is very light, then gradually becomes mottled and returns to another, lighter line directly below the dark center section. To achieve this mottling, you would tie very tightly, in the usual manner, adjacent to the dark part of the arrow. Then you would tie a little more loosely in the background areas, just enough to allow a little dye to permeate but not so much as to make a really dark value. To finish the wrap, you would tie tightly again. Thus, you could obtain dark, middle and light values in the dyeing. This method presents opportunities for textural effects in other designs.

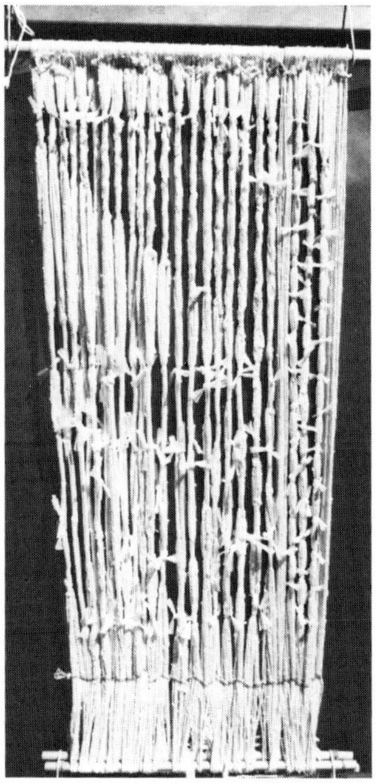

Figure 93. The Completed Wrapping. *When the resist ties are finished, you will have actually tied one quarter of the full design, Note the strong diagonal of the arrow and the spaced tying along the selvage.*

When you have finished the wrapping, dye the warp, dress the loom and weave. Begin by opening the first shed and inserting one of the thin plastic dowels; change the shed and insert another one, then continue with the weaving. When you have finished the weaving, add the third plastic dowel and complete the piece as you wish. The wall hanging in Figure 94 was finished by wrapping bundles of warp ends with gold gimp after the piece was removed from the loom.

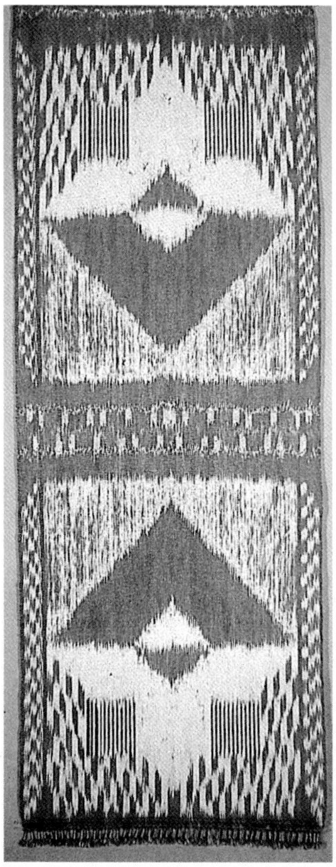

Figure 94. *(left)* Sumba Arrows. *The overall pattern for this wall hanging was tied without a cartoon, 23 x 61 in. (60 x 155 cm).*

Figure 95. *(above)* Sumba Arrows *(detail). Checks and blocks of narrow strips develop the diagonal motif to complement the lines of the arrow.*

Figure 96. *(left)* Varied Color Values. *In this sheer, handspun cotton fabric, two values of indigo were achieved by unwrapping sections of warp during the dyeng. Notice also the crepe effect, created by irregular sleying in the reed.*

Figure 97. Staggered Resists. *To create random stripes, stagger the resists. The wraps shown here vary in thickness because warp bundles (of 12 ends each) were wrapped in groups of two or three or more.*

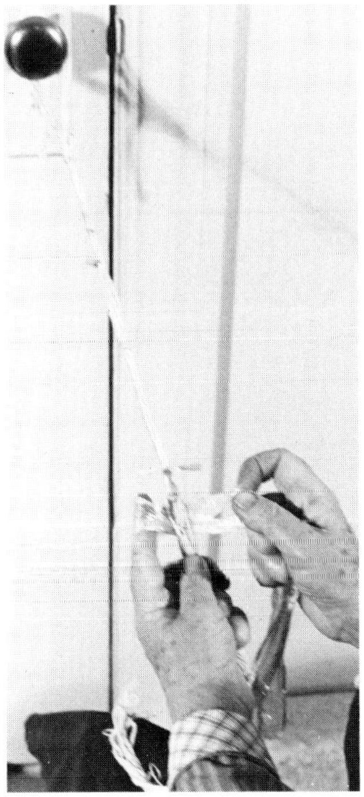

Figure 98. Tying the Resists. *To tie resists under tension, just hook the warp onto a door knob or other stationary object.*

Project 5

Random Warp-Ikat Stripes

My desire for a lightweight cotton shirt led to the contemporary interpretation of ikatted warp stripes shown in Figure 96. Bundles of warp were wound and wrapped individually, to create a random pattern of narrow stripes in shades of indigo and white. Being an avid hand-spinner, I chose to spin all the yarn for the shirt, and over a period of several months created a very fine singles yarn of long staple cotton. It is especially important to size handspun cotton with dilute liquid starch to reduce breakage during warping and weaving. If you use a commercial cotton yarn for this project, you may or may not need to size it. A fine wool yarn could also be used.

Materials

1. Cotton warp and weft for a fabric 24 in. x 5 yards (60 cm x 4.5 meters), fine enough to sley 36 e.p.i. and weave 24 picks per inch; choose yarns of the same weight and twist for both warp and weft
2. Two-harness loom, 12-dent reed, warping board and standard weaving equipment
3. Two colors of plastic tape for tying the resists
4. Indigo vat dye
5. Sizing for the yarn

Methods

Winding the Warp. Wind the warp in 47 individual bundles of 12 ends each. Tie the cross and the warp end loops. Set 24 bundles aside (later to be sized with the ikatted warp bundles prior to dressing the loom).

Tying the Resists. Lay the other bundles (you should have an odd number of them, one less bundle than will remain un-ikatted) out on a table in groups of two or three bundles. These will be wrapped to create intermittent warp stripes. To create a nonrepetitive pattern, stagger the bundles within each group so that when you tie them as a unit, the stripes will fall at different places on each bundle (Figure 97). Once you have done this, fold each group of two or three bundles back and forth several times to make a convenient size to wrap the ikat ties and create a repeat in each group. Try not to have your bundles in the wrapped parts exceed about the thickness of your finger. To facilitate tying all those narrow resists of many different lengths, tie each group independently. In Figure 98, you can see that innovation is called for. When wrapping individual bundles of unequal lengths, since you need to wrap under tension but won't be able to use a frame or warping board, hook each warp bundle onto something – I chose a door knob. Clasp the bundled warp in one hand as you tie the resists. You will remove a few of the wrappings during the dyeing process to get the lighter blue, so use two colors of plastic tape for wrapping the resists. One color will remain on through all the dyeing, while the other color will be removed during the dye sequence. The warp is now ready for dyeing.

Dyeing. The darker and lighter stripes of indigo visible in the detail shown in Figure 96 are accomplished by giving the warp two dips in the indigo vat dye, removing some of the ties, then dipping the yarn a third time. Wash the yarn, remove all the ties and wash again. It is best to size all your yarn at this point, especially if you are working with handspun yarn, and dry it under gentle tension. Sizing helps prevent yarn breakage during weaving.

Dressing the Loom. Lay the warp out on the floor, alternating an undyed warp bundle with an ikatted bundle. After they are smoothed out, you can see where the ikat stripes will fall. Change their positions to break up any visible repeats. This is the advantage of having all the warp in individual bundles. It is now very easy to dress the loom with alternating ikat and plain white stripes.

To enhance and complement the handspun cotton, I sleyed the yarn in such a way as to create a crepe effect in the weave. To do this, sley the first bundle of undyed warp at two ends per dent, and then use the following sequence for sleying the warp through the 12-dent reed: 3 ends of ikatted cotton per dent for 4 dents, for each ikat stripe; 2 ends of undyed cotton per dent, for 3 dents; 1 end of undyed cotton in each of the next 4 dents; 2 ends of undyed cotton in the next dent. Repeat this sequence across the 24-in. (60-cm) width of the reed. To make a firm selvage, sley 4 ends in each of the two outside dents on both sides. Tie onto the cloth beam and weave.

Weaving. The irregular sleying will create a crepe effect. Figure 96 shows this effect as well as the denser stripe of the ikat. The undyed sections of the more densely sleyed ikat stripe look whiter, a result of the washing during dyeing. This adds extra interest to the fabric.

Finishing. When you take the cloth from the loom, machine-stitch the ends to prevent raveling. If you want a wash-and-wear garment, treat the fabric just as you will when you wash it after it is worn. For my own handspun fabric, I set the washing machine for a gentle cycle, added the soap and fabric, started the machine and turned my back, not knowing if the fabric would be ruined or not, and when the washing was finished, I put it in the dryer! When it was almost dry, I pressed it with a warm iron – just enough to give the fabric a finished look.

Naturally, I was very interested in the shrinkage. I started with 5 yards (4.5 meters) of warp on the warping board. Counting loom waste, takeup in weaving and the loss in finishing, the lengthwise shrinkage totaled only a yard and 6 in. (slightly more than one meter), and widthwise, 4 in. (10 cm), which is remarkable for handspun cotton, considering the finishing treatment.

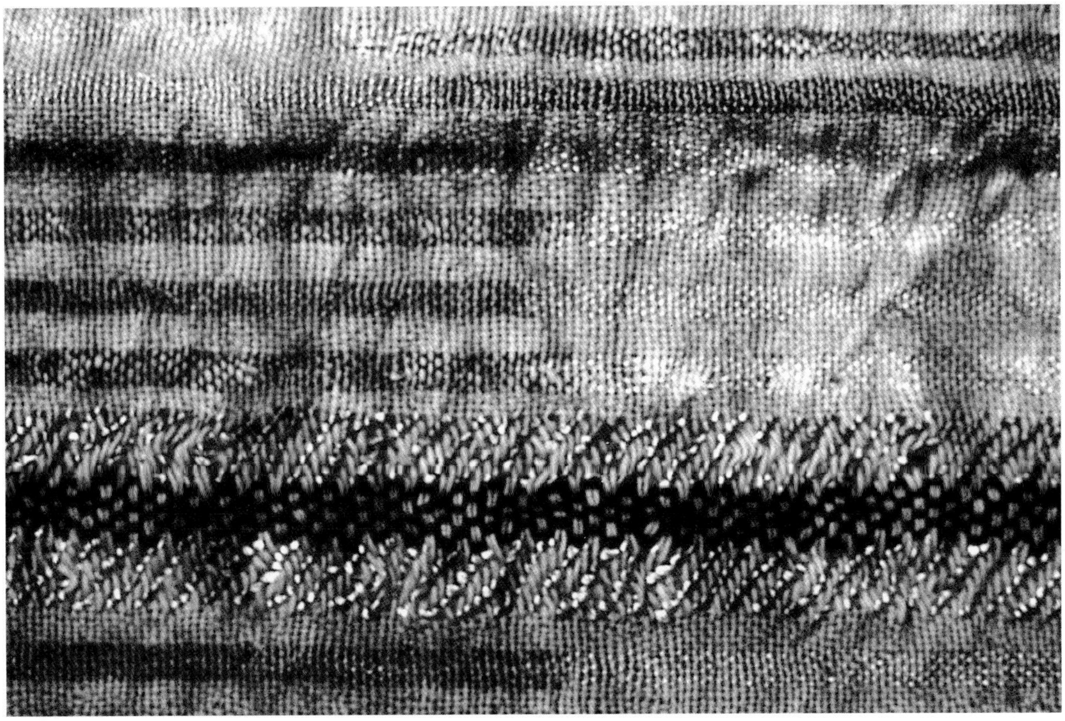

(Above) Lydia Van Gelder. Baulé 88. *Warp Ikat.*

(Left) Dyula, Ivory Coast. *Warp Ikat.*

Figure 99. *(left)* Swedish Apron. *Ikat-resist stripes and light-colored plain stripes are set off nicely by dark blue stripes.*

Figure 100. *(right)* Celebes Silk *(detail). This detail of the selvage illustrates how extra weft has been allowed so that each pick of weft resist can be positioned to match the pattern. These extra weft protrusions will be hidden by the seam when the fabric is made into a sarong for ceremonial occasions. The cloth is 24 in. (60 cm) wide and several yards long. Collection, Joseph Fischer.*

Chapter VI

Weft Ikat

In warp ikat, as we have seen in Chapter IV, the pattern is dyed into the warp before the weaving; once the warp is on the loom, the design is set and cannot be changed. Weft ikat allows greater latitude for fluidity of line and space as you weave.

During the weaving of a weft ikat, it is necessary to position each weft yarn precisely in relation to the preceding weft shot and to the ones that will follow. Any shifting of the patterned weft yarn will alter the design. All this demands a great deal of skill from the weaver.

Weft ikats have been made in most parts of the world where the ikat technique has been used. Among the few exceptions is West Africa, where only warp ikat is done. In Southeast Asia, many beautiful weft ikats have been produced. Particularly striking are the weft ikats from Bali where the pattern completely covers the width of the fabric. By contrast, in the silk weft ikats from Thailand (see Figure 7, page 12), the weft-resist pattern only partially covers the width of the fabric. Japan, with its high development of *kasuri*, as ikat is called there, produces both single-motif and allover patterning with weft ikat. India, which has an old and highly developed ikat tradition, is famous all over the world for the beauty of its ikats, particularly the weft ikats woven in the districts of Orissa and Andhra Pradesh.

Before starting a weft-ikat project, look at the two traditional weft ikats in Figures 99 and 100.

Ikat patterns have been found on Swedish textiles made from the end of the eighteenth century. The patterns are frequently found on woven textiles for everyday use, mainly bed ticks and aprons. The treatment of the fabric in Figure 99 is a simple weft-ikat stripe set off by solid-color stripes. Notice that the fabric has been used widthwise, so the weft stripes run vertically on the apron.

Figure 100 shows a close-up of an unusual form of weft ikat in a very fine silk fabric from Celebes, woven by the Bugis people. This silk has the rustle and crispness of taffeta. Notice the jagged line formed where the light weft-resist parts meet the dyed sections. These areas alternate with solid dyed sections in checkerboard fashion throughout the length of the fabric. The loops of yarn at the selvage are excess weft created as weft adjustments were made to preserve the pattern during weaving.

Figure 101. Lydia Van Gelder. Washboard, *23″ x 20″, Weft Ikat.*

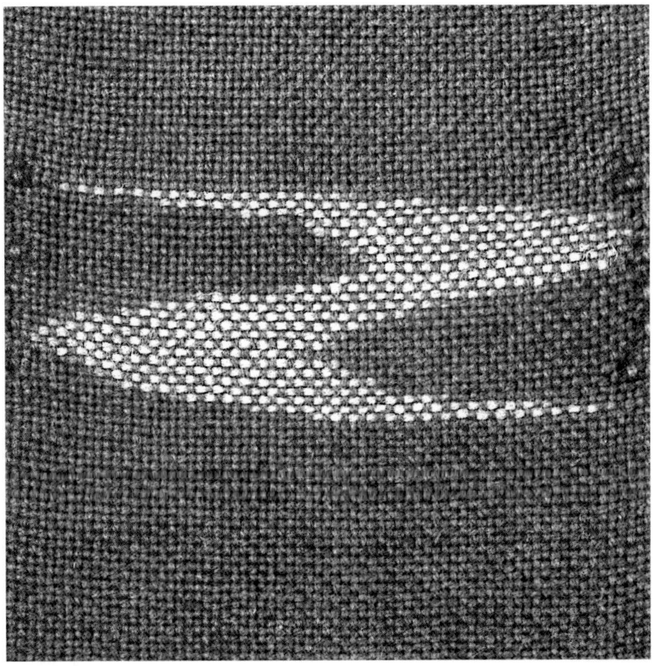

Figure 102. First Sample, Undulating Weft. *The ikat in this sample, woven in balanced plain weave, does not read as strongly as in the weave illustrated in Figure 104.*

Project 6

Simple Weft Ikat

The samples in this project are intended as experimental pieces, to give you a range of experience that you can utilize later in other projects as well as your own ikat designs.

Materials

1. Enough warp yarn to weave seven or eight samples 8 x 8 in. (20 x 20 cm); wool, cotton, rayon or a blend approximately 10/2 size; sett 12 e.p.i.
2. White weft yarn heavier than the warp, of wool, cotton, rayon or a blend: you will need enough for your weft plus enough to make an additional warp for an extra 6-in. (15-cm) sample
3. Four-harness loom, warping board and standard weaving equipment
4. Weft-winding device
5. Plastic tape for tying resists
6. Dye to suit your yarn

Methods

Winding the Warp. You will weave on two warps: one will be the same yarn as the weft and the other one will be a finer yarn. Wind enough of the finer warp yarn for seven or eight small sample pieces. Tie the cross and ends, and place figure-eight ties through the warp in preparation for dyeing. You do not have to dye this warp, but if you choose an already dyed warp, pick a color close in value (it need not be the same color) to

Figure 103. Weft Ikat. Thailand *(detail). The resist marking which forms a border near the selvage of this contemporary cloth assisted in placing the ikat pattern. The weft dominates because it is thicker yarn than the warp.*

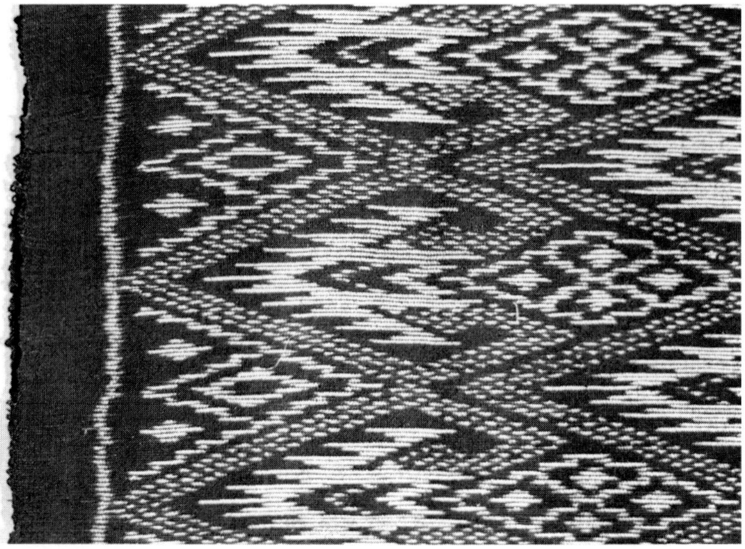

Figure 104. Second Sample, Variation of Undulating Weft. *The weft ikat design is stronger here than in Figure 102 because the weft has packed in more closely and covered more of the warp.*

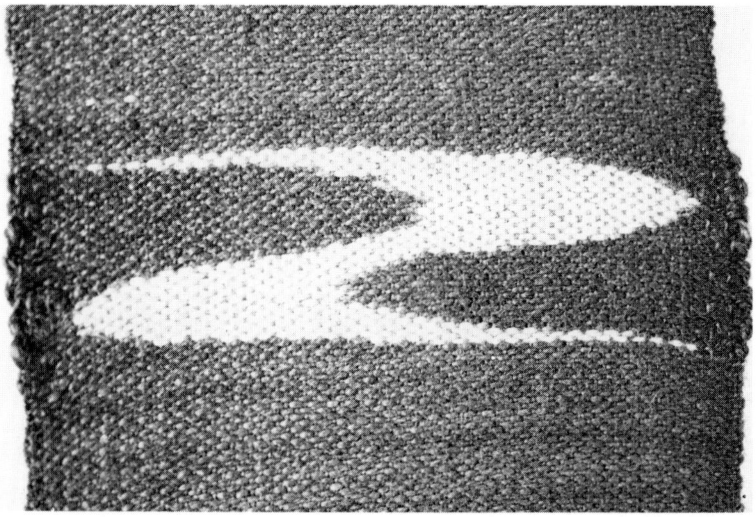

Figure 105. Guatemalan Weft Ikat *(detail). The extra weft has been woven back in near the weft stripes, causing a slight lumpiness at the selvage, Collection, Susan Richter.*

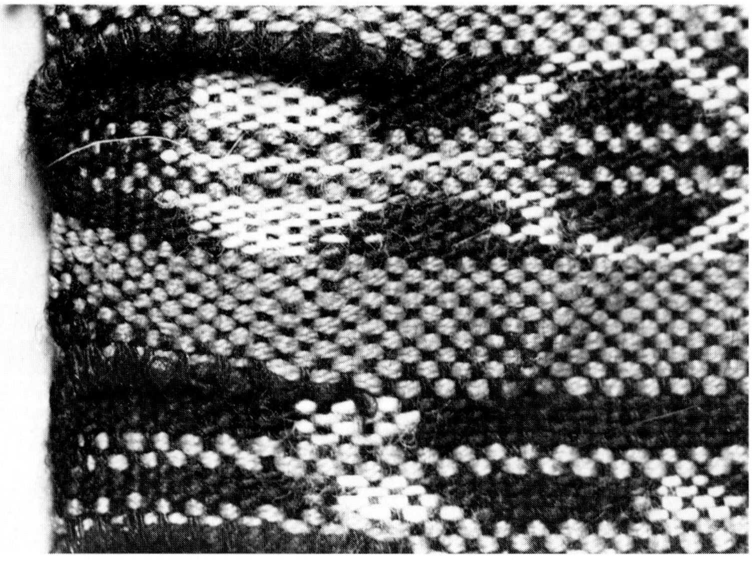

the dye you will use for the weft. This will give you the best results. Alternatively, you could use a white warp, which would combine with the resist-wrapped weft sections for a stronger white but would also show a little bit in the dyed weft areas. Put the warp on the loom, ready to weave.

Use your weft yarn to wind enough warp to weave about a 6-in. (15cm) sample. Tie the heavier yarn onto the finer warp on the loom, making sure that the added warp is long enough so that the knots where you tied onto the first warp will not advance through the reed during the weaving. This warp is only for your first small sample, which you will weave to see how the weight of the warp yarn in relation to the weft yarn influences a weft ikat.

Winding the Weft. Figure your weft-skein X measurement according to the Japanese method described in Chapter III. For each of the weft skeins you wind, you will set up your weft-winding device at X plus an additional amount; the excess weft is to allow for the shifting of each pick as you weave the samples in this project.

Skein 1. Set up your winding device at X + 4 in. (10 cm) and wind a skein of 30 ends. Secure a paper under the wound yarn. Mark on this paper the 8-in. (20-cm) weaving width in the middle of the skein. Now mark on the paper, and wrap, a 3-in. (8-cm) resist section in the center of the weaving width.

Skein 2. Leaving your winding device set up at X + 4 in. (10 cm), wind a skein of 40 ends. On this second skein, wrap the same 3-in. (8cm) resist in the center of the weaving width.

Skein 3. Wind a third skein at X + 4 in. (10 cm), but this time wind from 60 to 80 ends. Mark the paper 1½ in. (4 cm) in from each selvage of the 8-in. (10-cm) weaving width. Then mark 2½ in. (6 cm) in from the selvages. This should create two 1-in. (2.5-cm) resists with a 3-in. (8-cm) section of dyed yarn between them. Tie the two resists.

Skein 4. Now set up your weft-winding device at X + 2 in. (5 cm) and wind one skein of 60 to 80 ends. On the paper, mark one resist in the center of the 8-in. (20-cm) weaving width; tie the resist.

Skein 5. Set up the winding device at X + ½ in. (1.3 cm) and wind another skein of 60 to 80 ends. For this skein, mark two equal resists on the paper, separated by an unresisted section the same width as the resist on skein 4. Tie these two resists.

Plain weft skeins. Skein off enough yarn to weave between sections of ikat on the samples. Depending on the amount of plain weave you want to have between ikat motifs, you may need as much as four times the total amount you wound for all the patterned weft skeins. Since this yarn will not be shifted when woven, simply set up your winding device at the X measurement and wind.

Dye all the patterned and unpatterned weft skeins in the same dyepot. Wash, and dry under tension.

First Sample, Undulating Weft. Note the gracefully curving motif in Figure 102, woven with just one resist area in the weft yarn. Begin your sample by weaving in tabby for 2 or 3 in. (5 to 8 cm) with the dyed, unpatterned yarn, with a beat that will give you the same number of picks per inch as e.p.i. Wind all of the first ikat skein on one bobbin.

In Figure 102, notice how the first ikat pick is placed so the design starts near the right selvage. Open the shed and position your ikat yarn so the resist falls in a similar place. In the next shed, shift the ikat over a little to the left. In this sample, don't worry about the extra yarn that is left at the selvages. Following the picture, keep shifting the weft to correspond to the ikat design. By shifting first to the left, then to the right and back to the left, you will weave the flowing water motif of Japanese *kasuri.* If you watch how you lay the weft ikat into the shed, you can control the thickness and shape of the motif, from fine to thick to fine. When the motif is completed or the ikat bobbin is empty, weave 2 or 3 in. (5 to 8 cm) with the plain weft to finish the sample. Pull the warp knots through the reed and cut this sample off the loom. Tie the finer warp onto the cloth apron ready for the next sample.

Second Sample, Variation of Undulating Weft. Continuing in tabby, weave 2 or 3 in. (5 to 8 cm) with the unpatterned, dyed yarn. Beat firmly. Wind a shuttle with ikat skein 2 and weave the motif to correspond to Figure 104, making the undulation as similar to the first sample as possible. After this motif is completed, weave another 2 or 3 in. (5 to 8 cm) with plain yarn to finish the sample. Do not cut this sample

Figure 106. Weft Loops. *Loops of extra weft yarn from an undulating weft ikat can be utilized as part of your design Also see (top) how the dyed background yarn makes the ikat motif dominate whereas (bottom) in undyed background the dyed sections of the weft ikat skein dominate*

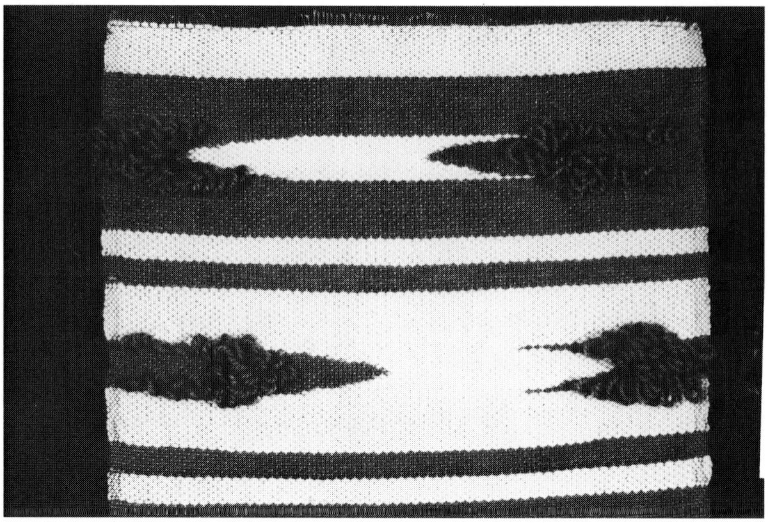

Figure 107. Circles Embellished with Texture. *The circles in this design were woven with two weft-ikat skeins in the shifting-weft technique, and accentuated with textural loops.*

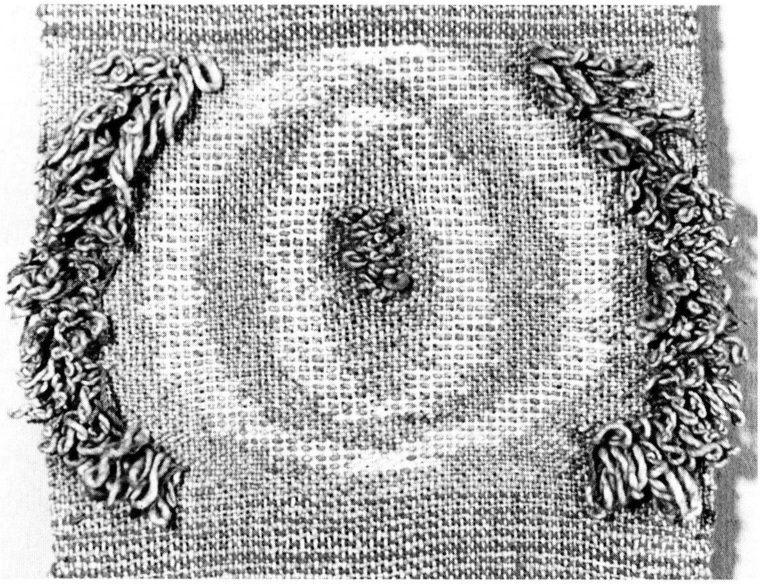

Figure 108. Yarn Adjustment, India. *Loops of excess weft are trimmed off close to the fabric.*

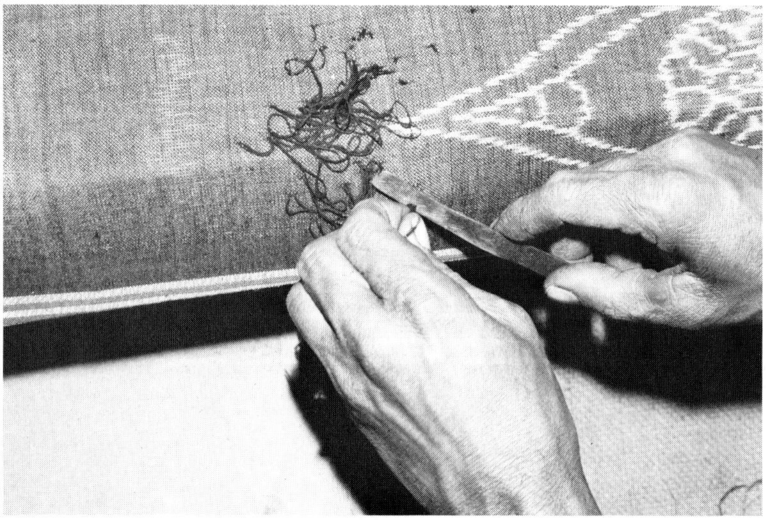

off the loom, as you will use the same warp to weave the remaining samples in this project.

Compare your first sample with the one you just finished. The ikat design in the second sample should be much stronger. Because the warp is finer, the weft can be more densely packed, accentuating the ikat pattern that it carries. The size of the weft yarn relative to the warp can greatly influence the way a design will look when it is woven, as can be seen in the fabric illustrated in Figure 103. In this contemporary weft ikat from Thailand, an exceedingly fine warp yarn was used at 60 e.p.i.; it was woven with a bulkier weft yarn at 22 picks per inch. In spite of the greater number of warp yarns, the larger weft yarn brought out the weft ikat strongly.

Treating the Selvages. If you examine Figures 102 and 104, you will notice a lumpiness in the selvages bordering the ikat design, but none of the loose weft loops that collected as you wove your two weft-ikat samples. The loops were dealt with by turning them to the back of the work and catching them in the weaving at every third or fourth shed.

This is not a new idea, as can be seen in Figure 105, a view of the wrong side of a weft ikat from the highlands of Guatemala, purchased at Zunil. The extra weft yarn was neatly tucked in during the weaving of the ikat stripes.

A different approach is to take advantage of this extra weft yarn and feature it in your design by forming loops with it. Figures 106 and 107 show examples of how this can be done. You may want to try it with one of the remaining samples in this project. To make the loops, lay the first ikat pick in the shed as it is to fall and beat the weft into place but do not change the shed. Pull the extra yarn back from the edge to make a snug selvage and use it to make a loop between the warp ends. Space the loops evenly as you weave, pulling them up over a pencil or some other gauging stick.

The design in Figure 107 shows how the weft, planned to be considerably longer than the weaving width, was looped to complement the curve of the ikat design. As the weaving progressed, the loops were carried along in a massive textural line. The ikat circles in the weft were done much as you will be doing your next samples. At the bottom of the outer circle, a shuttle with one central ikat resist moved just a little to the right and, in the next shed, just a little to the left, until the smaller circle came into the design. Then another shuttle with two ikat resists, one tied in the same place as the resist in the first skein and the other centered so that it would form the inner circle, was used to continue the weaving. The shifting of the weft to right and left shaped the two circles. A tufting was made in the middle of the small circle, also with some of the extra weft yarn. The selvage looks the way a regular selvage would when woven with a textured yarn because the extra weft was all taken up in the loops. The loops were laid in at the start of alternate sheds.

This need to make weft adjustments is a characteristic of weft ikat. In the carefully woven weft-ikat fabrics from India, this problem is met by weaving the excess yarn into the fabric and then trimming it. The weaver from Barpal, district of Sambalpur, Orissa, shown in Figure 108, is trimming the ends close to the fabric surface with a cutting knife. This trimming of the weft yarn is usually done near the selvage.

Another possibility for treating extra weft loops would be to let them all hang out at the selvages. When the weaving was finished, a suitable number of weft yarns could be bundled and wrapped to form a decorative or sculptural edge. You could color-relate the wrapping with the interior of the weaving, or add new yarns and textures.

Third Sample, Shifting Weft. Using your experience with undulating-weft ikat, move on to another type, shifting weft. This method, shown in Figure 109 on page 97, is still practiced in Japan and Okinawa as well as other places. Wind one shuttle with skein 3 and another with unpatterned yarn. You will follow an X-shaped motif derived from the Okinawan weaving in Figure 117 on page 99. This sample will be woven in a direct diagonal line, not undulated as in the preceding samples. In this and the remaining samples in this project, treat the selvages as you wish.

Weave 2 or 3 in. (5 to 8 cm) with the unpatterned yarn in tabby; beat firmly. Using the ikat shuttle, open the shed and place the first resist as far to the right as possible. Change the shed, beating firmly. In this second shed lay the resist as far to the left as possible. Change the shed. Lay the next resist on the right close to, but just a little to the left of, the last righthand resist. In the next shed, shift the lefthand resist just a little to the right. Keep shifting the weft ikat, a little to the left, then a little to the right, to form diagonals. You will see that where they cross, they form a solid white resist spot. The rest of the lines are striped because a resist alternates with dyed yarn in the sheds, as you can see in the Okinawan piece. This design is known as the scissors motif in Okinawa and Japan.

When the resists reach the opposite edge, reverse the direction of the shifts and return to the original positions. Weave until you use up your patterned weft or finish a motif, then weave 2 or 3 in. (5 to 8 cm) with the unpatterned weft to complete your sample.

Fourth Sample, Undulating and Shifting Wefts Combined. Wind one shuttle with skein 4 and another, with unpatterned yarn. As you weave this sample and the following one, notice how the difference in the length of your skein influences your pattern. Weave 2 or 3 in. (5 to 8 cm) with the unpatterned yarn, then begin the motif. Shift the resist to get first a circle and then a figure eight, using the same technique as for the scissors motif, except that here you will shift the resist in a circular line rather than on the diagonal. Finish with 2 or 3 in. (5 to 8 cm) of unpatterned weft.

Fifth Sample, Variation of Undulating/Shifting Wefts. Now wind a shuttle with the last resist skein. As before, begin your sample by weaving 2 or 3 in. (5 to 8 cm) with the unpatterned yarn. However, when you begin the motif, start at one side of the weaving width and shift the resist in only one direction and see what you get. Because the length of this skein (X+ ½ in. [1.3 cm]) is so much shorter than the previous skeins, the pattern that develops should be similar to the one illustrated in Figure 109.

The shifting-weft ikat shown in Figure 110 combines methods you have just used in the preceding samples. It is woven with handspun wool, dyed in natural indigo. I began the weaving with one shuttle; then, as the weaving progressed, I introduced another shuttle with the same weft-resisted yarn. I moved these shuttles independently of one another, one shuttle taking the pattern rapidly off to the right and the other progressing upward. Next I brought the resist areas on both shuttles together, which made the resist pattern a solid white again; then I wove for a while with one shuttle on which I had wound a skein resist-tied to alternate with the other resists. In the upper section, two shuttles were again in use, but they did not completely separate as they did in the lower part of the weaving.

Figure 115 is an example of some of the fine details found in present-day weaving from Okinawa. These delightful flying birds, woven with shifting wefts, are a good example of other design possibilities using this weft-ikat method. If you want to try this motif yourself, lay the edge of a ruler along the yarns going from the head to the tail and to the separation between the wings. You will be able to count the number of weft skeins needed for each change in the weft resists.

Sixth Sample, Weft Twill. This sample and the final one in this series will explore weaves other than the plain weave used for the samples completed so far. By now you should be able to choose which skein lengths you like best, and have some ideas of your own you would like to try. The pieces in Figures 111 through 114 suggest some possibilities.

The weft ikat in Figure 111 is a reverse 3/1 twill. As in a warp ikat woven in a warp-faced twill, the weft twill shown here brings out the weft ikat more strongly. You will notice, on either side of the white resist area, a narrow stripe of a lighter value than the background color. The separate tie for this stripe was removed just before the last dip in the indigo, resulting in the lighter value. The extra weft yarn has been tucked under alternating warp yarns on the wrong side of the fabric and then trimmed (Figure 112); the warps have been staggered in order to prevent undue tension on the warp and to reduce bulk.

Figure 113 also shows a weft ikat woven in a 3/1 twill. Two separate ikat patterns were tied, one with a single resist and a second with two resists. The extra yarn at the selvages was later wrapped with white accents and then trimmed. The 3/1 twill of the ikat sections contrasts with the plain weave used between them.

To make your sample, wind a weft skein to your own measurement, marking the same 8-in. (20-cm)

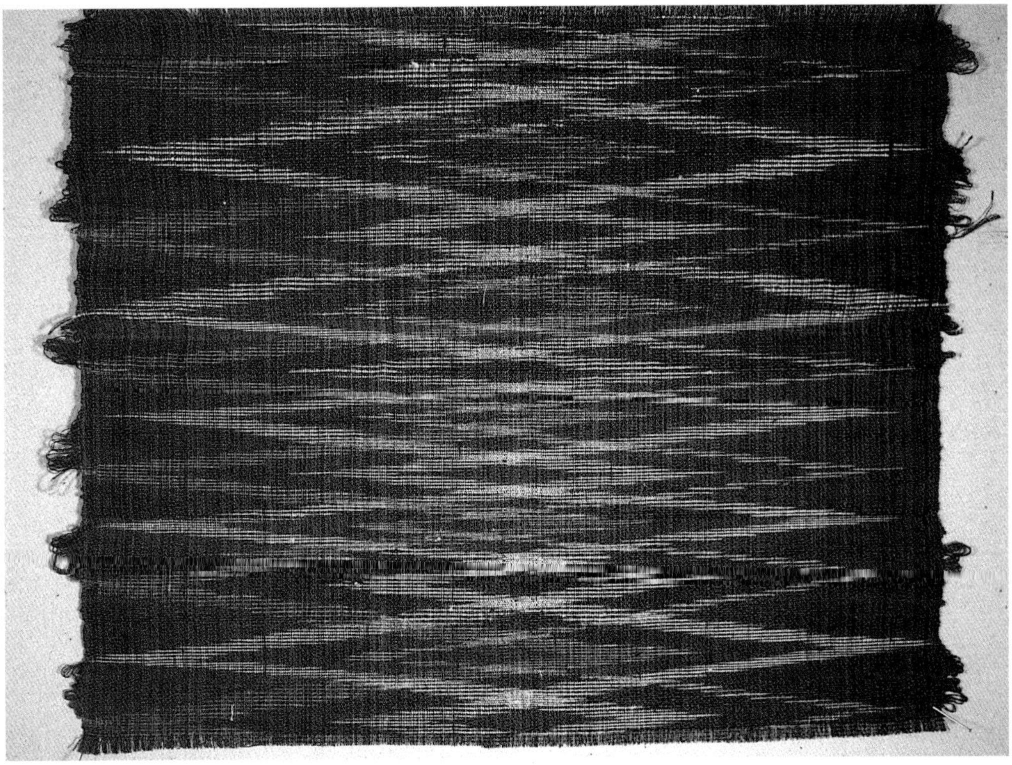

Figure 109. *(above)* Kimono Fabric, Japan. *Tsutuo Odani, a contemporary weaver in Kyoto, used the shifting-weft technique for this silk* kasuri *fabric. The excess weft at the selvages will be hidden by seams when the kimono is sewn together. Collection, Lydia Van Gelder.*

Figure 110. Shifting-Weft Ikat. *Careful planning of resist placement in two differently patterned ikat skeins and controlled shifting of the weft yarns resulted in the "three-eyed monster" pattern in this piece. The skeins with the three "eyes" were tied so as to coincide with the resists in the other skein.*

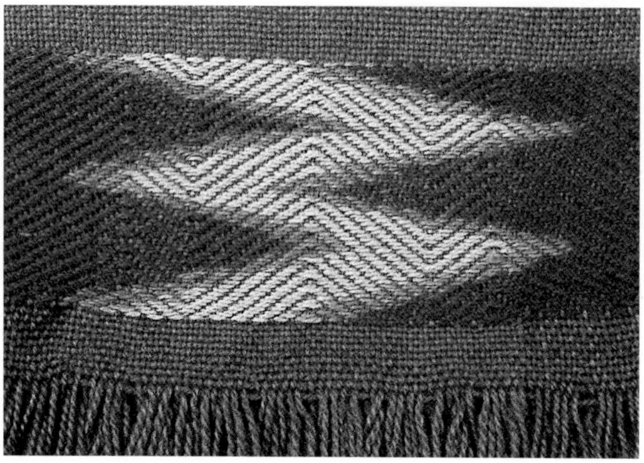

Figure 111. Weft Ikat, Reverse Twill. *The shifting of the weft ikat in a sharp diagonal complements the 3/1 twill, which creates a stronger ikat impression and adds surface texture.*

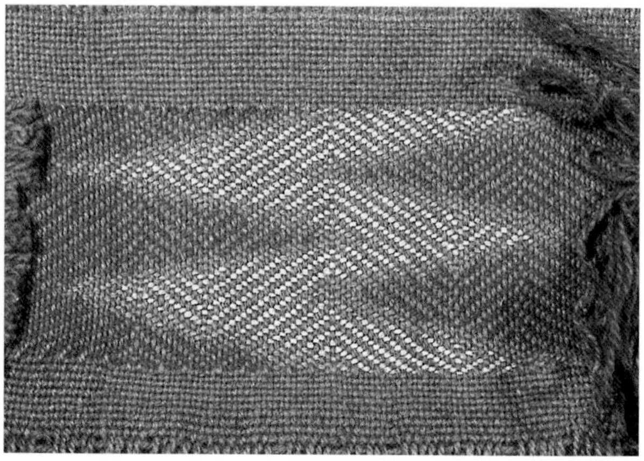

Figure112. Weft Ikat, Reverse Twill *(detail). The underside of the twill weave in Figure 101 shows how the excess weft has been turned under, caught in alternating warp ends and trimmed off.*

Figure 113. Weft Ikat, Block Pattern. *This weft ikat was not shifted or undulated. The twill texture in the ikat sections contrasts with the plain-weave background.*

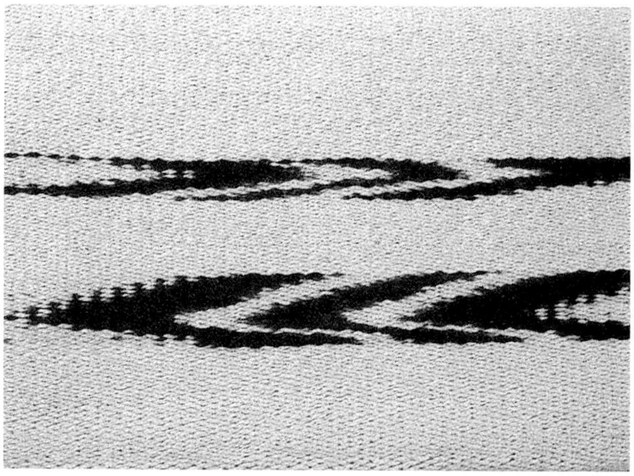

Figure 114. Weft-Faced Cloth. *In this weft rep, undyed yarn was used for the background; the dyed sections of the ikat weft, rather than the resisted* parts, form the pattern.

Figure 115. Flying-Bird Motif, Okinawa. *This tiny motif, enlarged many times in this photograph, appears in many Okinawan pieces. Collection, Lydia Van Gelder.*

weaving width on the paper as before. Make a single broad resist in the center, perhaps 4 in. (10 cm). Dye the skein, along with additional skeins of plain weft if needed, wash, and dry under a little tension. Weave a weft-twill sample, manipulating the ikat resists as you wish.

Seventh Sample, Weft-Faced Cloth. The cloth in Figure 114 was woven as plain weave, but the warp yarns were spaced widely enough to allow the weft to pack down and completely cover the warp. For your last sample, try a weft-faced plain weave, beating the weft down firmly as you weave.

For this sample, again wind a weft skein to your own measurement and use the 8-in. (20-cm) weaving width marked on the paper. This time try something different in the dyeing, using either three or five resists, each separated by an unresisted section of yarn. If you tie the skein with three resists, unwrap the center one after the first dyeing and dye it a second color or a lighter value of the dye used for the unresisted yarn. If you tie five resists, remove the wrapping from the two alternate resists after the first dyeing and redye the yarn either in the same dyepot or in another color.

When you weave the sample, use what you have learned to experiment freely with the shifting of the ikatted weft yarns. The way in which you have wrapped and dyed this weft skein may also lend itself to experimentation with the background color or the treatment of excess weft. The interesting variation of ikat in Figure 114 is a reversal of traditional ikat designs. The weft skeins were resist-tied and dyed in the usual way for ikat, but the use of undyed yarn for the background optically reverses the positive and negative areas in the pattern. This approach would make a marvelous rug, if you were to start out with a yarn that wasn't white. Notice that when the resist yarn is shifted rapidly, the lines are finer; when the shift is slowed, the resists become wider (and correspondingly, the dyed parts become finer or wider). Although the extra yarn could be brought up in loops for texture, the weft could also be planned, with a minimum of shifting and careful calculation of the X + measurement, so that there would be very little excess.

Figure 116. Cutting abaca fiber, Okinawa.

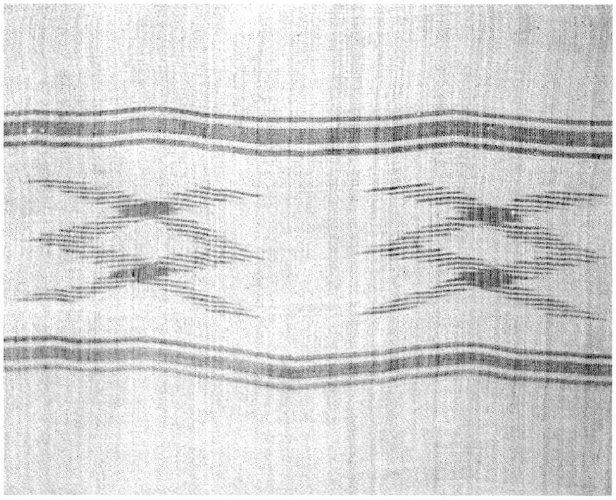

Figure 117. Scissors Motif, Okinawa. *This finely woven banana-fiber cloth departs from the usual ikat-resist pattern on a dark background; here, the background adjacent to the design area appears to have been resisted and then dip-dyed or spot dyed to achieve a dark motif on a light background. Collection, Lydia Van Gelder.*

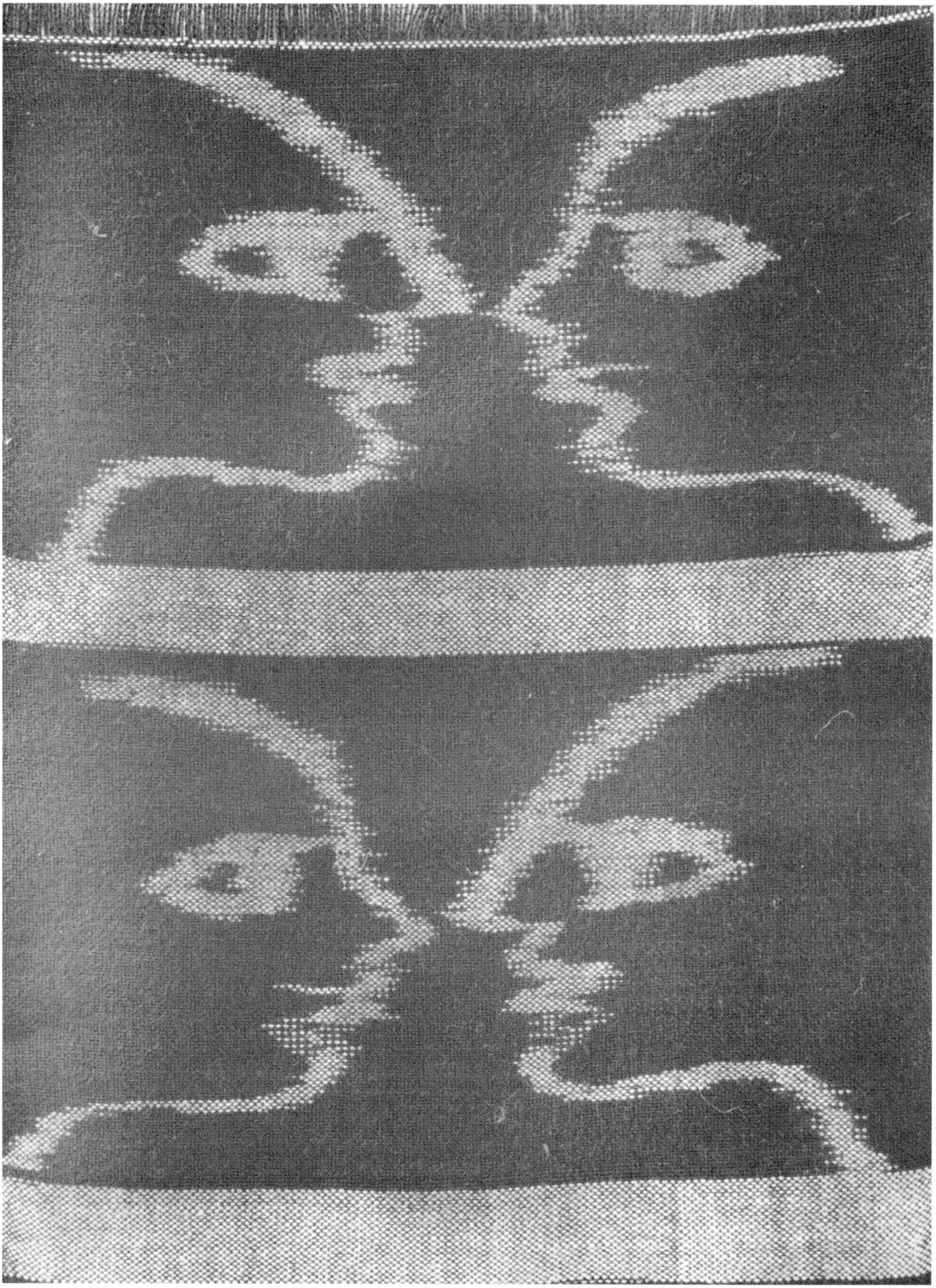

Figure 118. *(left) Ed Rossback.* Kasuri Heads II. *E-gasuri; motif in reverse repeat.*

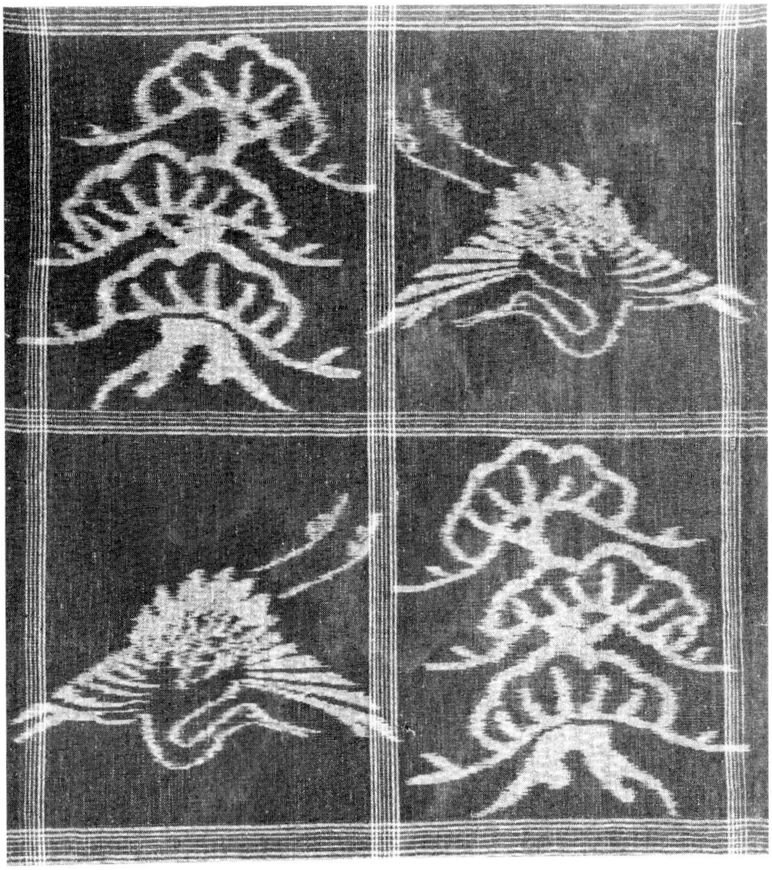

Figure 119. E-gasuri, Japan *(detail). The horizontal reverses in this nineteenth-century picture ikat were created by changing the direction of the shuttle during the weaving. 57 x 13¼ in. (145 x 34 cm).*

Project 7

E-gasuri

The origins and early development of kasuri (Japanese ikat) are veiled in mystery and supposition. There is a folk tale of a woman, Inoue Den, who is said to have created this technique in the early nineteenth century at Kurume on the Japanese island of Kyūshū. However, Professor Bühler mentions ikats which found their way into seventh century Japan from southeastern China; and it is known that *kasuri* has been woven in Okinawa since at least the fourteenth century. What is not certain is whether the technique was introduced in Okinawa through trade with Indonesia and other places, or whether ikat already existed there and was merely influenced, via trade goods, by techniques that had originated simultaneously elsewhere.

There are several classifications of *kasuri*, but our concern here will be with *e-gasuri*, or picture ikat, and geometric *kasuri*. *E-gasuri* is characteristic of Japanese ikat and is often combined with the more rigid geometric designs. Before starting the *e-gasuri* project, look at some fabrics from Japan using this weft-ikat technique.

Figure 119 shows a cloth depicting the crane (a symbol representing a thousand years) and the pine tree, which are combined here to symbolize longevity. It is a cotton cloth dyed with indigo for a *futon*, or bed covering, made in the mid-nineteenth century in Kurayoshi, Tottori Prefecture, on the island of Honshu. The design reverses itself on each horizontal row, a characteristic of the *e-gasuri* technique that will be explored in this project.

The example of *e-gasuri* in Figure 120 is unusual because the picture ikat is woven on a warp patterned to complement the theme of the weft design. The carp, with lines that simulate water curving over its body, is swimming over waves symbolized by the graduated vertical warp stripes. The gracefully drawn carp shows the exactness with which a drawing can be rendered in this weft technique. This combination of themes on the warp and weft creates a truly complete statement. Again, notice how the weft motif changes direction in each row.

The last illustration of *e-gasuri* (Figure 121) is a *mon*, or woven family crest, in which the popular three-commas motif (attributed to the royal family) is combined with the ideogram for longevity, to wish good luck and happiness.

In this project, a segment of the three-commas crest is the design motif, to be woven using the *e-gasuri* technique; the procedures that follow are based on material from Yoshiko Wada.

Materials

1. White cotton yarn for warp and weft, size 20/2, for a finished weaving 8 in. (20 cm) wide by at least 2 yards (2 meters) long – more, if you want to experiment further; sett 30 e.p.i. (The samples in Figures 124 through 127 were woven with a white two-ply, extra-fine cotton yarn.
2. Two-harness loom, warping board and standard weaving equipment
3. Celotex board, 12 x 18 in. (30 x 45 cm); heavy-duty pins (Bank pins are especially good); sketch paper; pencil; two felt-tip pens, black and red; notebook for weaving records; graph paper
4. Plastic tape for wrapping the resists (two colors, if you wish)
5. Vat dye
6. Liquid starch

Methods: Preparation of Warp and Weft

Preparing the Warp. Put all the cotton yarn (for both warp and weft) in a pot of cool water, bring to a boil and continue boiling for 20 minutes to clean and shrink. Rinse, and dry under a little tension to straighten the yarn. Wind your warp, size it, and dry under tension. Dress the loom.

Drawing Your Design. Since your weaving width is 8 in. (20 cm), start with a piece of paper 8 in. (20 cm) wide. Draw a comma design centered in the weaving width and reasonably narrow – 3½ x 1⅜ in. (9 x 3.5 cm) is a good size for a beginning project, as the 1⅜-in. (3.5-cm) measurement will keep the pattern thread relatively short. Now completely fill in the comma motif with the black felt-tip pen.

Finding Your X Measurement. Follow the Japanese procedure for determining the X measurement. Before unweaving, count the number of picks per inch and record this count.

Winding the *Tane-ito*, Japanese Method. This is the operation that makes *e-gasuri* unique among ikat techniques. The *tane-ito*, in literal translation, means seed-thread, and it is used as a guide for wrapping the resists. In Japan, this pattern thread is wound on a frame of fine bamboo reeds. Figure 122 shows a frame made by cutting in half a Japanese bamboo reed from a loom and then mounting the two halves in a frame. The pattern thread is wound back and forth between the reeds, and the pattern is inked on it.

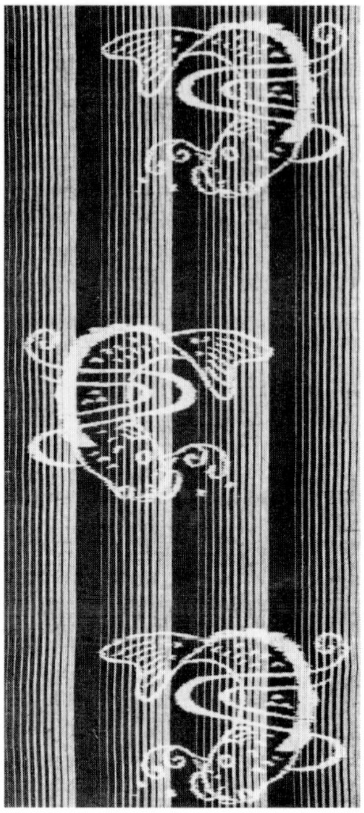

Figure 120. E-gasuri, Japan. *Late nineteenth century. 55 x 13¼ in. (140 x 34cm).*

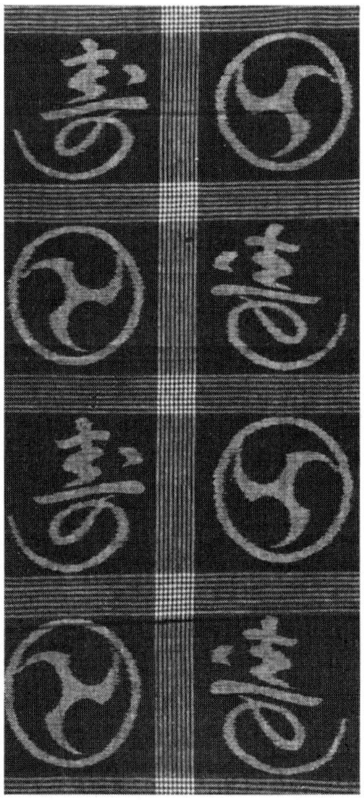

Figure 121. E-gasuri, Japan. *This picture ikat was woven in the nineteenth century, but the three-commas crest is of ancient origin.*

Adapting/Winding the *Tane-ito*. Lay a piece of graph paper on a Celotex board (see Figure 123). Determine your X measurement (A), then set heavy-duty pins (B) into the graph paper, exactly that distance apart. Next, line up pins on each side so that the number of pins on the right side is equal to half the number of weft picks in the pattern motif; the left side should also have pins equal to half the number of weft picks, plus one extra pin. If you have difficulty placing the pins closely enough to match the correct number of picks per inch, cut across the paper design from selvage to selvage in two or three places, evenly spaced; spread it out to meet the set of the pins and the correct weft count, tape the design to the graph paper and reset your pins.

Now you are ready to wind the *tane-ito*. It is important that you use a thread which has been well sized, so that your pattern thread will not stretch later in the process. Leaving an extra length of about 12 in. (30 cm) at one end of the pattern thread, tie the thread to a pin (C) some distance from your design. Bring the long end of your yarn down to the first pattern pin on the left (B) and wind the pattern thread back and forth between the pins. Do not skip a pin or take one out of sequence. Finish off the pattern thread by tying it to another pin (D) below the pattern, again leaving a little extra yarn beyond the pin.

Marking the *Tane-ito* with the Pattern. With the black felt-tip pen, mark all the threads wherever they pass over the filled-in motif on the paper: make sure the underside of each thread is also marked. Mark the selvages by running the red felt-tip pen along the inside of each row of pins. This will give you evenly spaced pairs of tiny red dots at each edge of your pattern thread; when you tie the resists, these can easily be distinguished from all the black markings.

Before the pattern thread is removed from the board, two very important markings remain to be made. Notice, at E, the long black mark on the thread leading to the pins. Make a similar long black mark on your pattern thread. At the other end of the pattern thread, mark three evenly spaced dots (see F). These dots designate the bottom end of the thread, while the top end of the thread is marked with one long mark.

Winding the Weft According to the *Tane-ito*. Carefully remove the pattern thread from the Celotex board. This pattern thread should measure about 9 yards 28 in. (approximately 9 meters). Since it is not a long weft, you can use a warping board, rather than a warping reel, to wind and tie the weft yarn. Use the extra yarn left at each end of the pattern thread to tie onto the pegs of the warping board, stretching the pattern thread out to its full length.

Now wind the weft yarn alongside the pattern thread, just as you would a warp, with a cross. Eight repeats of the pattern are used in the first two samples outlined in this project, so you will need to wind at least eight weft yarns. But you will undoubtedly want to try some combinations of your own, so wind at least 16; however, do not be overly ambitious because it is not advisable to have the weft bundle too thick for this fine patterning.

Tying the Resists for *E-gasuri*. In the Japanese method, the weft is next marked with a water-soluble ink, in a color similar to the one to be used for the yarn dyeing, just outside the blackened areas of the pattern thread. The weft bundle is then tied between the water-soluble marks, taking care not to include the marks (so that they will disappear when the yarn is dyed). The pattern thread may or may not be included in this tying.

I prefer to do it a little differently, and I recommend that you begin your wrapping this way. The pattern thread has been marked with pairs of tiny red dots evenly spaced along its length to indicate the selvages. Now cut off 8 or 9 in. (20 to 25 cm) of plastic tape (you will find the length that suits you best as you gain experience) and tear from this a strip about ¼ in. (0.7 cm) wide. Use this narrow strip to wrap selvage marks along the weft, following the red markings on the pattern thread. *Do not include the pattern thread in the wrappings;* check frequently on this. Wrap only the width of the selvage marks. When all the selvage marks have been wrapped, you are ready to wrap the pattern resists. I find that tying all the selvages first helps keep the weft yarns from shifting out of position during the rest of the tying.

It is helpful, but not necessary, to wrap the pattern with a different color of tape than the selvages. Cut a length of plastic tape, tear it in half or smaller, and wrap all the pattern resists. Vary the width of the plastic ties to suit the widths of the resists on the pattern thread. The accuracy of your tying determines the clarity of your woven design.

Dyeing and Sizing the Weft. Skein the tied weft bundle onto a niddy-noddy. Tie loose figure-eight ties through the skein to keep it from tangling during the dyeing. Wind the pattern thread around a card and keep it for your records. Skein enough extra weft to weave from 4 to 6 in. (10 to 15 cm) between the samples. Dye all the weft in the same dyepot. Wash the yarn. Remove all the resist ties and lightly wash again. Size the yarn, both patterned and unpatterned, in a liquid starch and dry thoroughly under tension. (*Funori,* or ogre starch, is recommended if you use the Japanese yarn from Kasuri Dye Works [see Suppliers List], which also sells ogre and the recipe; ogre is also available in health food stores.)

Methods: Weaving

In each of the samples illustrated in Figures 124 through 127, the design motifs appear in different positions. This change of position, which is one of the unique and charming qualities of *e-gasuri,* is achieved by changing the way in which an ikatted weft yarn is wound onto the shuttle (beginning with either the top or bottom end of the yarn) and the direction from which the pattern shuttle is inserted into the first shed when the pattern is woven. As you weave the samples in this project, be sure to record these procedures carefully in your notebook.

First Sample, Comma Motif. Wind a shuttle with dyed, unpatterned yarn and weave in tabby about 2 in. (5 cm). Wind another shuttle with one weft-ikat yarn, starting with the top end (marked by the single long resist) and finishing with the bottom end (with the three resist dots); cut off the weft yarn. Starting with the bottom motif, open the shed and insert the pattern shuttle *from right to left.* The bottom end of

Figure 122. Dorothy M. Miller. Winding the *Tane-ito,* Japanese Method. *In Japan, the* tane-ito *is wound on a frame made of fine bamboo reeds similar to this one, which was made from a Japanese weaving reed.*

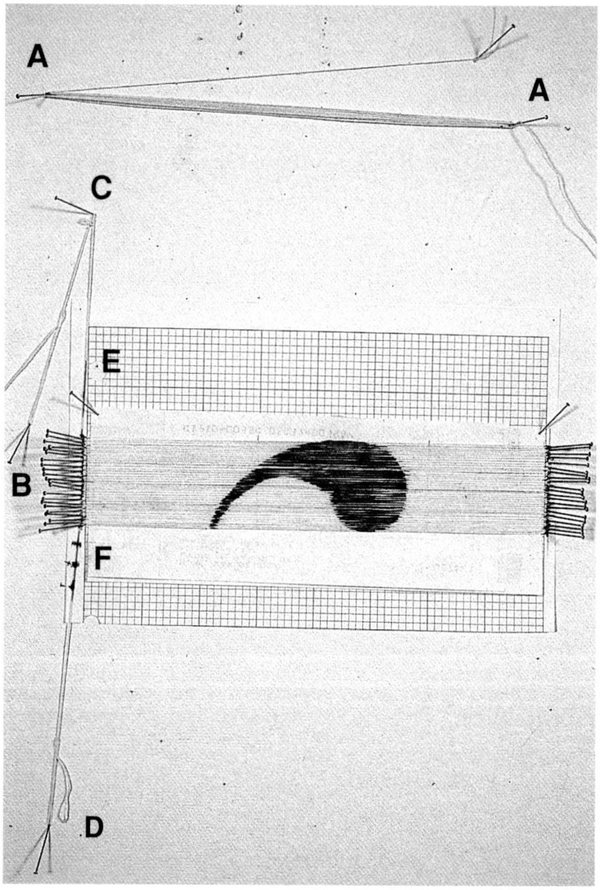

Figure 123. Adapting Winding the *Tane-ito. Mounted on a Celotex board are: (A) the X measurement; (B) pins placed for winding the pattern thread; the start (C) and end (D) of the pattern thread; (E) the marked top end of the pattern thread; (F) the bottom end of the pattern thread, marked with three dots.*

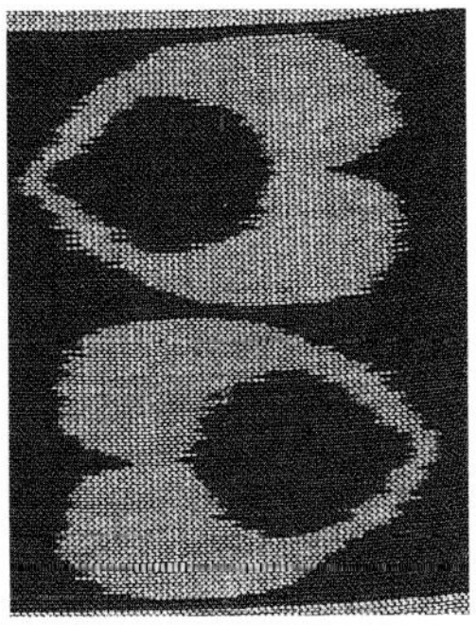

Figure 124. *(above left)* First Sample, Comma Motif. *All of these comma motifs were woven from identically patterned weft-ikat skeins. The variation in their placement on the cloth results from changes in the way the shuttle is wound and the direction in which the shuttle begins weaving. The motifs start from the bottom in this photograph, in the order in which you will weave them.*

Figure 125. *(above right)* Second Sample, Comma Motif. *Refer to your records for the first sample to weave this heart-shaped variation of the same motif.*

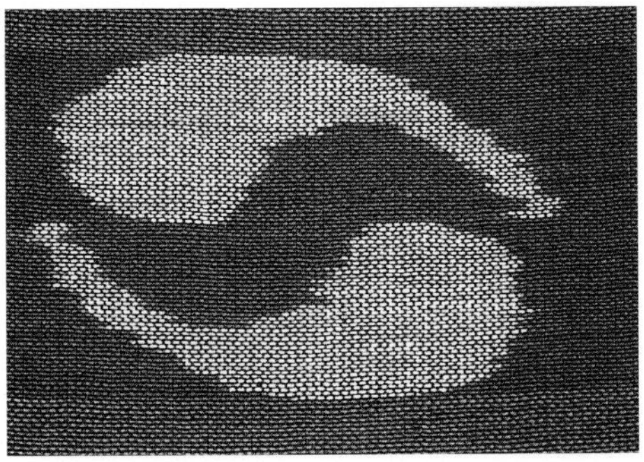

Figure 126. *Inverted Commas.* Different combinations of the motif change the design feeling completely. This sample was begun with a band of plain weft and then the third and first motifs were woven. The reversal of this design could be completed by continuing with 20 picks of unpatterned yarn, weaving the fourth and second motifs, and finishing with another band of plain yarn.

Figure 127. *Butterfly.* Another weaving sequence resulted in this stylized butterfly: the second and third motifs were woven, separated by a narrow band of weft with a single resist to represent the body and head of the butterfly.

the weft, with the three dots, should be at the right selvage. Place the first pick of the comma motif so that the selvage resist marks align at right and left with their respective selvages. Use the selvage marks as guides, checking to see that the pattern resists also fall properly, and weave the first motif. Leave the top and bottom ends of the weft hanging out of the weaving as a reference. Weave about ½ in. (1.3 cm) with the unpatterned yarn.

For the second motif, wind another shuttle with the patterned yarn, again starting with the top end and finishing with the bottom end (indicated by the three dots). This time, however, insert the shuttle in the shed *from left to right* to reverse the comma. Using the selvage marks as a guide, weave the second motif. Weave about ½ in. (1.3 cm) with the unpatterned weft yarn.

Notice that the third motif from the bottom in Figure 124 flips over. This change is made by winding the shuttle from the bottom end of the patterned weft yarn to the top, finishing with the long resist marking. Insert the shuttle *from left to right* in the first shed. Aligning the selvage and pattern resists, weave the motif, ending with the bottom end of the ikat yarn. Weave ½ in. (1.3 cm) with unpatterned weft.

The last motif of the first sample is wound on the shuttle in the same way as the third motif, from the bottom end of the patterned yarn to the top end. To weave this motif, insert the shuttle *from right to left* in the first shed. Weave the comma and finish by weaving about 2 in. (5 cm) with unpatterned weft yarn. Record all of the directions for comma motifs 1, 2, 3 and 4 in your notebook.

Second Sample, Comma Motif. By weaving the comma in different positions, you can create several designs from the same motif. The sample shown in Figure 125 resembles two heart shapes, reversed. To frame this motif nicely, weave a few picks of white weft yarn and then three picks of dyed, unpatterned yarn. Referring to your records for the previous sample, weave the third motif followed by the second motif. Then weave three picks of dyed, unpatterned yarn. Now weave the fourth motif and, lastly, the first motif, finishing with three picks of dyed yarn and a few picks of white yarn. Record this in your notebook.

Figures 126 and 127 suggest other ways to weave the comma motif. If you decide to experiment further, be sure to record your procedures for reference.

Third Sample, Abstract Design. In the abstract design shown in Figure 131, it is interesting to see what happens when the pattern is off-center. The blocks of striped lines make interesting groups when the position of the motif is altered in the weaving. You will see many applications of this striped accent in *e-gasuri* fabrics.

For this design, draw an abstract motif on paper. The motif should measure about 5¾ in. (14.5 cm) by 1¼ in. (3 cm) and have one block of fine lines and another block of stronger lines (you need not draw the lines in detail, but indicate where they are to be placed in the design). To transfer this design to a pattern thread, follow the same procedures for establishing your X measurement, marking your pattern thread, and winding and tying the weft resists as for the *e-gasuri* comma motif. However, this time do not center your design but position it on the Celotex board about ¼ in. (0.7 cm) from the left selvage. Mark your design on the pattern thread as before, except for the areas designated for blocks of stripes. To mark these fine lines, slip a piece of paper under every other pattern thread and mark only those yarns on top of the paper. For stronger lines, use the same method but slip the paper under and over the pattern threads by twos, so that you will have alternating pairs of marked and unmarked yarns.

If your design does not exceed a height of 1¼ in. (3 cm), on a weaving width of 8 in. (20 cm), your pattern thread should measure about 8 yards 12 in. (7.5 meters), and the weaving can be done on the same warp as the comma motif. You will need to wind and tie four patterned weft yarns for this sample, plus at least eight more if you want to experiment further.

To start, weave about 3 in. (8 cm) with plain dyed yarn. Then wind an ikat shuttle for the first motif, beginning with the top end of the patterned weft yarn. Open the shed and insert the shuttle from right to left. Place the selvage resist marks, and remember that this design will be off-center. Weave the first motif, then weave about 1 in. (2.5 cm) with plain, dyed weft yarn.

The second motif is now shifted to start at the other side of the fabric. Wind the shuttle as for the first motif, starting with the top end. Open the shed and insert the shuttle from left to right. Weave the motif, then weave about 1 in. (2.5 cm) with plain, dyed weft yarn.

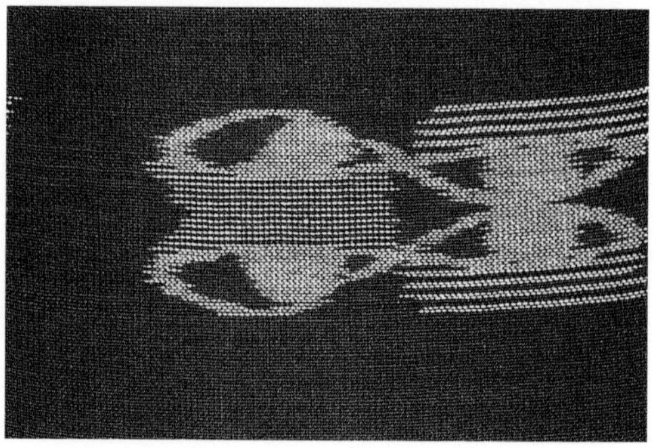

Figure 128. Detail of Third Sample, *showing design unit on the right.*

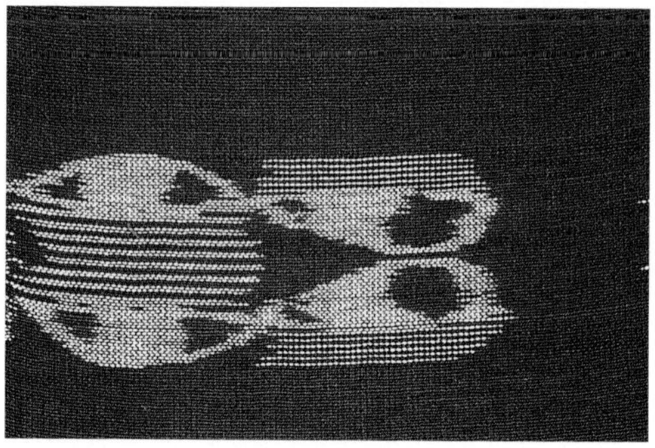

Figure 129. Detail of Third Sample, *showing design unit on the left.*

Figure 130. Detail of Third Sample, *showing design unit going from selvage to selvage.*

In the third motif, the design shifts back to the other side, but it also turns upside down. To get this reversal, wind the shuttle starting with the bottom end. Open the shed and insert the shuttle from right to left, adjusting the pattern according to the selvage marks. Weave the motif, plus about 1 in. (2.5 cm) of unpatterned weft yarn.

For the last of the alternating abstract motifs, again wind the shuttle beginning with the bottom end of the patterned weft yarn. Open the shed and put the shuttle through from left to right. Weave the motif and finish the sample by weaving about 3 in. (8 cm) with the plain dyed weft. Record all of the directions for abstract motifs 1, 2, 3 and 4 in your notebook.

Experiment further with your abstract design, using what you have already learned from weaving the comma motifs. With an off-center motif, the design possibilities seem to be limitless. For example, you could weave a single motif in such a way as to fill the full width of the fabric. To do this with your abstract motif, you would first weave a little with plain, dyed weft; then you would weave motifs 1 and 4, and finish with the unpatterned weft. An important principle in Japanese weaving is to attain the greatest design potential with the least preparation. It is a good principle to keep in mind as you explore the possibilities of *e-gasuri* in your own weaving.

Script in *E-gasuri*. The *e-gasuri* technique offers a versatility in ikat that is truly unique, and there is one more design possibility that should not be overlooked. Because it is possible to use such fluid lines in *e-gasuri,* you can literally write in weaving. To do this, you would follow the same procedures as for the comma motif. With a written word, you can also weave its mirror image, both upside down and in reverse, by controlling the winding of the shuttle and the direction from which you begin weaving the motif.

Figure 132. Mirror-image *words in* e-gasuri.

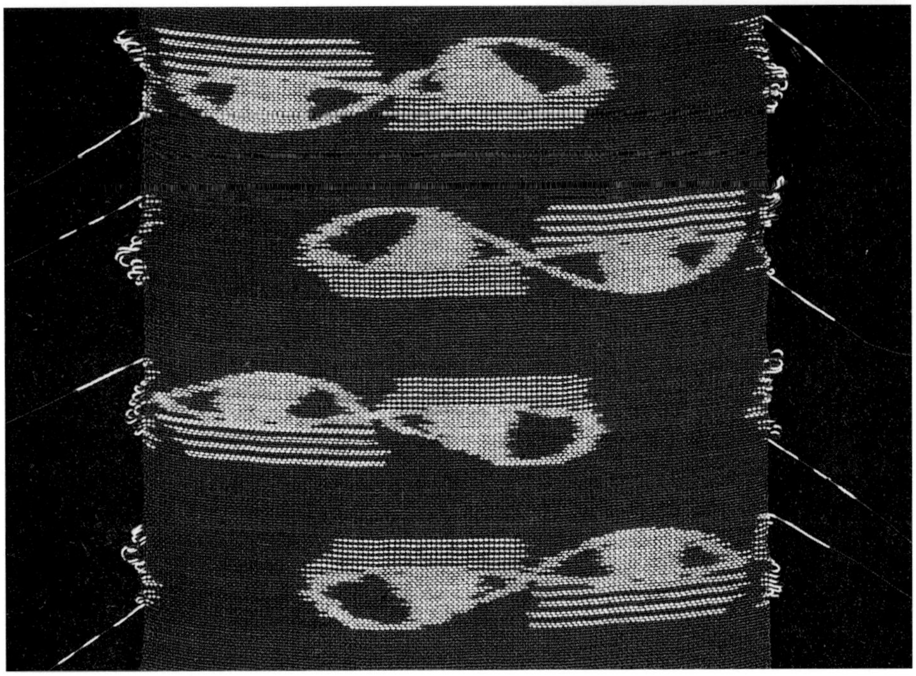

Figure 131. Third Sample, Abstract Design. *The sample in this photograph "reads" upward from the bottom, beginning with the first off-center motif. Notice that the top and bottom ends of the pattern thread, visible near the selvages, begin and finish on opposite sides. This is because there is an odd number of picks in the motif; the comma motif (Figures 124 – 127) has an even number of picks.*

Figure 133. *(left)* Traditional Overshot, Wheel of Fortune. *Ikatting the pattern weft can add new dimension to colonial overshot weaves like this one.*

Figure 134. *(below)* Marking the Pattern Weft. *One repeat of the* Wheel of Fortune *has been woven, and the weft picks to be ikatted have been marked with three different colors of felt-tip pens. This sample will be unwoven and the marked wefts used as pattern threads. This design has three separate pattern threads.*

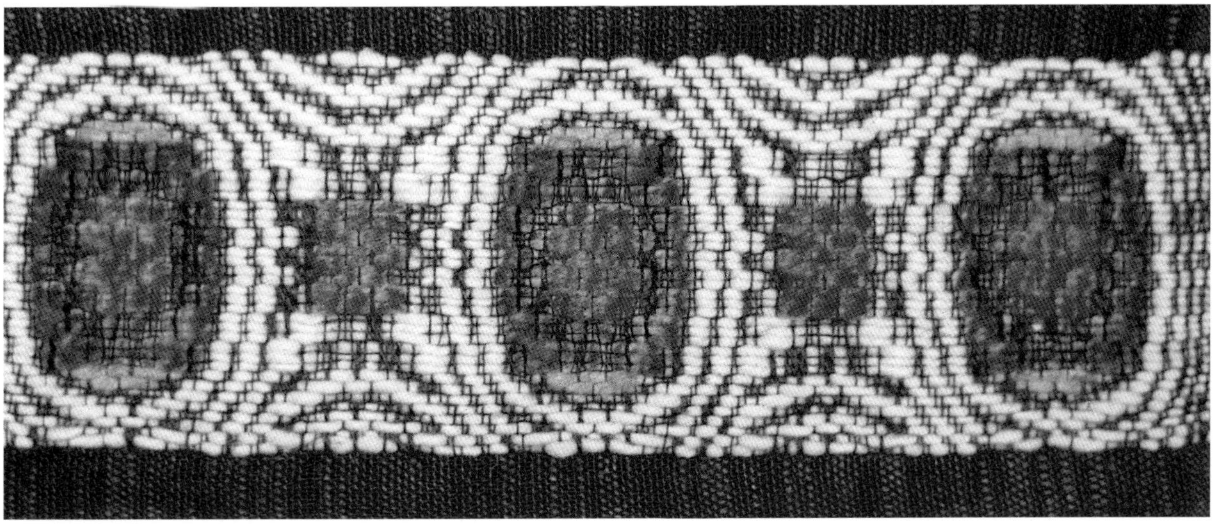

Project 8

Traditional Overshot

Traditional overshot weaves from Europe and Colonial America continue to have, besides their historical significance, a great deal of charm. You can take a new approach to their weaving by ikatting certain parts of the overshot pattern weft.

Any overshot pattern can be used for this project, but the Wheel of Fortune (Figure 133) was selected for the sample. The original draft has been reduced in scale (see Figure 136) to make the units applicable to this small sample.

Materials

1. Warp yarn, size 10/2, for a finished weaving 3 yards (2.5 meters) long by 15 in. (40 cm) wide; sett 12 e.p.i.

2. Yarn for the tabby inter-weft, 10/2 as for warp

3. Soft, fluffy yarn (either wool or cotton) for the overshot weft, to weave 8 to 10 picks per inch

4. Four-harness loom, 12-dent reed, warping board, weft-winding device and standard weaving equipment

5. Draft of an overshot pattern (if you do not use the Wheel of Fortune, Figure 136)

6. Felt-tip marking pens in three colors

7. Plastic tape for tying the resists

8. Dye to suit the pattern yarn

When selecting yarn colors, consider their relationship to each other in the weaving and dyeing. The warp and tabby weft could be either white or a very light color. In the sample shown in Figure 133, the warp and tabby weft yarns are about the same value as the pattern yarn that was dyed. The pattern weft yarn could be white, or a very light value of the color it will be dyed. For example, a very light green could be overdyed a dark green.

Methods

Plan your pattern to get several horizontal repeats of your design. For the Wheel of Fortune sample, the design was drafted to be centered on the fabric, with five full units across the fabric and no broken or unbalanced units at the sides.

Warping. Wind the warp for your sample, put it on the loom and weave a few inches (cm) with the tabby inter-weft yarn in plain weave. Wind a shuttle with the undyed, thicker pattern yarn and weave one full repeat, using both the pattern and inter-weft yarns as you will be when you weave the finished piece. Weave a few picks of plain weave with the thinner tabby yarn, to hold the pattern in place as you work with it. Cut the woven sample off the loom and lay it out on a table to mark the yarns. I recommend pinning it to a Celotex board to hold the weaving taut.

Marking the Pattern. Markings will not be made to indicate where to ikat the pattern yarn. With one of your colored pens, mark the 12 overshot picks in the centers of the five design motifs. With a second color, mark all the remaining overshot picks within and including each of the three ovals except the two top and bottom rows, which you will now mark with the third colored pen. Mark the outer turnings of the weft at the selvages with one of the colored pens. Rub the color into the yarn as firmly as you can in order to get an accurate mark on the yarn. Figure 134 shows how the woven, marked pattern weft should look.

If you are weaving an overshot pattern of your own choosing, select and mark off units within the design to complement the pattern, as has been done with the Wheel of Fortune.

Winding the Weft for Ikat. You will wind off and wrap three separate resist bundles for each row of motifs: a bundle of 12 picks (the central oval) marked with the first and second colors of pen; another bundle of 12 picks (six above and six below the central oval) marked only with the second pen color; and a bundle of four picks (two above and two below the central oval) marked with the third color of pen.

Before proceeding, count the number of pattern shots needed to complete one whole motif and record it for use in calculating how much pattern weft you will need to complete the project.

Then separate your pattern threads for ikatting by carefully unweaving your sample until you reach the marked weft yarns. Cut off and lay aside the two picks of weft marked with the third pen; separate the next six wefts and lay them aside; take out the center 12 picks of weft and lay them aside. In the following instructions, they are referred to as the third, second and first resist ties.

To find your X measurement, use a section of the unwoven weft which you marked at the selvage turnings. Then set up your adjustable weft-winding device to the X measurement in order to wind the skeins and tie the weft resists. As in Figure 135, tie the first pattern thread between the two holding blocks, using the selvage marks to place it accurately. Now wind the skein for the first tying, which is the center section of the motif. Wind multiples of 12 (the number of picks you need for each motif), but it is best to wind more than one skein so that the bundles to be tied are not overly thick. Smaller skeins tie much more accurately.

Tying the Resists. Tie the skein according to the markings on the pattern thread. Wrap *very tightly* those resists marked with the first pen color, as they are the motif. Where you have marked the pattern thread with the second color, make a looser wrapping to create a partial resist. This will result in shading in the finished piece.

When you have finished tying all the skeins for the center motifs, remove the first pattern thread and replace it with the second pattern thread. Repeat the process of winding weft and tying resists, but make all these wraps loose to create partial resists. Follow the same procedure for the third pattern thread, again wrapping the resists loosely.

Skein off enough of the same yarn as the pattern weft to weave the areas that will not be ikatted, and dye all the overshot-weft skeins in the same dyepot. Before you wash and dry the weft skeins, mark each one according to its ikat pattern, using a tie of colored yarn or other device.

Load shuttles with the dyed, unpatterned weft, and with each type of ikat skein; mark the loaded shuttles to differentiate between the resist patterns. Weave a few inches (cm) with the tabby yarn in plain weave, then start the design. Remember that these Early American patterns are woven with one shot of tabby inter-weft between overshot picks.

Several variations are possible with this overshot pattern. Try weaving just blocks of resist using only the center, or first, resist tying. Vary your treadle combinations and weave in blocks. Or alternate bands of ikatted overshot weaving with plain weave. There are any number of interesting possibilities.

Figure 135. Tying the Pattern Weft. *The weft skein in this photograph has been tied according to the colored markings on the pattern thread, which is visible underneath the skein. Two kinds of resist wraps are shown here: the darker wrapping is the usual tightly wrapped ikat resist; the white plastic tape is loosely wrapped to create a partial resist.*

Figure 136. Reduced Draft, Wheel of Fortune.

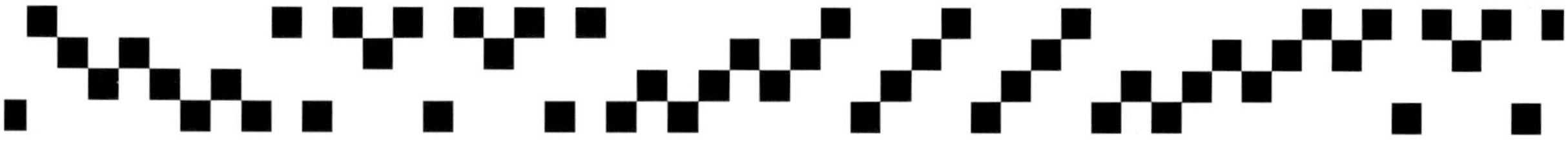

Figure 137. First Sample, Plain Weave. *Weave this preliminary sample in plain weave to develop the undulating-weft design.*

Figure 138. Second Sample, Overshot Weave (detail). *This close-up of Figure 139 shows the undulation of the weft motif and the juxtaposition of the pattern overshot and foundation weave.*

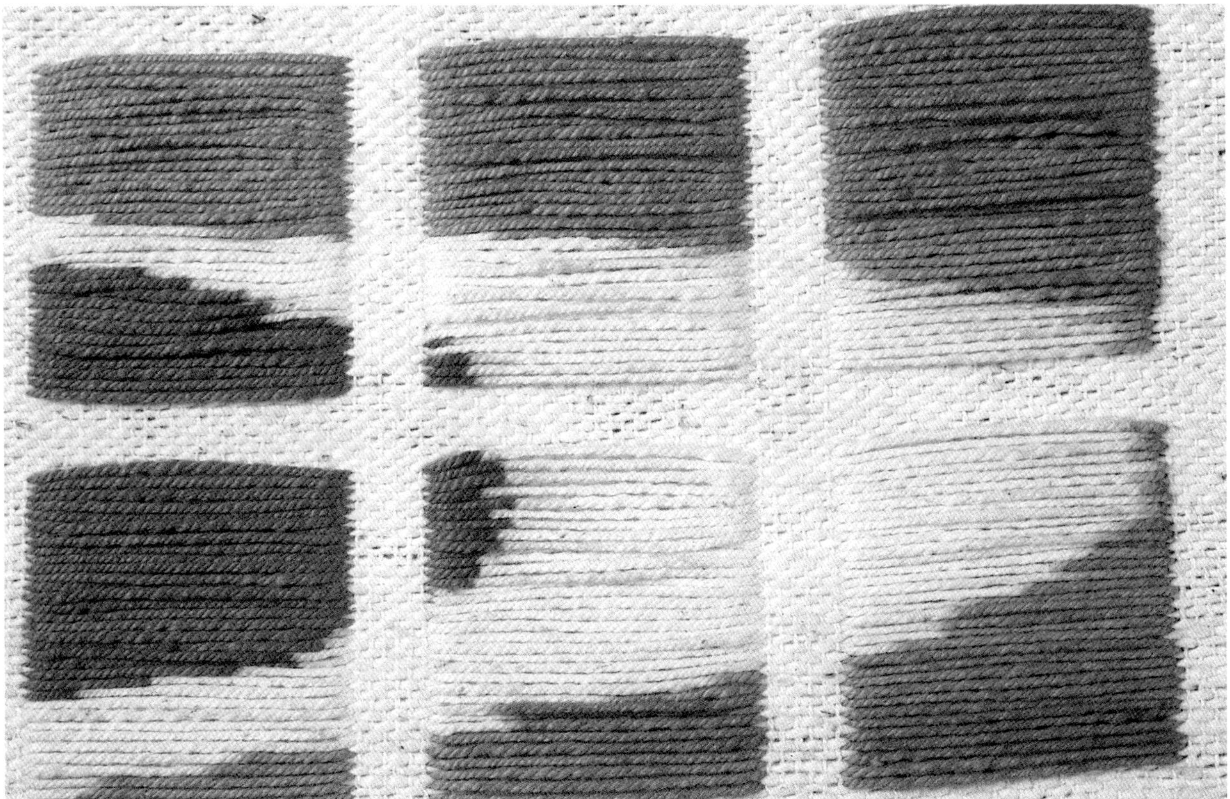

Figure 139.
Contemporary Overshot

Project 9

Contemporary Overshot

There are still more directions you can explore with loom-controlled overshot weaving techniques. In this project. overshot is used in the contemporary wall hanging shown in Figure 139, which suggests clouds seen through a window. The ikatted overshot weft, woven in the undulating-weft technique from Project 6, is combined with plain-weave areas that form the window frame and panes.

Materials

1. Warp, enough 10/2 white cotton for at least a 2-yard (2-meter) length 18 in. (45 cm) wide (you will weave at least three 18 x 18 in. [45 x 45 cm] samples); sett 12 e.p.i.
2. Tabby weft, enough soft, one-ply white cotton to weave three 18-in. (45-cm) squares
3. Overshot weft, enough soft cotton carpet warp to weave three 12-in. (30-cm) squares in undulating-weft ikat (see section on winding the weft, below)
4. Four-harness loom, 12-dent reed, warping board, weft-winding device and standard weaving equipment
5. Plastic tape for tying the resists
6. Dye to suit the yarn used for the overshot (Procion was used in the samples illustrated)
7. Sketching materials, paint, brush and paper, graph paper (optional)

Methods

Drawing the Design. Using the methods discussed in Chapter I, block out an 18-in. (45-cm) square on newspaper and make a rough sketch of the design in Figure 139, including the 12-in. (30-cm) overshot square and the undulating-ikat design within it. Refine the drawing until you are satisfied with the cartoon.

Winding the Weft. Before you set up your weft-winding device, decide how much you want the ikat motif to undulate, which will determine how much extra weft you allow beyond the 12-in. (30-cm) weaving width. Take a piece of string about 28 in. (70 cm) long; in the center mark off 12 in. (30 cm) and in the center of that measurement, mark a 3½-in. (9-cm) length. The 3½-in. (9-cm) measure will be the length of the ikat resist. Hold the marked string taut over the drawing of your design. Play the string back and forth, horizontally and vertically, and estimate how much beyond the 12-in. (30-cm) marks you will need to allow in your weft skein for the undulation. Use this estimate to set up your weft-winding device. Wind three weft bundles, to weave three separate samples. Position and tie a 3½-in. (9-cm) resist on each bundle. Wind off six more small skeins, two for each sample.

Dyeing the Weft. In the piece in Figure 139, two different hues of orange were used. On one side of the resist, the yarn was dyed a red-orange; on the other side, a yellow-orange. The values are so close that only a change of hue is evident. With cold-water Procion, it is possible to dip one end of an ikatted skein in the first dye while holding the other end out. After the first end is dyed, wrap it in a plastic bag and dip the other end in the second dye. The resist separation is ample to assist in this procedure. Dip three of the small skeins in each dye. Wash and prepare these skeins for weaving.

Winding the Warp. Wind the warp and dress the loom, using the following order for drawing in:

1, 2: repeat for 40 ends
Repeat four times: 3,4 (repeat for 24 ends), 1, 2 (repeat for 6 ends)

3, 4: repeat for 24 ends
(to complete the five overshot squares)

1, 2: repeat for 40 ends

First Sample, Plain Weave. After the loom is dressed and the weft skeins dyed, try the ikat motif first in plain weave. This will give you a feel for this particular ikat resist, and, as you weave, you will undoubtedly discover other design possibilities. Figure 137 shows an example.

Weave 2 or 3 in. (5 to 8 cm) with the unpatterned weft which has been dyed the color that will be on the *left* of the ikat motif when it is woven. Start the undulating-weft motif and weave, following the undulation drawn on your cartoon. When you finish the motif, change to the solid color that is on the *right* side of the ikat motif, and weave to finish off the sample.

Second Sample, Overshot Weave. As you weave the design in the overshot squares, refer to your cartoon for pattern and color placement. You will, of course, manipulate each pick of the overshot weft to achieve the undulation you want. Start your weaving with the white cotton tabby weft, working in plain weave (1-3, 2-4) until you have balanced the border width, plus a little more to turn under for a finish. The instructions that follow are for a rising-shed loom. To weave the overshot squares, treadle 1-2 and place your first pick of overshot weft; treadle 1-3, using the tabby weft (same as the border weft); 1-2, overshot weft; 2-4, tabby. Repeat these four picks until you have squared the overshot-weave areas. (To see whether you have woven a true square, release the tension on the warp; if necessary, weave another pick or two of overshot to complete the square.) Then weave in plain weave with the tabby weft to make the narrow horizontal stripes that form the window pane. Alternate the overshot squares with plain-weave stripes until you have five repeats of the overshot squares. Finish with the same amount of plain weave as you wove at the beginning of the design.

The detail in Figure 138 shows clearly the juxtaposition of the pattern overshot and foundation weaves. The design carries on in spite of the cross structure of vertical and horizontal lines. Although their values are close, the two oranges form a strong contrast against the white background.

Third Sample, Overshot Variation. Another design interpretation using the same ikatted weft is shown in Figure 140. A different color of background tabby weft has been used, and the overshot weft undulated differently. For your third sample, experiment to achieve a variation of your own.

To finish, you can mount your samples on stretcher bars and turn under the selvages and ends. The excess overshot weft at the selvages is of no consequence, since it will not show.

Figure 140. Third Sample, Overshot Variation. *Several design interpretations can usually be woven from the same weft-resist pattern. Here, the ikat flows upward rather than undulating.*

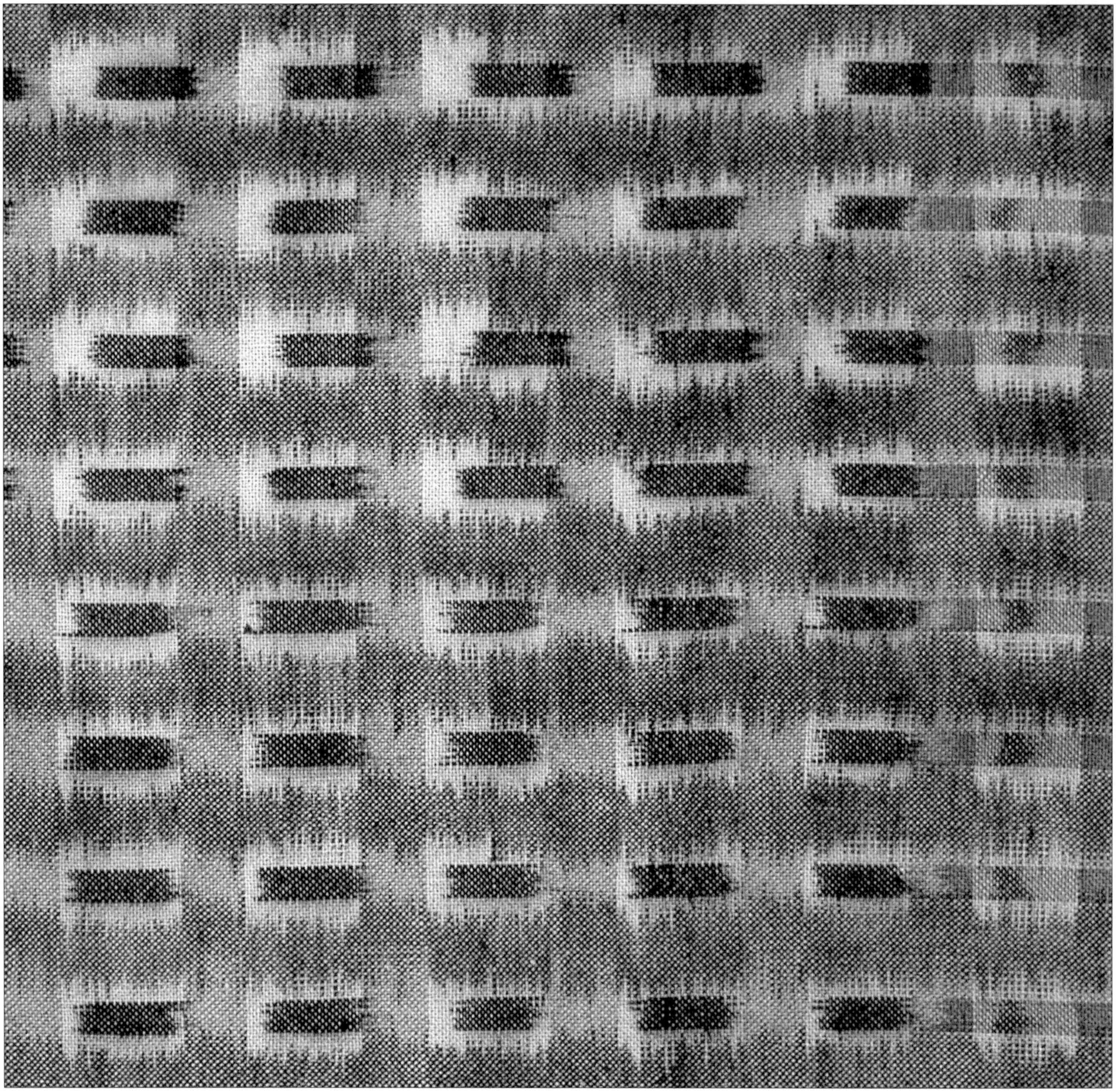

Figure 141. Virginia Davis. Serranda 4 *(detail) Double Ikat, linen.*

Figure 142. *Patolu* Sari, Gujarat *(detail). A* patolu *design typically consists of a border of stripes and resist-dyed patterns around a central field that is either plain or densely patterned. This sari has geometric motifs in a square grid.*

Chapter VII

Double Ikat

In double ikat, resist patterns on the warp and weft yarns are identical and fall on top of each other in the woven cloth. The method results in strong pattern definition, as shown in Figure 142 , an example of double ikat from India.

The colorful warp, weft and double ikat saris from Andhra Pradesh are famous all over India and are especially popular in the big towns. According to Dr. Marie-Louise Nabholz-Kartaschoff, specialist in Indian ikat, they are produced by weavers belonging to the Sali community who live in Pochampalli and the surrounding villages near Hyderabad. But the most beautiful and technically the most interesting of all Indian ikat textiles are the *patola* from Gujarat, done in the intricate and rare double-ikat technique. The design on a *patolu* consists essentially of a border of stripes and ikat patterns framing a field that is either plain or densely patterned. The traditional motifs are flowers, leaves, flowering trees, parrots, elephants, tigers, dancing ladies and geometric designs such as triangles and crosses. These precious silk textiles are used at weddings and other important festivities as well as for religious purposes such as clothing for cult figures and canopies for small altars.

The process of creating double ikats, as described by Dr. Nabholz, is infinitely complicated and time-consuming. Undyed warp and weft yarns are counted, bundled and folded with meticulous care according to the pattern wanted. The weavers are so familiar with the traditional designs that they usually wrap the ikat patterns from memory. Only for new or modified designs do they use graph-paper drawings. The bundles are dyed with synthetic dyes in three successive baths. (Natural dyes are no longer used.) Between dyebaths, new sections are wrapped and others are unwrapped. The usual colors of the finished *patola* are white, yellow, orange, red, blue, green or bluish green, dark brown or black.

Another center of double-ikat production is the island of Bali. The *geringsing* cloths, woven only in the mountain village of Tenganan Pergeringsingan, hold great significance for the Balinese. The name translates as without sickness or without evil, *gering* meaning sick and *sing*, without. The cloths are woven in various sizes in about twenty different patterns, some of which have names, while others had names that have long since been forgotten.

Following is a somewhat detailed look at the traditional methods employed in creating a *geringsing*, based on material supplied by Dr. Urs Ramseyer and his wife, Nicole Ramseyer-Gygi. With Prof. Bühler, they co-authored the catalog that accompanied the exhibit "Patola and Geringsing" at the Museum für Völkerkunde in Basel, Switzerland, 1975 to 1977.

The Ramseyers spent a year and a half filming a Balinese woman preparing and weaving a single *geringsing;* Figures 144 through 147 have been taken from this film.

Three general categories of pattern are used on *geringsing* – figures, floral patterns and geometric motifs. Figure 143 shows a geometric *geringsing* with the fringe uncut, just as it was taken from the backtension loom on which all *geringsing* are woven. Some *geringsing* cloths remain in this uncut, circular state and others are cut, but all have religious or ceremonial significance.

After the handspun cotton is skeined, it is mordanted so that the red coloring, an adjective dye, will adhere to the yarn. The indigo, a vat dye, does not require a mordant. The mordant is a solution of oil and ashes of a nut in water. After treatment, each skein is placed to soak in a jug inside a large vessel. A lid is put on the jug and wrappings are placed around and on top of the jug. A ritual period of 42 days is required for the soaking, followed by another period of 42 days during which the yarn is hung on a bamboo pole to dry. The yarn is then ready to be wrapped and dyed for use as either warp or weft.

The warp for the *geringsing* double ikat is wound in a different manner than for the pieces from Sumba and Borneo discussed in Chapter IV. In some ways making a *geringsing* is very complex, and in other ways it is direct and simple. The warp is wound on a frame consisting of two posts set in a piece of lumber, shown in Figure 144. The distance between the posts is half the length of the continuous warp. The warp is wound in a figure eight between the posts, thus establishing the cross. Enough warp to weave five cloths is usually wound at one time.

The warp for this piece was divided into seven sections: two borders and five pattern divisions (as can be seen in the finished piece in Figure 143). This division of the warp corresponds to the warping in separate bundles that you have done for earlier projects in this book, except that the separations are made on the frame, without cutting the warp.

As she winds, the Balinese weaver also separates the warp into two sizes of groups that will come into play as she ties the resists for her ikat pattern. Here, the two poles of her warping frame play a unique role, for she can separate warp ends into a relatively few large groups on the lefthand pole and subdivide these into smaller groups on the righthand pole. In Figure 144, notice the difference in spacing of the warp groups on the two poles.

When all the yarns are wound, she can refine the grouping of the yarns by shifting the groups up or down the poles according to the sequence of her pattern. She then twines between the groups at each edge. The warp remains on this frame for the tying.

Next the warp is marked with vertical black lines that will be used as a guide in wrapping the pattern. A notched palm leaf is used to mark the placement of the lines at top and bottom of the warp. A straight-line grid is created by rubbing the string of a bow in soot, then aligning it with the markings at top and bottom all across the warp.

Using a moistened strip of palm fiber, the resist wrapping is now begun. From memory, using only the divisions marked on the warp, the pattern is wrapped as shown in Figure 145. The weaver wraps all of the parts to remain white and all that are to remain red. Only the parts to be dyed indigo are left unwrapped.

In Figure 146, the warp has been removed from the warping and tying frame. Before removing the yarn from the frame, a strong palm-fiber cord was run through the warp ends along the posts. Parts are being wrapped which will later become the chessboard pattern. This is an excellent method of wrapping a resist at the fold. The warp bundles, now wrapped, are laid aside to be dyed with the weft.

The weft is wound on an ingenious weft-winding frame shown in Figure 147. It rotates much like our warping reels. Two rods are set in two pieces of lumber, with a space between the two rods that is the proper width of the fabric. Running lengthwise through the center of the frame is a longer rod that extends beyond the frame. It rests on supports that hold the frame at working level, and it forms the axis upon which the weft frame is turned. From a large spool rack holding fifty spools of cotton yarn, fifty ends are gathered together into one bundle and wound spirally onto the weft frame, automatically dividing the weft into bundles of fifty ends. The groups are now separated by twining. The weft-winding frame is awkward to use for tying, so the heavy rods are replaced with smaller ones that are lashed into a new frame to hold the weft yarn under tension.

Markings are made on the weft bundles in the same manner as the warp, with a bow string brushed with soot. Again the resist ties are done from memory.

The yarn is dyed in two colors, blue and red. Over the long processing period, the mordant changes the white cotton to a warm tan (which also takes on a reddish tone from the red dye). The effects of the mordant, and of the overdye of red on the indigo blue, produce the deep, rich colors of the *geringsing* cloths. The indigo dyeing is done first. Successive dippings and airings bring out the desired deep blue. Then the resist wrappings are removed from the sections to be dyed red. The red dyeing is a much more complicated process. Partially crushed bark and roots of one plant and the bark of another are prepared with a little water. The repeated dyeings and airings needed to bring out the depth of red desired can take as long as five years. The red overdye on the indigo produces a rich, deep warm black that some people call a black violet.

When the yarn is ready for weaving, the bundles of yarn are separated. The continuous warp has string heddles attached to one shed, and the various rods and rollers of the backstrap loom are inserted. At this time, also, the selvage stripes of natural white and indigo are added. The extra little sticks at the back of the warp are used to adjust the pattern placement and tension on the warp. The cloth beam is attached with cords to the carved stick behind the weavers back. The other end of the continuous warp is held between two sturdy posts.

The cloth is woven in plain weave, in a ratio of three weft yarns to every five warp yarns within the patterned area. The dark blue and white selvage stripes are warp-faced, a result of the denser sett of the warp yarns here. Each pick of the weaving is examined and individual adjustments of the yarns are made, in order to keep the yarns within the motifs in their proper pattern positions.

In Figure 143, you can see the spacing of the yarns in the patterned plain-weave sections. The pattern holds together well, with the excellent resist parts contrasting sharply with the dyed parts. The very nature of the slow-working red adjective dye and the special action in the indigo vat dye contribute much to the success of these traditional, fast-disappearing *geringsing* ikats from Bali.

Figure 143. *Geringsing* from Bali. *Production of these cloths involves so many processes of mordanting, resist tying, dyeing and detail weaving that a period of up to eight years is required to complete a* geringsing. *72 x 9 in. (186 x 23 cm) excluding fringe. Private Collection.*

Figure 144. Winding the Warp. *The weaver is wearing a* geringsing *breast cloth with her batik sarong. She divides the warp into groups as she winds.*

Figure 145. Tying the Marked Warp. *The bundles of warp have been marked for tying with a taut bow string rubbed in soot; now the resists will be wrapped with a palm-leaf bast. The palm leaf running under the warp ends along the pole aids in slipping the wrapped warp off the frame.*

Figure 146. Wrapping the Center Fold. *The alternate wrappings for the chessboard pattern are partially completed in this photograph. Before the warp was removed from the warping and tying frame, a strong cord of palm fiber was run through the end loops along each post, The resist wrap on the warp was started just below this cord, then a figure-eight wrap went back and forth over the top of the yarn, taking in the cord each time.*

Figure 147. Weft-Winding Frame. *This frame swivels as the yarn is wound onto it. Before the weft is removed to a tying frame, the proper series of yarn bundles will be marked with strips of palm fiber.*

Figure 148. Diagonal Weave. *Though not a true diagonal weave; a diagonal selvage develops during the weaving of this triangular fabric. The ikat is planned so that it: crosses itself to produce a double ikat.*

Project 10

Simple Double Ikat

From the foregoing description, you might well wonder how the double-ikat technique used on *geringsing* ikats could relate to your own weaving and dyeing. By now, however, you should be able to use your knowledge of warp and weft ikat to create a double ikat just by having the resists coincide in the warp and weft. If you were to weave a precise, controlled geometric design in double ikat, you would chart your design on graph paper according to the methods described in Chapter II. Each square of the graph would represent X number of warp ends and X number of weft picks (the sett and pickage would be determined by weaving a sample with the yarns you planned to use for the fabric). Then you would wind the warp and weft, tie, and dye and weave your fabric according to the design already established in your graph. However, for a less complicated first project, I suggest you try this simple double ikat.

The fabric woven for this project, shown in Figure 148, is a head or neck scarf woven with handspun wool and dyed in natural dyes. The effect of a double ikat is achieved in the outer border and inner triangle through manipulation of the weaving process rather than precise dyeing of warp and weft. For want of a better name, I call the process a diagonal weave. As the weaving progresses, each warp yarn in succession becomes a weft yarn, producing a triangular fabric. The warp is ikatted so that the double ikat appears in the bands and in the triangle in the middle of the fabric.

Materials

1. A soft, fluffy white wool warp yarn no heavier than 4-ply knitting worsted for a finished weaving 24 x 24 in. (60 x 60 cm) plus fringe; sett 8 e.p.i., well spaced for a soft fabric (no weft yarn is used)

2. Two-harness loom, 8-dent reed, warping board and standard weaving equipment

3. Dye suitable for wool

4. Plastic wrap and string, paper for marking the resist pattern

Methods

Warping. Wind the warp in three groups:

Group 1. Two skeins of 6 ends each – 12 ends. This group will be dyed with the patterned yarns in group 3.

Group 2. Two skeins of 32 ends each – 64 ends. This group will remain undyed.

Group 3. Three skeins, of 36 ends, 48 ends and 36 ends, respectively – 120 ends. These will be tied for resists.

Making a Diagram. Cut a strip of paper about 30 in. (75 cm) long, to make a diagram as shown in Figure 150. Along one edge of the paper, draw a line the length of your warp and mark off the lengthwise warp resists as follows: Mark a 6½-in. (16-cm) resist in the center, divided by a dotted line as shown; on each side of the center resist, allow for a 4¾-in. (12-cm) unresisted space; and at each end of the warp, mark a 4½-in. (11-cm) resist. The measurements of these resists are slightly larger than the width of the warp stripes as they will be threaded through the reed, to allow for the fact that the warp will be stretched and tied under tension.

Next, draw a line which is parallel to the first one and is also divided by the dotted line. Along the second line, which represents the width of the warp in the reed, mark off the width and placement of the warp stripes as follows: Again working from the center, mark off a 6-in. (15-cm) stripe of ikatted warp (48 ends, at 8 e.p.i.); on each side of this stripe, mark off a 4½-in. (11-cm) ikat stripe (36 ends each; these will have different resists from the central stripe); next, mark a 4-in. (10-cm) stripe of white (32 warp ends); and finally, at each end, a ½-in. (1.3-cm) stripe (6 ends) of red. This portion of the diagram will serve as your guide when you dress the loom.

Tying the Resists. Now tie a marking string loosely around the middle of the skein of 48 ends in warp group 3. Next tie all three skeins in group 3 together by their ends and put this group under tension. Following the instructions for wrapping long resists in Chapter III, wrap the two 4½-in. (11-cm) resists at each end of the warp skeins; including all three skeins in this warp. Then wrap a 6½-in. (16-cm) resist only on the skein with 48 ends, first removing the marking tie. Figure 150 shows how your wrapped warp should look. By first tying the resists at the ends of all three skeins, there is less likely to be a shifting of the yarns when you tie the middle section.

Dyeing. Dye the skeins from groups 1 and 3 in the same dyepot. The scarf illustrated here was dyed in cochineal mordanted with tin (stannous chloride), oxalic acid and cream of tartar. The result was a brilliant flag red. You may wish to use some other dye source.

This scarf had a second dye application, which you may wish to try if you are comfortable with the techniques of yarn dyeing for ikat. Use a dye with a lighter or much darker value than the first dye to get the sharpest possible contrast between dark/light values. The lighter stripes in this example were dyed a strong light yellow from field mustard, with tin and cream of tartar as mordants. After the first dyeing, wrap resists over the sections already dyed red and remove the resists from the end wrappings. Leave the middle section wrapped; it will remain white. Dye group 3 and group 2 in the same dyepot. Do not include group 1 in this dye, as it will remain red.

Dressing the Loom. After dyeing, prepare the yarn for weaving and dress the loom. Put the warp on the loom in this order:

6 ends of red (one skein from group 1)
32 ends of white (one skein from group 2)
36 ends of ikat (one skein from group 3)
48 ends of ikat (the skein from group 3 with the center resist)
36 ends of ikat (the third skein from group 3)
32 ends of white (one skein from group 2)
6 ends of red (one skein from group 1)

Weaving. The weaving will go very fast, and it is exciting to see the shape develop. With a filler yarn (which will be removed when the weaving is finished), weave in tabby the amount you have allowed for the fringe, say 4 in. (10 cm). Now comes the fun part. Reach around to the back of the loom and cut the first warp yarn on the right as close as possible to the knot at the warp apron. Pull this cut warp yarn to the front of the loom, through the heddle and reed. Open the shed and lay this warp yarn into the shed, using it as a weft yarn. Change the shed, reach in back of the loom and cut the next warp yarn on the right, pull it to the front, and lay it in the next shed. Continue cutting and weaving one warp yarn for each succeeding shed. As you are weaving, remember that the warp is under tension, so allow for the warp collapse, which will increase the number of picks per inch when the scarf is removed from the loom. The double-ikat pattern will develop automatically as you weave. After a few inches are woven, you will need to add a supporting tape to hold the warp apron and cloth apron under tension on the right side of the loom (see Figure 149). Tie a tape or cord to the warp apron close to the right selvage edge. Bring this tape forward through a dent in the reed, but not through a heddle eye. Tie the tape to the cloth apron and tighten it to approximate the tension on the warp.

At the left selvage, tie the extra weft hanging from the weaving (which will later become part of the fringe) in soft, temporary knots to hold the selvage warp yarns in place. These knots will be taken out later. Do not tighten the diagonal selvage edge or your triangle will be distorted.

When the weaving is completed, remove it from the loom and untie the weft knots at the left selvage. Unweave the warp fringe allowance and tie both the warp and weft ends hanging out along the two straight sides in an overhand-knotted fringe. This treatment of the fringe is similar to the way Ecuadorian and Mexican shawls are finished.

This contemporary handling of ikatted yarns, in which warp yarns become weft, could be carried much further in other projects.

Figure 149. Weaving. *Each warp yarn is cut free and woven in sequence to develop the diagonal selvage.*

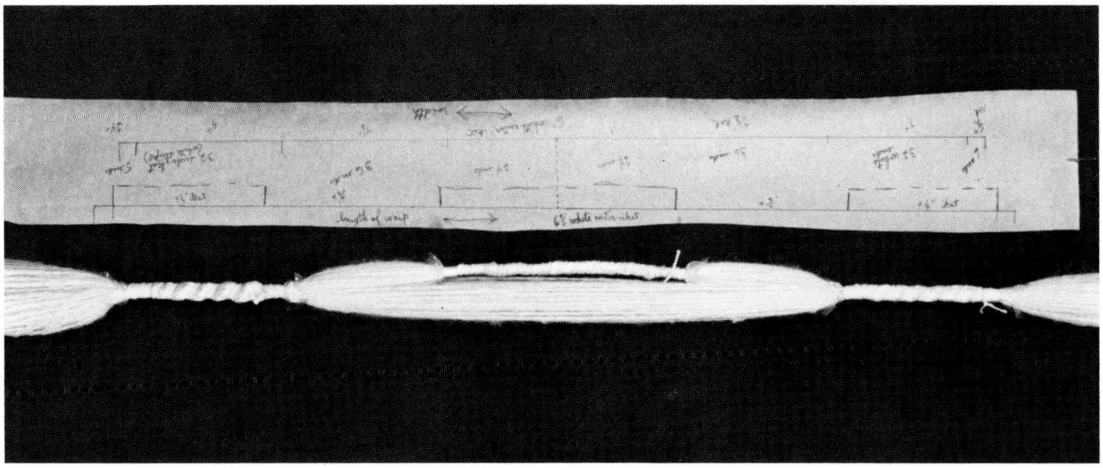

Figure 150. Tying the Resists. *Using a paper pattern as a guide, tie all three skeins as a unit at each end, but tie the special center resist on only one skein.*

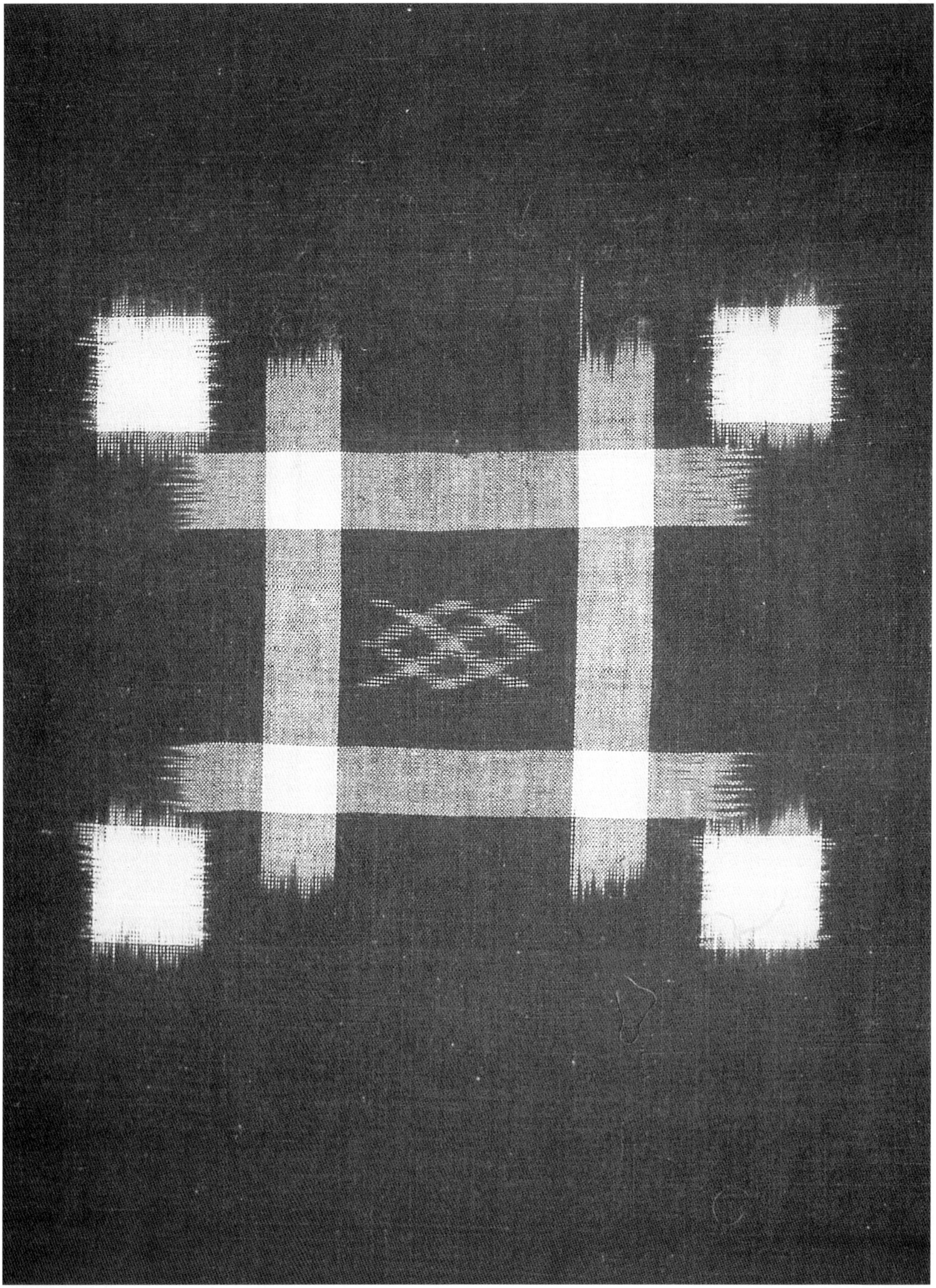

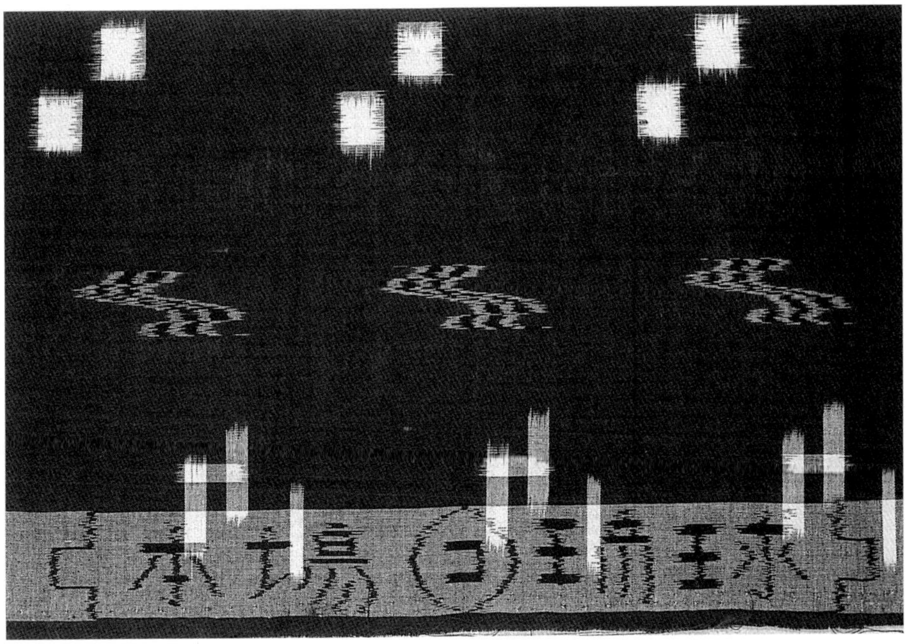

Figure 151. (left) Japanese Geometric Double Ikat. *Bold patterns of white resist against dark indigo-dyed cotton are typical of Japanese* kasuri. *Collection, Yoshiko Wada.*

Figure 152. *(right)* Okinawan Ikat (detail). *The character writing in* e-gasuri *says* honba Ryukyu, *which translates simply as "genuine Okinawa." Bold squares of double ikat contrast with the delicate shifting-weft ikat, a symbol of streams of water. Collection, Lydia Van Gelder.*

Project 11

Geometric Double Ikat with Weft Ikat

Before starting a project combining double ikat with weft ikat, let us look at two examples – one from Okinawa and one from Japan – which unite these techniques.

The fabric shown in Figure 152 is typical of current Okinawan weaving, which uses motifs of flowers, birds, water (represented by wavy lines) and scissors (represented by crossed lines). This fabric is not particularly complicated except for the strip of character writing across the width of the fabric, put in with the *e-gasuri* technique discussed in Project 7. The black warp is crossed with a very dark turquoise, giving the background a beautiful blue-black color. The stark white double-ikat areas were established in the warp, and the weft skeins were tied to coincide with those places. The wavy lines of weft ikat in the center, depicting flowing water, seem to have been done in the *e-gasuri* method rather than by shifting the weft, since there are faint selvage marks on the right side of the fabric.

In Figure 153, the *kasuri* fabric from Japan has a pattern with two alternating motifs, one geometric and one figured. It has the traditional white resist on cotton dyed with indigo, and it is woven in plain weave. The motifs in this type of pattern are symbolic and may take plant, animal or geometric forms.

E-gasuri tiger and bamboo patterns are combined here to symbolize security. The double-ikat squares and the central stripe of warp ikat were done in the *kasuri* technique. The resist marks on the selvage show only in the *e-gasuri* wefts, the measurements of the double-ikat areas having been planned so well that these weft yarns needed no aid at the selvages. The grace of line drawing in the tiger and bamboo contrast nicely with the rigid lines of the *kasuri* pattern.

Now begin the project, in which you will combine geometric double ikat and weft ikat.

Materials

1. White cotton yarn, size 20/2, for warp and weft; your planned weaving width should be about 8 in. (20 cm) wide; sett 30 e.p.i.

2. Two-harness loom, warping board and standard weaving equipment

3. Plastic tape for wrapping the resists

4. Vat dye, liquid starch

Methods

Preparing the Warp. Shrink the warp and weft yarn, following the procedures outlined in Project 7, and size these yarns. You do not have to size the yarn, but sizing helps to eliminate elasticity in the yarn and you will be able to wrap your resists more accurately. Wind enough warp to weave at least two blocks of each 2¾-in. (7-cm) square design motif, separated by 8 to 10 in. (20 to 25 cm) of solid-color warp. Make whatever additional allowances are necessary for loss to the loom tie-on.

Examine the two designs in Figures 154 and 155. In the first, there is a square block of warp resist. In the second, a stripe of dyed warp separates the warp-resist areas. Plan and wrap the warp for the pattern shown in Figure 154 and two warp stripes for the design in Figure 155. Tie the cross and the uncut loops at the ends of the warp. Dye the yarn and size it again before weaving. Dress the loom and weave a few inches in plain weave to establish your X measurement for the weft.

Preparing the Weft. For these two designs, you will need five weft skeins, to tie with five different resist designs with the selvage marks, plus one skein to be dyed without resists. The number of weft shots per unit within the design will depend on the number of warp yarns per unit, since you will square the weft ends with the warp ends. Make the weft skeins, using your X measurement, as follows:

Skein 1. Wrap this resist the width of the warp resist in the reed.

Skein 2. Wrap three resists separated by two unresisted spaces, which will form the four smaller squares within the large square.

Skein 3. Tie these resists as you did for skein 2; but also tie off sections to form the lower part of the stylized leaf on one side, ten weft shots for each design.

Skein 4. Tie resists as for skein 2, and also tie the central part of the leaf, ten weft shots each design.

Skein 5. Tie resists as for skein 2, and add the stem of the leaf, four weft shots each design.

Skein 6. Wind enough weft to weave the start and end of the warp, the plain areas between each design, and the central stripe in the second design; dye this skein without resists.

Figure 153. Japanese Ikat. *This nineteenth-century* futon *fabric combines double and warp ikat with* e-gasuri. *The selvage marks that assisted in placing the* e-gasuri *wefts are visible.*

Weaving. With the plain dyed weft yarn, weave up to the warp-ikat motif in plain weave. To weave the motif in Figure 154:

1. With skein 1, weave enough weft shots to square the border stripes of white.

2. With skein 2, weave up to the point where twelve shots of weft are needed to square the first two inner squares.

3. With skein 3, weave five weft shots.

4. With skein 4, weave five shots of weft.

5. With skein 5, weave two shots of weft. (The inner motifs should be square; if they are not, unweave and adjust the number of weft shots to make squares.)

6. With skein 1, square the central white warp stripe.

Starting with step 5, reverse these directions to complete the motif, then finish the design by weaving a few inches with the plain dyed yarn.

To weave the second design, follow steps 1 through 5 above, then proceed as follows:

6. Weave two or three shots of skein 1.
7. Weave a few shots of the unpatterned dyed weft yarn to square the stripe of dyed warp.
8. Repeat step 6, then follow the directions in reverse from step 5 back to step 1, to complete the motif. Finish the design with a few inches of plain dyed yarn.

A note: The weaving completed in steps 6, 7, 8 should equal the width between the two squares within the motif.

These two designs, simple though they are, take you through the steps for one method of combining geometric and weft *kasuri*. The *e-gasuri* method can also be used, following the directions in Project 7.

We now have examined examples of weft ikat woven independently of the geometric double ikat (Figure 153), and weft ikat woven in the same tying with the geometric double-ikat pattern (Figures 154 and 155). Figure 151 shows a Japanese fabric in which areas of double ikat frame the very popular scissors motif. You have already mastered the processes for producing the double-ikat geometric pattern. The four outer squares are tied for double ikat, while the frame is created by tying warp-ikat stripes and weft-ikat stripes. Where these stripes cross, a double ikat of sorts is produced, with extremely sharp outlines that contrast with the "legs," or feathered outlines, seen in the double-ikat squares. The whole design is extremely well balanced and organized.

One of the charms of the design, is the effective utilization of the shifting-weft scissors motif, which you wove in Project 6. In this example, the scissors motif appears to have been woven with a skein tied with two resists. As in Project 6, the shed was opened and the resists placed first to the right, with the left-hand resist directly in the center of the weaving width. The movement first to the right and then to the left continued. The resists crossed, still moving in the same direction, until they appeared to have resumed their original positions. Then the directions were reversed and the motif completed.

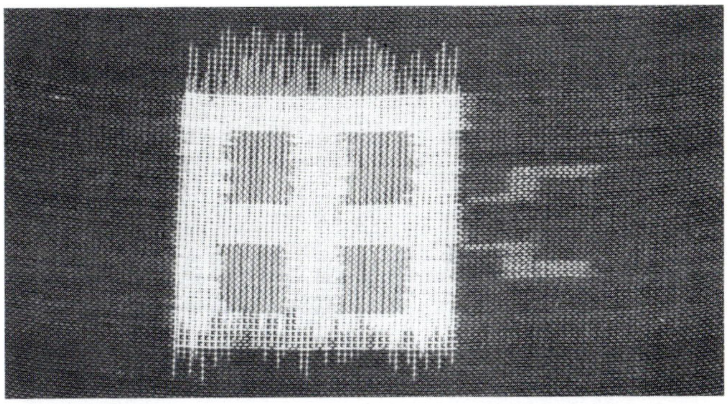

Figure 154. *(top)* Geometric and Weft Ikat Motif. *A square of resist-dyed warp crosses ikatted weft to form a simple design. Some of the weft yarns were tied with resists to form the stylized leaf next to the geometric motif.*

Figure 155. *(bottom)* Geometric and Weft Ikat Variation. *A warp stripe of dyed, unpatterned yarn has been added to the design shown in Figure 154. This motif is woven the same as the first one, except for the addition of a weft stripe in the center to balance the design.*

Figure 156. *(left)*
Compound Ikat, India. *The warp-ikat selvage border of this sari, which is shown horizontally in this photograph, is independent of the weft-ikat areas. Collection, Dorothy Miller.*

Figure 157. *(right)*
Compound Ikat.
India *(detail).*

Chapter VIII

Compound Ikat

You have worked with warp ikat, where only the warp yarns are resisted and carry the pattern; weft ikat, where only the weft yarns are wrapped to resist the dye and form the pattern; and double ikat, where resists on the warp and weft yarns are planned to coincide and result in a pattern. Compound ikat combines warp and weft ikat methods. In compound ikat, the ikatted warp and weft yarns do not coincide, but rather form independent, complementary patterns.

Two fabrics, one from India and the other from Indonesia, illustrate compound ikat. The sari from Orissa, India, in Figure 156 has weft-ikat motifs that include the typical flowers on the ornamental ends, plus *tumpals* (a triangle-shaped motif of ancient origin), flowers, elephants and *nabagunjara* (a mythical animal from Orissa, India) in the center field of the sari. The warp is shown crosswise in this illustration; warp-ikat motifs can be seen in the selvage stripe of floral motifs embellished with warp brocade. The weft-ikat areas in the main field and the ornamental end section were probably tied on separate frames, and the warp ikat at the selvage edge on still another frame.

Figure 157, a detail of Figure 156, allows us to see several interesting things more clearly. The first thing to notice is the obvious contrast between the warp- and weft-ikat patterns. The softer, watercolor effect of the triangular weft-ikat motifs is quite different from the stronger, bolder flowers in the warp. The warp-brocade border at the selvage has additional fine white warp yarns added within the brocade. We can see the intentional accents of the resist ties in the stair-step line of the *tumpal* motif; the two longer sides were tied in groups of twelve ends, stepping up to a group of twenty ends for the tip of the triangle. These white resists were used not only to separate the dye areas, but to form a definite part of the overall design. The resist line at the base of the *tumpal* is a marking made to assist in placing the pattern during the weaving. A similar assist is sometimes used in *e-gasuri* weaving. The spot-dyeing method of spooning on dye was undoubtedly used to color special sections in the main field, as in the *tumpal* shown here.

The compound ikat from Indonesia in Figures 158 and 159 are similar to pieces I have seen with labels indicating they come from Java. Whether they are woven there or just exported by a company with offices in Java is not known.

The overall design strongly suggests an influence from India, in the use of floral motifs and in the internal divisions of the patterns. However, there are Indonesian characteristics as well, particularly in the serrated stripes bordering the ornamental end section with the signature "Roket". These serrated stripes in warp- as well as weft-ikat yarns are found in many fabrics woven in the Indonesian archipelago. It has been suggested that this motif could have originally come from India, at a very early date, via trade goods. See the similar treatment in the Indian compound ikat in Figure 156, where serrated stripes border the ornamental end section of the sari. The one, two, three sequence of colors in the bands of floral motifs in the center field would have been tied the same but in three individual bundles, and then each skein dyed in one of the three colors. The ikat selvage, which is shown in the detail in Figure 158, has a closer sett than the rest of the warp. It is also possible that another type of yarn was used in this selvage band, which appears to draw the fabric up slightly, as can be seen at lower left in Figure 159.

The detail of the Indonesian fabric in Figure 158 shows the contrast in the direction of the warp and weft ikat. Here it is very clear that you get stronger horizontal lines in a weft ikat and stronger vertical lines in a warp ikat. Compare the warp ikat in the selvage border with the horizontal lines of the letters in the signature.

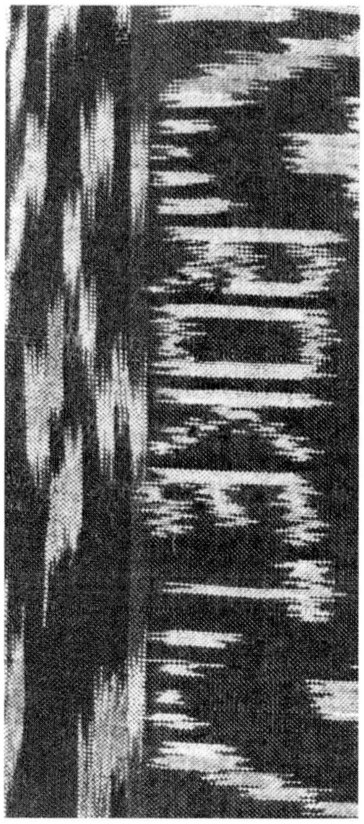

Figure 158. *(above)* Compound Ikat, Indonesia *(detail). The way in which warp and weft ikats work independently of each other to create a compound ikat is apparent here.*

Figure 159. *(right)* Compound Ikat, Indonesia. *The quality of this fabric, shown with the warp running vertically, indicates that it was woven for export. Labels on similar pieces show that a company in Java distributes these fabrics as far away as West Africa. Collection, Dorothy Miller.*

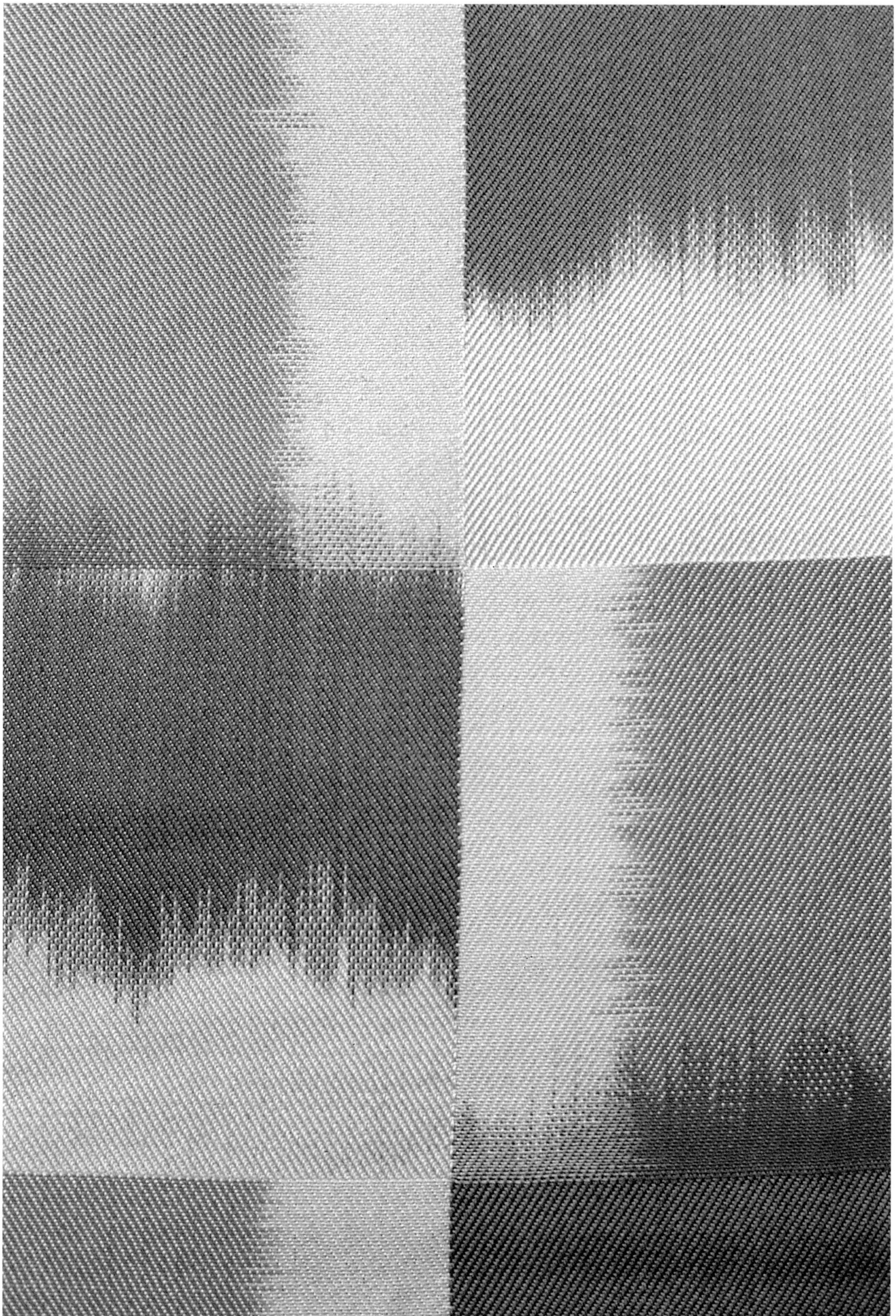

Figure 160. *(left)* Compound Ikat *(detail).*

Figure 161. *(right)* Compound Ikat, Orissa India. *Collection, Lucille Michie.*

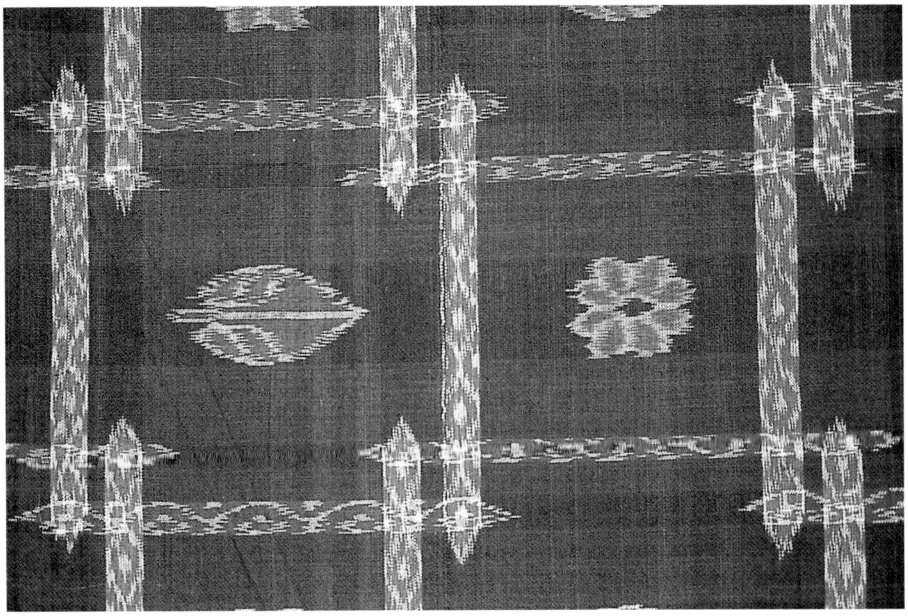

Project 12

Compound Ikat

For this project, you will weave a weft-ikat pattern set in alternating squares of a plaid or grid which is composed of warp- and weft-ikat lines. Using the basic linear components of fabric construction (vertical, represented by the warp, and horizontal, represented by the weft), plan a design. Figure 4, page 10, shows a simple application of compound ikat. The two examples from India and Indonesia already analyzed in this chapter have more complicated patterns, but their basic structural qualities could also be utilized in your design. You should design in terms of contrasting vertical and horizontal lines or masses which are, at the same time, in harmony with each other. Whether you make some notations on paper, draw a complete cartoon or use graph paper to chart your pattern will depend on your design. By now you should be sufficiently comfortable with ikat techniques to design a larger fabric, perhaps one with multiple repeats in both warp and weft.

In the weaving of compound-ikat fabrics, when the warp ikat falls in a selvage border it is often sleyed more densely in the reed than the main part of the fabric, where the weft ikat usually falls. This has the effect of strengthening the ikat design in the border. It is usually better to use the same yarn throughout the warp and emphasize the warp ikat by altering the sett in the reed, rather than using a heavier warp yarn for these portions. Differences in the weight and elasticity of the warp yarns would be apt to distort and pucker the fabric. On the other hand, you may want to explore the interesting effects that can be achieved by deliberately combining a very springy yarn with one that has very little elasticity, such as linen. To do this, you would alternate bands of the different yarns at equal intervals across the width of the fabric. You could plan a weft-ikat pattern that would fall within bands of the springy yarn and a warp-ikat pattern for the less stretchy bands. When the tension was released and the fabric removed from the loom, an intriguing texture could result.

Materials

1. Cotton yarn for warp and weft, size 20/2 (similar to the yarn used in Project 7)
2. Two-harness loom, weaving accessories, reed to accommodate both 30 e.p.i. and 40 e.p.i.
3. Warping board to serve as warp-winding and warp-tying frame
4. Weft-winding device
5. Vat dye
6. Plastic tape for tying the resists

Methods

This design has a grid pattern in which warp-ikat bands outline alternating squares of plain weft and shifting-weft ikat patterns. Plan the warp-ikat sett at 40 e.p.i., with the remaining unpatterned warp sett at 30 e.p.i. The width of the fabric is approximately 12 in. (30 cm).

Warping. Wind the warp long enough to weave at least one or two repeats of the complete design. Wind the following independent bundles:

Group 1.	32 ends
Group 2.	20 ends (ikat)
Group 3.	20 ends (ikat)
Group 4.	105 ends
Group 5.	20 ends (ikat)
Group 6.	20 ends (ikat)
Group 7.	105 ends
Group 8.	20 ends (ikat)
Group 9.	20 ends (ikat)
Group 10.	32 ends

The 40 ends in each warp-ikat band have been broken into two groups of 20 ends each, so that you will be able to stagger the ikat pattern by shifting the warp, as you did in Project 1. Wind and tie the crosses and end loops of each group separately; however, when you tie the resists, you may tie groups 2 and 3 together, 5 and 6, and 8 and 9 – and then separate them again when you are ready to shift the ikat bands in dressing the loom. Groups 1, 4, 7 and 10 are not tied for resists but are dyed in the same dyepot as the ikatted warp chains and all the weft skeins.

Winding the Weft. Plan the weft-ikat pattern so it falls into only one of the two squares of 105 warp ends. Lay a paper under your weft-winding device and mark the placement of the righthand square of 105 ends, which will be approximately 3½ in. (9 cm) wide. Allowing for a small border of unpatterned weft, plan a shifting-weft motif that will fall within this 3½-in. (9-cm) square.

Between bands of shifting weft, there should be a weft-ikat stripe to correspond to the warp ikat. When woven, these will set off and complete the grid effect. Wind these skeins on your weft-winding device, using the Japanese method of calculating the weft measurement.

Dye all the patterned and unpatterned wefts in the same dyepot with the warp yarns. Wash and size the yarn, and dry it under tension.

Dressing the Loom and Weaving. Sley the ikatted warp groups in the reed at 40 e.p.i. and all the others at 30 e.p.i., double-denting the two outside dents on each side.

When you weave the shifting weft, alternate the direction in which the shuttle is inserted in the shed at the beginning of each band of shifting-weft ikat, in order to place the weft motif first in the righthand square and then, in the following band, in the square on the left. This is the same method you used in alternating *e-gasuri* motifs in Chapter IV.

Weave this compound ikat in tabby with a firm beat. Since the warp sett is 30 e.p.i. in the weft-ikat areas, you should have at least 30 picks per inch in the weft. Correspondingly, the weft stripe which finishes the grid pattern should be beaten firmly enough to approximate the 40 e.p.i. in the warp stripe.

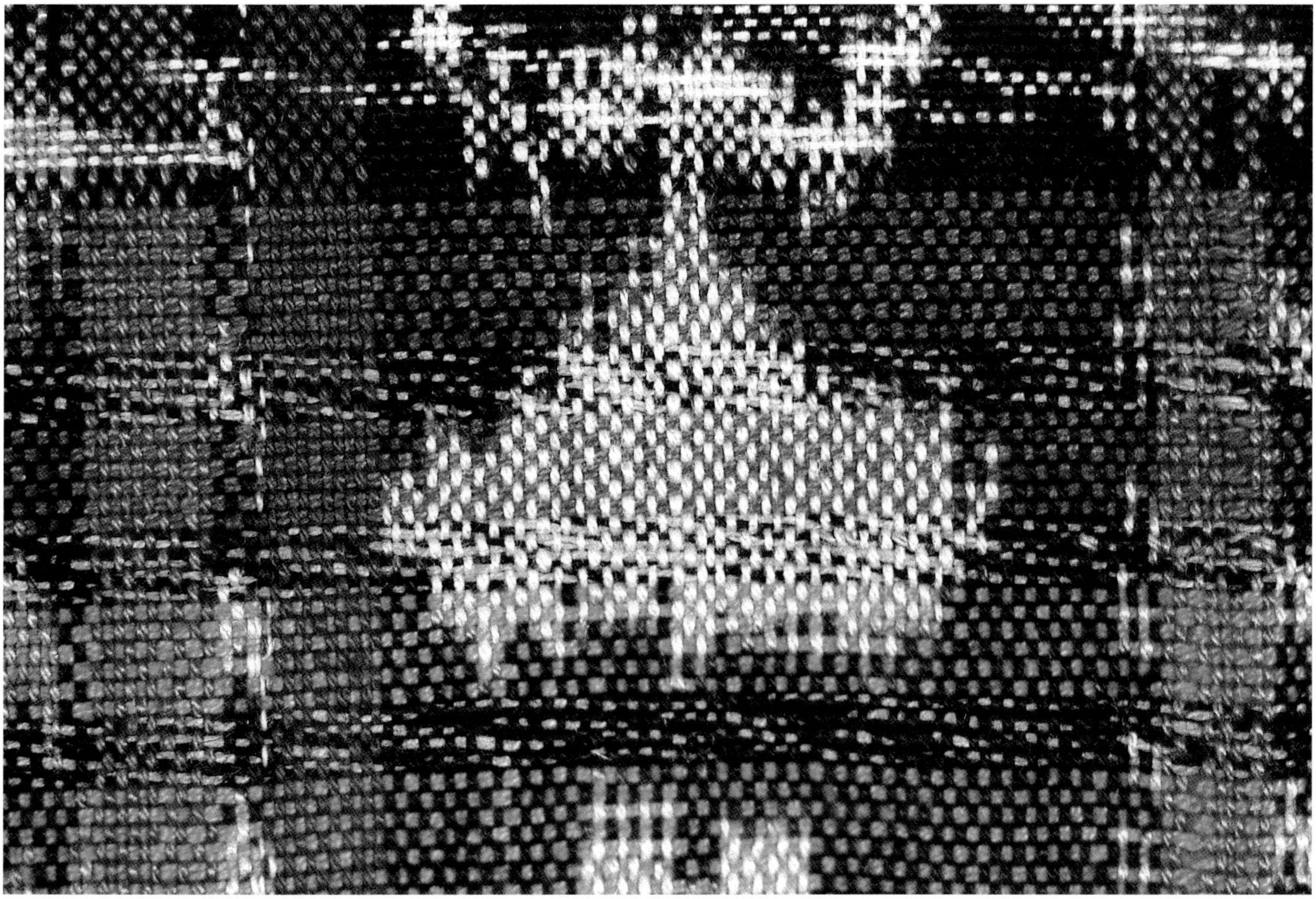

Figure 162. Compound Ikat, Guatemala.
Collection, Susan Richter.

Figure 163. *(left)*
Lydia Van Gelder.
Mt. Unzen. *Shifu, ikat, shibori. Collection, Mr. and Mrs. Keoki Raymond.*

Figure 164. *(right)*
Silk warp/paper weft vest (detail).

Chapter IX

Shifu: The Art of Japanese Paper Spinning and Weaving

The making of paper cloth robes began about 988 by a priest, Shoku. About 1638 a cloth was woven with spun paper yarn. First made by Japanese peasant spinners and weavers, *shifu* ("shi"-paper, "fu"-cloth) soon became popular with the nobility. A brief description of the process of *shifu* follows:

Most any sheer, fibrous paper can be used, but first consider using paper made from *kozo* fibers, the white bark of the *kozo*, a variety of the mulberry tree. Dress patterns and tissue paper may be tried as well.

First, fold the paper in half once; fold it again, leaving a 1-in. (2.5-cm) allowance at the top. Make a very light ¼-in. (0.7-cm) pencil mark across the first fold. Using a cutting board and a Great Neck, a book binder's knife, or an Exacto knife, with a T-square as a guide, cut down through the first and second folds. Do not cut through the 1-in. (2.5-cm) allowance at the top (Figure 165). Open and lay the cut paper out flat (Figure 166). Roll in a damp (not wet) cloth towel, and lay aside for a few minutes.

Next, on a damp towel or a cement block, with damp hands, roll the paper firmly away and gently back a few times; roll softly in the center and hard at the sides. The paper will begin to resemble yarn.

Place a damp paper towel in the bottom of a basket in preparation for tearing the sheet into one long strip. Following the drawing in Figure 167, tear through one uncut margin at the top, then through the bottom margin, between the next pair. Continue alternating top and bottom until you reach the end. Fold and twist the continuous strip as illustrated in Figure 171. The twisting is where the distinguished "slub" characteristic of *shifu* is formed (Figure 170). As you work, allow the twisted paper to fall lightly into the basket.

The *shifu* yarn may be spun on a spindle spinning wheel, a flyer wheel, a Charkha, or even a bobbin winder. The important point is that the piece of equipment has a very light draw in tension.

After spinning, wind the *shifu* yarn on a tying device, tie for ikat patterning, and then dye. Any dyes which will dye cellulose fibers are usable. During weaving, the shifu yarn must be kept slightly damp; this is for both warp and weft shifu.

The *shifu* pieces shown in Figures 163 and 172 were in the preparation stages when the volcano erupted on Mount Unzen in Shimabara in southwestern Japan. The photographs showing that violent disaster so impressed me that it carried into these pieces — what better way to express this than with *shifu,* a technique and a material from Japan. There are three pieces in all and each piece is 32 in. x 24 in. x 5 in. (80 cm x 60 cm x 12.5 cm), each was done with a silk warp and paper weft.

"Mt. Unzen" is mounted with the silk warp laying horizontal and jutting out from the weaving, denoting the violence at the time the volcano erupted. The paper weft is vertical. The blue in the ikat suggests the sky, the brown the muddy waters and the flaming reds the fire from the volcano. The brown and red were treated with a shibori clamp resist. "Night Storm," with its shifting weft ikat, is reminiscent of the darkness of the night. The extra shifting weft produced textured loop areas, which again express the violence of the eruption. "Flowing Colors," depicting the red of the flames flowing into the blue of the sky and water, has the silk warp vertical and the *shifu* weft ikat horizontal. Again, extra weft was planned to form textured loops at the sides.

The *kinujifu* vest shown in Figure 164 has a silk warp horizontal and a *shifu* weft ikat vertical. This detail shows the black and white weft ikat *shifu* set off by added colored stripes of silk and metallics.

If you decide to experiment with *shifu,* you will probably encounter some of the following terms:

momenjifu = cotton warp/paper weft

kinujifu = silk warp/paper weft

morojifu = paper warp/paper weft

asajifu = linen warp/paper weft

Figure 165. *(top)* Cutting the Paper. *This shows the paper being cut through the first and second folds.*

Figure 166. *(middle)* The Paper After Cutting. *Here the paper is placed flat on a damp towel.*

Figure 167. *(bottom)* Tearing the Sheet Into One Strip. *This illustration shows the proper method used for tearing the paper.*

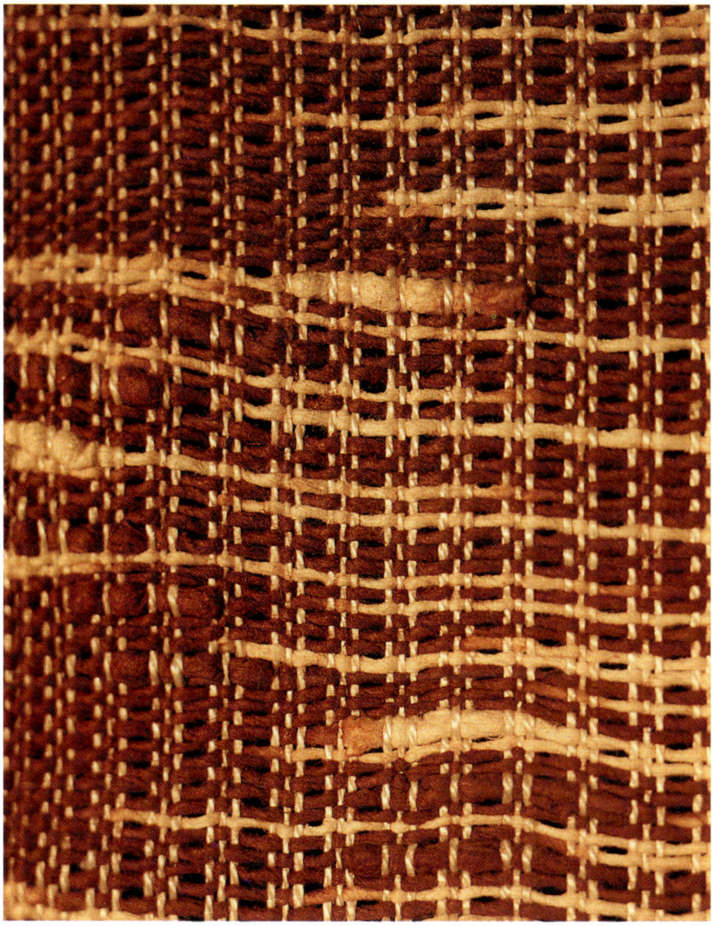

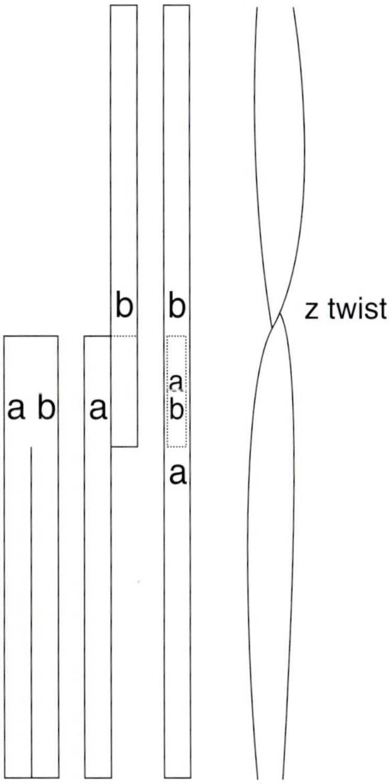

Figure 168. *(top left)* The Torn Strips. *As the paper is torn, the strips should fall into a basket lined with moist paper towels.*

Figure 169. *(middle left)* Spinning the "Yarn." *Note the Z twists.*

Figure 170. *(bottom left)* Louise Yale. Shifu *fabric showing the slubs.*

Figure 171. *(top right)* Folding and Twisting the Paper. *This schematic shows how the paper should be folded and twisted in preparation for spinning.*

Figure 172. *(bottom right)* Lydia Van Gelder. Night Storm *(detail). Shifting weft ikat, shifu. Collection, Dr. and Mrs. Craig Campbell.*

Figure 173. *(left)*
"Flame" Yarn Stockings. *Ikat knitted, Scandinavian, circa 1700. Collection, Mary Walker Phillips.*

Figure 174. *(right)*
Ikat Knitted Sweater. *The same ratio of stitches as in the sample were cast on for this; thus, the block pattern was created.*

Chapter X

Ikat Knitting

Introduction

In the "History of Ikat" (page 9), Prof. Bühler outlined the beginning of the ikat technique in ancient times. This, however, only refers to ikat in weaving, very little, in fact, has been written about the origins of ikat knitting.

Cynthia LeCount in her book, *Andean Folk Knitting*, states that it wasn't until the Europeans introduced the technique of knitting that a few pieces used ikat patterning in the *chullo*, a knitted cap. Prof. Bühler mentions, in *CIBA Review #44*, that some ikat was done in wool knitting in England early on. And, according to *Textiles of Ancient Peru and Their Techniques* by Raoul D'Harcourt, "Future researches on this subject may, however, hold surprises in store for us."

Ikat for Hand and Machine Knitting

Before we go into knitting a controlled design, let's explore the freedom and fun of knitting a free "hit and miss" pattern. Any holding device, a niddy-noddy for example, which will hold the yarn taut while tying the resist will suffice. Figure 175 shows handspun yarn resist tied and dyed. One end of the yarn bundle was dyed in a warm brown using walnut-hull dye, the other end in walnut hull with an iron mordant that gives the darker brown coloring.

Whether you are knitting by hand or knitting with a knitting machine, the principles of planning the design are the same. There are variables, however, in the elasticity of the yarn and tension. One suggestion for using handspun yarn on a knitting machine is to eliminate the overhead tension feeder and feed the cams by hand. This provides better control of the ikat pattern.

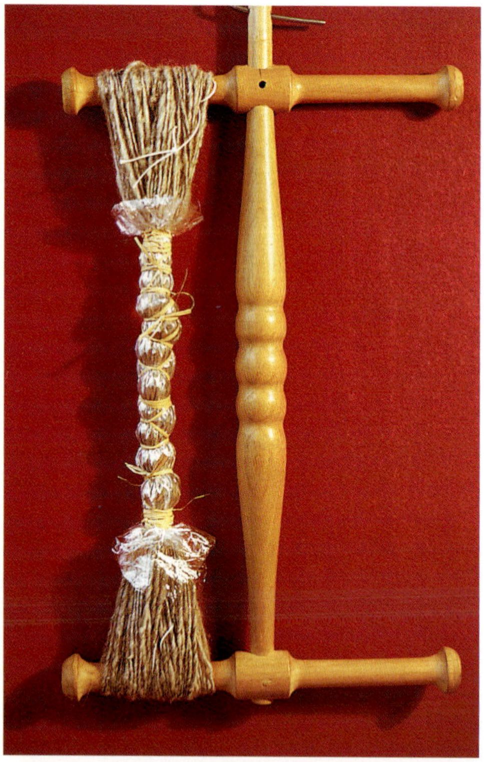

Figure 175. *(top left)* The Yarn after Tying and Dyeing. *This shows the handspun yarn resist tied and dyed.*

Figure 176 and 177. *(top right and bottom left)* Visualizing and Marking the Pattern. *The top photograph shows cut, colored pieces of paper placed where the patterning is to go. Six rows of the sample have been marked with the marking pen in the bottom photograph.*

Figure 178. *(right)* Marking the Pattern. *The left and right margins of the pattern are marked between the stitches.*

A Knitted Horizontal (Weft Direction) Pattern

When planning your design, remember that the horizontal lines (also referred to as weft direction) will be the strongest. Vertical lines (warp direction) will be fuzzy and not as sharp. If you wish to make a strong vertical definition, plan for this by turning the *finished* fabric so the strong horizontal line becomes a strong vertical line.

Knit a sample (either by hand or machine) approximately 6 to 10 in. (15 to 25 cm) in the chosen stitch. Do not slip the selvage stitches. Read "Calculating the Weft Length for Weft Ikat: Determining the X Measurement" in Chapter III. Cast off and pin the sample to a board using a T-square or a sheet of paper to true it up. Count and record the number of stitches for one or two inches (2.5 or 5 cm) across, horizontal. Count and record the number of rows for one or two inches (2.5 or 5 cm) up and down, vertical.

Cut some pieces of colored paper to visualize where you want the ikat patterning to fall (Figure 176). Move these cut patterns around to get a feel for what you want in your design; this helps you visualize where you want the design (pattern) to fall. Pin to the knitting.

Figure 179. *(below right)* A Tension-Holding Device. *The marked yarn is unraveled on a tension-holding device.*

Figure 180. *(below left)* The Master Yarn. *A piece of paper has been placed under the master yarn to mark where the pattern falls and resist will be tied.*

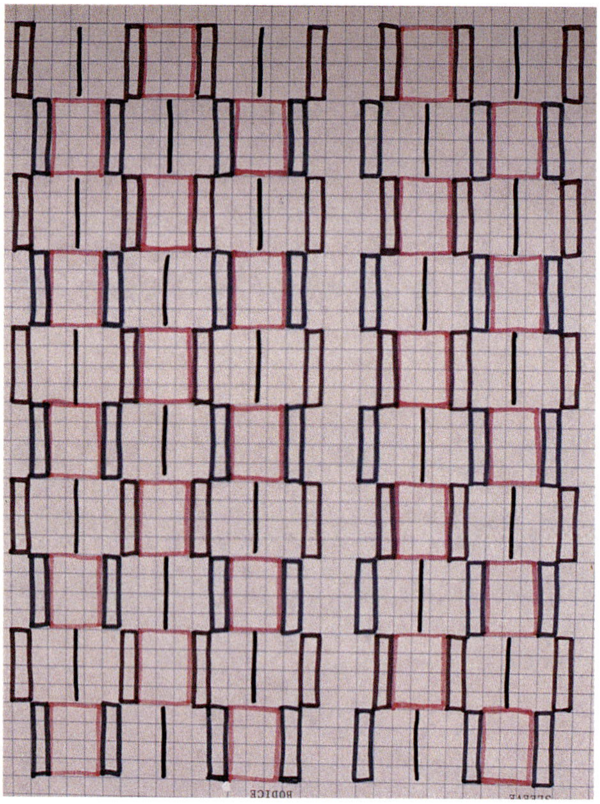

Figure 181. *(above)* Charting. *This is the chart, drawn on graph paper, for a knitted sample.*

Figure 182. *(below)* Sweater Back. *This is the back of the sweater featured in Figure 76 showing the color changes.*

With a water-soluble fabric marking pen, mark the right and left margins of the pattern, marking only the joining yarn *between* stitches (Figure 178). Mark for at least 6 rows, vertically (Figure 179). In another color, mark the outside turn of the yarn at the selvage of each of the rows. On a tension-holding device (Figures 180 and 181), preferably one where the yarn will go in a straight line, unravel the marked knitting. At the same time, wind onto the holding device. Line up the marks as best you can; make sure the selvage marks true up together around the outer curve of the pegs.

On a strip of paper secured under the master yarn (Figure 180), take the mean average, marking on the paper where the pattern falls and consequently where the resist will be tied (see Chapter II). It is a good idea to keep the master yarn for more tyings; in addition; the colored markings on the master could bleed into the yarn during dyeing.

From your notes, wind enough yarn for your pattern. Resist tie the outer turn of the selvage marks with a very fine plastic strip (see Chapter VII). Next, resist tie the pattern motifs (see Chapter III). Dye the yarn. Be sure to include enough yarn for your background knitting, although all background yarn does not need to be dyed.

If the same ratio of stitches are cast on for the ikat knitted piece as in the sample, the pattern will develop into blocks (Figure 174). If, however, there are a few more stitches (+2) or a few less (-2) than were cast on for the sample swatch, the ikat will develop into a shifting weft pattern (see Chapter VII). Examples of shifting weft design are shown in Figures 173 and 186.

A Knitted Vertical (Warp Direction) Pattern

Following a chart drawn on graph paper, knit a sample in the chosen pattern stitch (Figures 181). Record the stitch and row count per inch (cm). Knit the full measurement, i.e., if this is to be a sweater, measure from the shoulder line to the waist; the width of the sample will be this measurement. When finished, it will be turned so the strong horizontal line becomes a strong vertical line. The sweater will be knitted from the cuff of one sleeve, crosswise, to finish off with the cuff of the second sleeve; the design motif will be knitted in the measurement – shoulder line to waist (Figure 174. The color changes are noted and the ikat bundles have been tied and dyed.

Starting with the cuff, knit the first sleeve, adding extra stitches for the front and back. As you knit, cast off stitches to allow for the neck opening. Continue knitting and include the ikat patterned yarn in the waist front. At the center back (Figure 182), where there is a color change, use one of the ikatted yarns. As added interest, enough pattern yarn was allowed so some could be knitted into one sleeve.

Figure 183. *(above)* Sweater Front. *(detail).*

Compound Ikat Knitting: Vertical and Horizontal Combined

The design for this came from a motif in a weaving from India (Figure 185). Cast on stitches to equal 7 in. (17.5 cm) and knit upwards 10 in. (25 cm) in the chosen stitch. Record the yarn and needle size. Count and record the number of stitches for one or two inches (2.5 or 5 cm) across (horizontal); count and record the number of rows for one or two inches (2.5 or 5 cm) up and down (vertical).

Cut colored paper to emulate the design you will follow. Move these around, cutting or adding to them (Figure 188). On the knitted sample, following your horizontal and vertical stitch count, indicate where the design will fall with a fabric marking pen (Figure 191). On graph paper, chart out this design exactly (Figure 187). You will need this graph when you wind the yarn and tie for the colored resists (Figures 189 and 192). Continue with the knitting. Extra length was allowed in the weft skein to be dyed a solid color (brown or black) and the placement of the motif was changed in the knitting from one side to the other for added interest.

A note: If you have trouble hitting the ikat just right in your knitting, try changing to a smaller or larger needle for the ikat parts. If, for example, you used a #8 needle, drop to a #5

Figure 184. *(below)* Weaving from India. *The motif in this design was the inspiration for the compound ikat knitting featured in Figure 91.*

for the ikat areas, and return to the #8 for the remainder of the garment. A smaller needle tightens the stitches; a larger one, loosens the stitches. Surprisingly enough, the change will not show in the final knitted piece.

One final note on ikat knitting. When planning a design, remember that any shaping (such as armholes, necklines, and increases or decreases) will alter your stitch count and will throw the ikat pattern off. Allow for this.

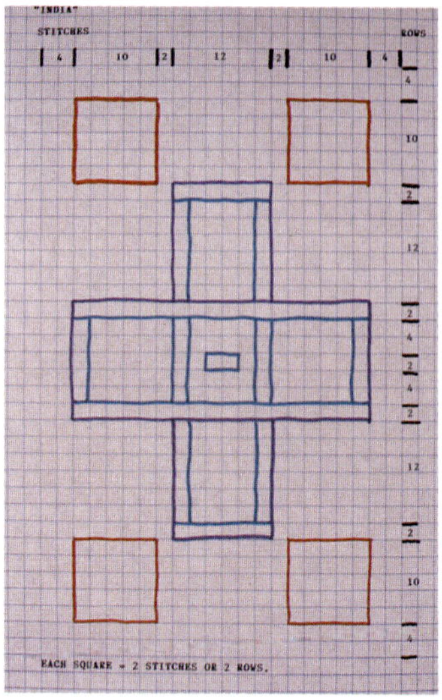

Figures 187 and 188. *(left and below)* The Motif. *These show the motif drawn on graph paper and the corresponding colored paper placed on the knitted sample.*

Figures 185 and 186. *(above and right)* Diane Cutler. *Two examples of matching knitting ikat with yarn.*

Figure 189. *(below top)* Tying the Resist. *The resist is tied according to the drawing on graph paper.*

Figure 190. *(left)* The Finished Design. *This shows the placement of the motif.*

Figure 191. *(right)* Marking the Sample. *The design is marked on the knitted sample and then transferred to the graph paper.*

Figure 192. *(below right)* Tied Resists. *All the resists have been tied and are ready for dying.*

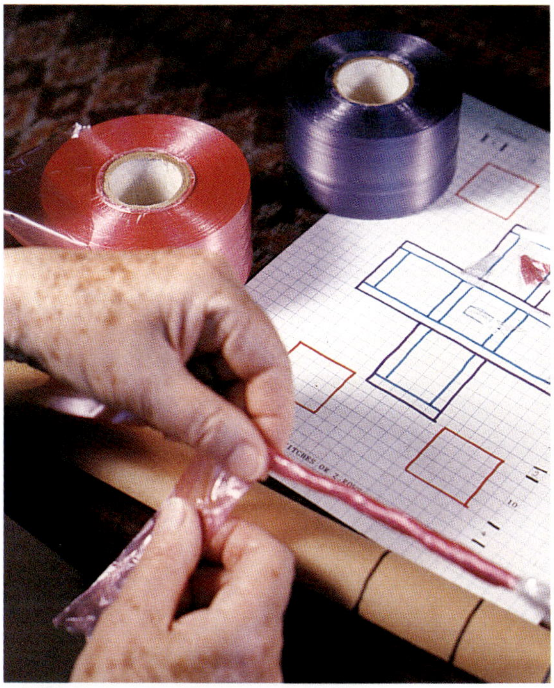

Figure 193. Ikat Rug, Sumba Method.
Collection, Dr. Peter Van Gelder.

Figure 194. *Detail of rug showing the extended loop and the fringe.*

Chapter XI

An Ikat Rug, Sumba Method

Although the design of the rug shown in Figure 193 doesn't look like the fabrics woven on the island of Sumba (see Project 3), the execution of the design is the same. This warp-faced rug was woven from two ikat warp-patterned widths; when the two widths were joined together, the design was reversed on one width as is done on Sumba. The following outlines the process:

A wool warp yarn was wound with enough warp bundles for one width. A second width was wound and placed on top of the other half. Each section (side) was identified with a loose figure-eight tie, and each bundle within the section with a cross. The left-side bundles were placed on top of the right-side bundles. A casual string marker (Figure 195) was tied where the resist patterning should occur, and the warp was placed, under tension, on a tying reel (Figure 196). The resists were tied (Figure 197), dyed, and removed. One warp side was put on the loom and woven. A heavy cord-like, single-ply wool yarn was used for the weft.

As the rug was woven, a generous, extended loop was made at each selvage. These were incorporated in the center joining and outer selvage accent. After the second width was woven, the two were joined together with the designs reversed. A wrapping of yarns brought the weft selvage loops together, down the center of the rug (Figure 194). The fringe was knotted off with a "Neolithic Knot."

Figure 195. *(top right)* The String Marker. *The string was tied where the resist patterning was to occur.*

Figure 196. *(left)* The Tying Reel. *The warp is placed on the tying wheel under tension.*

Figure 197. *(bottom right)* The Tied Resists.

Suppliers List

Bryant Laboratory
880 Jones Street
Berkeley, CA 94710
Chemicals; write for mail-order catalog and price

Cerulean Blue Ltd.
119 Blanchard Street
Seattle, WA 98121
(Mailing Address: P.O. Box 21168
Seattle, WA 98111-3168)
Dyes and chemicals

Diane Cutler
7392 Palm Avenue
Sebastopol, CA 95472
(707) 823-5909
Instruction in machine knitting with commercial and handspun yarn

Dharma Trading Company
1604 Fourth Street
San Rafael, CA 94902
(Mailing Address: Box 916
San Rafael, CA 94902)
(415) 456-1211
Spinning, dyeing, and weaving supplies

Handweavers Guild of America, Inc.
3327 Duluth Highway
Suite 201
Duluth, GA 30136-3373
(770) 495-7702

Kasuri Dye Works
1959 Shattuck Avenue
Berkeley, CA 94704
(Mailing address: P.O. Box 7101
Berkeley, CA 94707)
(510) 527-4997
Resist-dyeing supplies from Japan

Pro Chemical & Dye, Inc.
P.O. Box 14
Somerset, MA 02726
(508) 676-3838
Fax: 508-676-3980
All dyes and chemicals

Riley Street Annex
130 Maxwell Court
Santa Rosa, CA 95401
(707) 526-2416
Kozo paper, dyes

Straw Into Gold
3006 San Pablo Avenue
Berkeley, CA 94702
(510) 548-5241
Spinning, weaving, and dyeing supplies

Unicorn Books and Crafts, Inc.
1338 Ross Street
Petaluma, CA 94954
(707) 762-3362
(800) 289-9276
Fax: (707) 762-0335
Textile books; weaving supplies; distributor of Rupert, Gibbon, & Spider dyes and chemicals

Art:
Susan Hodges. Warp Ikat, Sumba Technique.

Ikat Collections

Listed here are only a few of the museums with collections of ikat fabrics. Many valuable collections are in private hands. If you plan to visit any of these museums for research study, an advance appointment is advisable.

The United States and Canada

Artweave Textile Gallery, New York
The Brooklyn Museum, Brooklyn, New York
Cleveland Museum of Art, Cleveland
Cooper-Hewitt, National Design Museum, Smithsonian Institution, New York
Costume and Textile Study Center, University of Washington, Seattle
Field Museum of Natural History, Chicago
The Fine Arts Museum of San Francisco, M.H. De Young Asian Arts Museum, Golden Gate Park, San Francisco
Indianapolis Museum of Art, Indianapolis
Los Angeles County Museum of Art, Los Angeles
Montreal Museum of Fine Arts, Montreal, Quebec
Museum of Fine Arts, Boston
Museum of the American Indian, Heye Foundation, New York
National Museum of Natural History, Smithsonian Institution, Washington, D.C.
Peabody Museum of Archaeology and Ethnology, Harvard University, Cambridge, Massachusetts
Robert H. Lowie Museum of Anthropology, University of California, Berkeley
Royal Ontario Museum, Toronto, Ontario
Seattle Art Museum, Seattle, Washington
The Textile Museum, Washington, D.C.

Worldwide

Calico Museum of Textiles, Ahmedabad, India
Göteborgs Historiska Museum, Göteborg, Sweden
Horniman Museum and Library, London
Kunstgewerbemuseum der Stadt Zurich, Zurich
Musée de l'Homme, Paris
Musée de l'Impression sur Etoffes, Mulhouse, France
Museum für Völkerkunde und Schweizerisches Museum für Völkskunde, Basel, Switzerland
Museum of Mankind, London
Nationalmuseet, Copenhagen
Nordiska Museet, Stockholm
Pitt Rivers Museum, Oxford, England
Röhsska Konstsljödmuseet, Göteborg, Sweden
Staatliches Museum für Völkerkunde, Munich
Tokyo National Museum, Tokyo
Tropenmuseum, Amsterdam
University Museum of Archaeology and Ethnology, Cambridge, England

Bibliography

CIBA Review

The *CIBA Review* (published 1936 - 1969 by CIBA Ltd., Basel, Switzerland), available only through major libraries, is one of the best sources of information for students of the fiber arts. The following issues pertaining to fibers, dyeing and weaving are relevant to ikat techniques.

2 India, Its Dyers and Its Colour Symbolism
4 Purple
7 Scarlet
9 Dyeing and Tanning in Classical Antiquity
10 Trade Routes and Dye Markets in the Middle Ages
11 The Early History of Silk
12 Weaving and Dyeing in Ancient Egypt and Babylon
30 The Essentials of Handicrafts and the Craft of Weaving Among Primitive Peoples
36 Indian Costumes
39 Madder and Turkey Red
40 Turkestan and Its Textile Crafts
44 Ikats
49 Flax and Hemp
52 The Ship of the Dead in Textile Art
68 Dyeing Among Primitive Peoples
85 Indigo
95 Cotton
104 Plangi Tie and Dye Work
1961/6 Textile Arts of the Araucanians
1964/2 Dyeing Theory
1965/2 Flax
1967/4 Japanese Resist Dyeing Techniques

General

Adrosko, Rita J. *Natural Dyes in the United States.* United States National Museum Bulletin No. 281. Washington, D.C.: Smithsonian Institution Press, 1968.

Birrell, Verla. *The Textile Arts.* New York: Harper & Row, 1959; Schocken Books, 1973.

Bühler, Alfred. *Ikat Batik Plangi: Reservemusterungen auf Garn und Stoff aus Vorderasien, Zentralasien, Südosteuropa und Nordafrika.* 3 vols. Basel: Pharos-Verlag Hansrudolf Schwabe, 1972.

Cannon, Lynda. "Plant Dyes". *Journal of the Chicago Horticultural Society,* vol. 3, no. 1 (1976).

Collingwood, Peter. *The Techniques Of Rug Weaving.* New York: Watson-Guptill Publications, 1968. London: Faber & Faber.

Emery, Irene. *The Primary Structures of Fabrics: An Illustrated Classification.* Washington, D.C.: The Textile Museum, 1966.

Handweavers Guild of America and Weavers' Guild of Pittsburgh, Pa. *Fiber Structures.* Exhibition catalog. Introduction by Irene Emery. New York: Van Nostrand Reinhold Co., 1976.

Held, Shirley E. *Weaving: A Handbook for Fiber Craftsmen.* New York: Holt, Rinehart & Winston, 1973.

Larsen, Jack Lenor, with Bühler, Alfred; Solyom, Bronwen; and Solyom, Garrett. *The Dyers Art: Ikat, Batik, Plangi.* New York: Van Nostrand Reinhold Co., 1976.

Lindahl, David; Knorr, Thomas; and others. *Uzbek: The Textiles and Life of the Nomadic and Sedentary Uzbek Tribes of Central-Asia.* Exhibition catalog. Basel: Zbinden Druck & Berlag, AG, 1975.

Mirsky, Jeannette. "Discovering Ancient Treasures in 'Caves of the Thousand Buddhas.'" *Smithsonian,* May 1977, vol. & no. 2.

Moser, Reihnard-Johannes. "Die Ikattechnik in Aleppo." In *Basler Beiträge zur Ethnologie,* vol. 15. Basel: Pharos-Verlag Hansrudolf Schwabe, 1974.

Pettit, Florence H. *America's Indigo Blues.* New York: Hastings House Publishers, 1974.
Phillips, Mary Walker. *Creative Knitting: A New Art Form.* New York: Van Nostrand Reinhold Co., 1971.
Regensteiner, Else. *Weavers Study Course.* New York: Van Nostrand Reinhold Co., 1975.
Robinson, Stuart. *A History of Dyed Textiles.* London: Studio Vista, 1969.
Weigle, Palmy. *Ancient Dyes for Modern Weavers.* New York: Watson-Guptill Publications, 1974.

The Americas

Bird, Junius. "A Pre-Spanish Peruvian Ikat." *Bulletin of the Needle and Bobbin Club,* vol. 31, nos. 1 - 2 (1947), pp. 72 - 77.
Boyd, E. "Ikat Dyeing in Southwestern Textiles." *El Palacio,* vol. 68, no. 3 (1961), pp. 185-189.
—. *Indigo.* Exhibition catalog. Sante Fe, N.M.: The Museum of International Folk Art, Museum of New Mexico, 1962.
Burnham, Harold B., and Burnham, Dorothy K. *Keep Me Warm One Night: Early Handweaving in Eastern Canada.* Toronto: University of Toronto Press with the Royal Ontario Museum, 1972.
Foster, George M. *Culture and Conquest: Americas Spanish Heritage.* Viking Fund Publication in Anthropology No. 27. New York: Wenner-Gren Foundation, 1960.
Grossman, Elfin F. "Textiles and Looms from Guatemala and Mexico." *Handweaver and Craftsman,* vol. 7, no. 1 (1955), pp. 6 - 11.
Hatch, David Porter. "Mexico, Land of Weavers." *Handweaver and Craftsman,* vol. 6, no. 2 (1955), pp. 10 13.
Harcourt, Raoul d'. *Textiles of Ancient Peru and Their Techniques.* Grace G. Denny and Carolyn M. Osborne, eds. Seattle: University of Washington Press, 1962.
King, Mary Elizabeth. A *New Type of Peruvian Ikat.* Workshop Notes, Paper No. 17. Washington, D.C.: The Textile Museum, 1958.
Lopez, Beatriz. "The Jaspé Process: The Guatemalan Tie-Dye and Weaving Technique." *Shuttle, Spindle and Dyepot,* vol. 8, no. 3 (Summer 1977), pp. 54 - 57.
O'Neale, Lila Morris. *Handbook of South American Indians,* vol. 5. Julian H. Steward, ed. Bureau of American Ethnology Bulletin No. 143. Washington, D.C.: Smithsonian Institution, 1949.
—. *Textiles of Highland Guatemala.* Publication No. 567. Washington, D.C.: Carnegie Institution of Washington, 1945.
Osborne, Lilly deJongh. *Indian Crafts of Guatemala and El Salvador.* Norman, Okla.: University of Oklahoma Press, 1965.
Rowe, Ann Pollard. *Warp-Patterned Weaves of the Andes.* Washington, D.C.: The Textile Museum, 1977.
Tidball, Harriet. "Jaspé." *Shuttle Craft Bulletin,* vol. 34, no. 1 (1957).
Vanstan, Ina. "A Peruvian Ikat from Pachacamac." *American Antiquity,* vol. 23, no. 2 (1957), pp. 150 - 159.

Europe

Nabholz-Kartaschoff, Marie-Louise. "Ikatgewebe aus Nord- und Südeuropa." In *Basler Beiträge zur Ethnologie,* vol. 6. Basel: Pharos-Verlag Hansrudolf Schwabe AG, 1969.
Wintzell, Inga. *Sticka mönster: Historiskt om stickning i Sverige, Nordiska museet, Stockholm.* Uddevalla, Sweden: Tryckt hos Bohusläningens AB, 1976.

Africa

Boser-Sarivaxévanis, René. "Recherche sur l'histoire des textiles traditionnels tissés et teints de l'Afrique occidentale." *Verhandlungen der Naturforschenden Gesellschaft von Basel,* vol. 86, nos. 1 - 2 (1975).
—. *Textilhandwerk in West-Afrika: Weberei und Farberei.* Basel: Museum für Völkerkunde und Schweizerisches Museum für Völkskunde, 1972-73.
Gardi, Renée. *African Crafts and Craftsmen.* Translated by Sigrid MacRae. New York: Van Nostrand Reinhold Co., 1969.
Kent, Kate P. *Introducing West-African Cloth.* Denver, Col.: Denver Museum of Natural History, 1971.
Lamb, Venice, and Lamb, Alistair. *The Lamb Collection of West-African Narrow Strip Weaving.* Washington, D.C.: The Textile Museum, 1975.
Musée des Arts Decoratifs. Art *Textile D'Afrique Occidentale.* 1977. (Available from the museum at Villamont 4, Lausanne, Switzerland.)
Sieber, Roy. *African Textiles and Decorative Arts.* New York: The Museum of Modern Art, 1972.

India

Arness, Judith Russell. "Tie-Dyeing in India: Weavers in Barpali Revive Traditional Craft." *Handweaver and Craftsman,* vol. 14, no. 1 (1963), p. 6.

Bühler, Alfred, and Fischer, Eberhard. *The Patola of Gujarat.* 2 vols. New York: The Rock Foundation, and Basel: Museum für Völkerkunde und Schweizerisches Museum für Völkskunde, 1979. (Available from G. Krebs AG, St. Alban-Vorstadt 56, CH-4052 Basel, Switzerland).

Bühler, Alfred; Fischer, Eberhard; and Nabholz, Marie-Louise. *Indian Tie-Dyed Textiles.* Ahmedabad, India: Calico Museum of Textiles.

Bühler, Alfred; Ramseyer, Urs; and Ramseyer-Gygi, Nicole. *Patola und Geringsing: Zeremonialütcher aus Indien und Indonesien.* Exhibition catalog. Basel: Museum fr Völkerkunde und Schweizerisches Museum für Völkskunde, 1975.

Chandra, Moti. "Costumes and Textiles in the Sultanate Period." *Journal of Indian Textile History,* vol. 6 (1961), pp. 5 - 61.

De Bone, Mary Golden. "Dhabla Weaving in India." *Shuttle, Spindle and Dyepot,* vol. 8, no. 3 (Summer 1977), p. 9.

—. "Patolu and Its Techniques." *Textile Museum Journal,* vol. 4, no. 3 (1976), pp. 49 - 62.

Fischer, Eberhard, and Shah, Haku. *Simple Weft Ikat from South Gujarat, India.* Ahmedabad, India: Calico Museum of Textiles.

Gulati, A.N. *The Patolu of Gujarat.* Bombay: Museums Association of India, 1951.

Jayakar, Pupul. "A Neglected Group of Indian Ikat Fabrics." *Journal of Indian Textile History,* no. 1 (1955), pp. 54 - 65.

Mehta, R.N. "Bandhas of Orissa." *Journal of Indian Textile History,* no. 6 (1961), pp. 62 - 74.

Mohanty, Bihoy Chandra, and Krishna, Kalyan. "Ikat Fabrics of Orissa and Andhra Pradesh." In *Study of Contemporary Textile Crafts of India,* vol. 1. Ahmedabad, India: Calico Museum of Textiles, 1974.

Indonesia

Adams, Marie Jeanne. "Classic and Eccentric Elements in East Sumba Textiles." *Needle and Bobbin Club Bulletin,* vol. 55 (1972), pp. 3- 40.

—. "Designs in Sumba Textiles, Local Meanings and Foreign Influences." *Textile Museum Journal,* vol. 3, no. 2 (1971), pp. 28 - 37.

—. "Dress and Design in Highland Southeast Asia: The Hmong (Miao) and the Yao." *Textile Museum Journal,* vol. 4, no. 1 (1974), pp. 51 - 66.

—. "Indonesian Textiles at the Textile Museum." *Textile Museum Journal,* vol. 3, no. 1 (1970), pp. 41 - 44.

—. *System and Meaning in East Sumba Textile Design: A Study in Traditional Indonesian Art.* Southeast Asia Studies Cultural Report Series, No. 16. New Haven: Yale University Press, 1969.

—. "Tie-Dyeing, an Art on the Island of Sumba." *Handweaver and Craftsman,* vol. 22 (1971), p. 9.

Bodorogi, Tibor. *Art of Indonesia.* Boston: New York Graphic Society, 1972.

Bühler, Alfred. "Patola Influences in Southeast Asia." *Journal of Indian Textile History,* vol. 4 (1959), pp. 4 - 46.

Bühler, Alfred; Ramseyer, Urs; and Ramseyer-Gygi, Nicole. *Patola und Geringsing: Zeremonialtücher aus Indien und Indonesien.* Exhibition catalog. Basel: Museum für Völkerkunde und Schweizerisches Museum für Völkskunde, 1975.

Gill, Sarah. "Selected Aspects of Sarawak Art." Ph.D. dissertation, Columbia University, 1968.

Gitringer, Mattiebelle S. "A Study of the Ship Cloths of South Sumatra: Their Design and Usage." Ph.D. dissertation, Columbia University, 1972.

—. "Additions to the Indonesian Collection." *Textile Museum Journal,* vol. 4, no. 3 (1976), pp. 43 - 48.

Groslier, Bernard Philippe. *The Art of Indochina.* New York: Crown Publishers.

Haddon, Alfred C., and Stuart, Laura E. *Iban or Sea Dayak Fabrics and Their Patterns.* Cambridge: The University Press, 1936.

Honolulu Academy of Arts, Spaulding House. *Textiles of the Indonesian Archipelago.* Exhibition catalog. Honolulu, 1973.

Howell, W. "The Sea Dayak Method of Making and Dyeing Thread from Their Home-Grown Cotton." *Sarawak Museum Journal,* vol. 1, no. 2 (1912), pp. 62 - 66.

Ikle, Charles F. "Ikat Technique and Dutch East Indian Ikats." *Bulletin of the Needle and Bobbin Club,* vol. 15, nos. 1 - 2 (1931), pp. 2 - 59.

Kahlenberg, Mary Hunt. *Textile Traditions of Indonesia.* Exhibition catalog. Los Angeles: Los Angeles County Museum of Art, 1977.

Langewis, Laurens, and Wagner, Frits A. *Decorative Art in Indonesian Textiles.* Amsterdam: C.P.J. van der Peet, 1964.

Newman, Thelma R. *Contemporary Southeast Asian Arts and Crafts.* New York: Crown Publishers, 1976.

Solyom, Garrett, and Solyom, Bronwen. *Textiles of the Indonesian Archipelago.* Asian Studies at Hawaii, No. 10. University Press of Hawaii, 1973.

Van Gelder, Lydia. "Indonesian Ikat Fabrics and Their Techniques." In *Threads of Tradition: Textiles of Indonesia and Sarawak.* Exhibition catalog. Joseph Fischer, ed. Berkeley, Cal.: Robert H. Lowie Museum of Anthropology and the University Art Museum, University of California, 1979.

Wagner, Frits A. *Indonesia, the Art of an Island Group.* New York: McGraw-Hill, 1959.

Japan

Bühler, Alfred. "Shibori und Kasuri: Zwei traditionelle japanische Musterungsverfahren fur Stoffe." *Folk,* vol. 5 (1963), pp. 45 - 64.

Dusenbury, Mary. "Kasuri: A Japanese Textile." *Textile Museum Journal,* vol. 17 (1978).

Munsterberg, Hugo. *The Folk Arts of Japan.* Preface by Soetsu Yanagi. Published with the cooperation of the Japan Society, Inc., New York, by Charles E. Turtle Co., Rutland, Vermont, and Tokyo, Japan.

Muraoka, Kageo, and Okamura, Kichiemon. *Folk Arts and Crafts of Japan.* New York: Weatherhill, 1973.

Noma, Seioku. *Japanese Costume and Textile Arts.* New York: Weatherhill, and Tokyo: Heibonsha, 1974.

Ritch, Diane, and Wada, Yoshiko. *Japanese Ikat: Warp, Weft, Figure.* Berkeley, Cal.: Kasuri Dye Works, 1975.

Robinson, Irma. "Kasuri and I." *Shuttle, Spindle and Dyepot,* vol. 1, no. 2 (March 1970).

Royal Ontario Museum and University of Toronto. *Japanese Country Textiles.* Exhibition catalog. Toronto, 1965.

Suzuki, Hisao, and Sugimura, Tsune. *Living Crafts of Okinawa.* New York and Tokyo: Weatherhill, 1973.

Tomita, Jun, and Tomita, Noriko. *The Techniques of Kasuri.* 7-11 Nakagawasono-Machi, Takaoka, Toyama, Japan. English text 1979.

Wilson, Sadye Tune. "Fundraising Brings Kasuri Kimono Weaver to Nashville Workshop." *Shuttle, Spindle and Dyepot,* vol. 9, no. 2 (Spring 1978), pp. 4 - 7.

Index

Picture Credits

The samples in this book come from various sources. If they have not been done by the author, the artist or the museum source is cited. Photographs are reproduced courtesy of the following individuals and museums:

American Museum of Natural History, New York: ~Figure 25 (Photo: Ruta)

Dorothy Beebee (drawings): Figures 18, 27, 28, 64

Marian Clayden: Page 23 (top)

Lia Cook: Pages 22, 24 (Photo: Van Gelder)

Field Museum of Natural History, Division of Photography, Chicago: ~Figure 13

Göteborgs Historiska Museum, Göteborg, Sweden: ~Figure 88

Museum für Völkerkunde und Schweizerisches Museum fr Völkskunde, Basel, Switzerland: ~Figures 8 (neg. #IIa 6026), 14 (#IIa 2045), 15-17, 49 (V;VI 16531), 123 (#IIa 6974), 124 (#IIa 2835); E. Eschler/M. L. Nabholz: ~Figures 24 (print from slide #T 5006), 26 (#IIa 2851), 34 (#IIa 2917), 42 (#IIa 2860), 96 (#IIa 2740); P. Hornet: pages 18-19 (top: neg. #IIa 6415), ~Figure 125 *(Patola und Geringsing* catalog #77); M.L. Nabholz: ~Figure 43 (print from slide:#T 4599); H.W. Van Gelder: page 18 (bottom, left; neg. #III 20257), ~Figures 1 (# IIe 569), 4 (#III 16601), 6 (#IIe 2038), 11 (#V122648), 12 (#20237), 31 (#IIc 1415), 46 (#IIe573), 47 (#III 20233), 62 (#VI 16518), 65 #III 20257); B. Waldis: ~Figures 33 (Inv. #EXH. OK. 8), 126 (#EXH. AK. 5), 127 #EXH. AK. 19), 128 (#EXH. AK. 26), 129 (#EXH. AE. 2), 130 (#EXH. W. 17).

Mary Walker Phillips: Page 29 (Photo: D.R. Long)

The Smithsonian Institution, Washington, D.C.: Page 7

Jean Stamsta: Page 28 (top)

Joan Sterrenburg: Pages 20, 21

The Textile Museum, Washington, D.C.: Figures 3 (Photo: Woltz), 91 (Photo: Van Gelder)

H.W. Van Gelder: Pages 17, 18 (top, left), 25, 26, 27 (both), 28 (bottom); ~Figures 5, 7, 9, 19-23, 28 32, 33, 35-41, 44., 45, 48, 50-61, 63, 66-87, 89, 90, 92-95, 97-104, 108-115, 117-122, 124, 131-135, 137-145.

Victoria and Albert Museum, London: Figures 2, 10, 105-107, 136

Special Acknowledgments

Sincere thanks to all who graciously provided photographs of art from their private collections for inclusion in this book. I am especially indebted to Jack Lenor Larsen and the Smithsonian Institution for their assistance, especially for supplying two particular photographs: Ethel Stein's piece on pages 2 and 3, which is in the collection of Jack Lenor Larsen and Mary Walker Phillips' piece on page 58, which is in the collection of the Smithsonian Institution.